Kam Cheong Li   Tak-Lam Wong
Simon K.S. Cheung   Jeanne Lam
Kwan Keung Ng (Eds.)

Technology in Education

Transforming Educational Practices with Technology

First International Conference, ICTE 2014
Hong Kong, China, July 2-4, 2014
Revised Selected Papers

Springer

Volume Editors

Kam Cheong Li
The Open University of Hong Kong, China
E-mail: kcli@ouhk.edu.hk

Tak-Lam Wong
The Hong Kong Institute of Education
Hong Kong, China
E-mail: tlwong@ied.edu.hk

Simon K.S. Cheung
The Open University of Hong Kong, China
E-mail: kscheung@ouhk.edu.hk

Jeanne Lam
HKU School of Professional and Continuing Education
Hong Kong, China
E-mail: jeanne.lam@hkuspace.hku.hk

Kwan Keung Ng
Caritas Institute of Higher Education
Hong Kong, China
E-mail: sng@cihe.edu.hk

ISSN 1865-0929 e-ISSN 1865-0937
ISBN 978-3-662-46157-0 e-ISBN 978-3-662-46158-7
DOI 10.1007/978-3-662-46158-7
Springer Heidelberg New York Dordrecht London

Library of Congress Control Number: 2015931400

Typesetting: Camera-ready by author, data conversion by Scientific Publishing Services, Chennai

Communications in Computer and Information Science 494

Preface

This edited volume consists of extended papers selected from the International Conference on Technology in Education (ICTE 2014). As the conference theme highlights, the contents of the papers discuss issues of "Transforming Educational Practices with Technology."

Technology has become an integral part in virtually all aspects of education, broadly covering curriculum planning, content development and delivery, assessment, program evaluation, and communication among learners, instructors, and institutions. In conventional universities, open learning institutions, as well as continuing education organizations, technology has become an irreversible force driving changes and transforming practices. New approaches, methods, procedures, and tools are emerging and therefore to contribute as a timely academic platform

In this volume, the papers are organized into four groups: namely "Application of Mobile Technologies in e-Learning," "Technology Advancement in e-Learning Systems," "Innovations in e-Learning Pedagogy," and "Open Education and Institution e-Learning Policy."

Our many sincere thanks go to the Organizing Committee of the conference for their effective administration and unfailing support. Our great thanks also go to the Program Committee. The high quality of this book could not have been maintained without their professional comments and advice in the paper-review process.

October 2014

Kam Cheong Li
Tak-Lam Wong
Simon K.S. Cheung
Jeanne Lam
Kwan Keung Ng

Preface

The edited volume consists of extended papers selected from the International Conference [illegible] ICTCS [illegible]. At the [illegible] [illegible]

[illegible] ways, [illegible] formats, [illegible] transactions, and [illegible] as well as [illegible]

[illegible] [illegible] Processing Entry.

Our [illegible] thanks go to the Organizing Committee of the conference for their [illegible] and unflagging support. Our great thanks also go to the [illegible] without which this book could not have been [illegible]

[illegible]

Organization

Organizing Committee

Chairs

Kam Cheong Li	The Open University of Hong Kong, Hong Kong
Jeanne Lam	HKU School of Professional and Continuing Education, Hong Kong

Members

Melani Au	HKU School of Professional and Continuing Education, Hong Kong
Oliver Au	The Open University of Hong Kong, Hong Kong
Radar Chan	HKU School of Professional and Continuing Education, Hong Kong
Simon K.S. Cheung	The Open University of Hong Kong, Hong Kong
Reggie Kwan	Caritas Institute of Higher Education, Hong Kong
Wing Leung	HKU School of Professional and Continuing Education, Hong Kong
Kwan Keung Ng	Caritas Institute of Higher Education, Hong Kong
Philips Wang	Caritas Institute of Higher Education, Hong Kong
Beryl Wong	The Open University of Hong Kong, Hong Kong
Tak Lam Wong	The Hong Kong Institute of Education, Hong Kong

International Program Committee

Chairs

Tak Lam Wong	The Hong Kong Institute of Education, Hong Kong
Simon K.S. Cheung	The Open University of Hong Kong, Hong Kong

Members

Zoraini Wati Abas	Universitas Siswa Bangsa Indonesia, Jakarta
Oliver Tat Sheung Au	The Open University of Hong Kong, Hong Kong
Gary Cheng	The Hong Kong Institute of Education, Hong Kong

Organizers

香港公開大學
THE OPEN UNIVERSITY
OF HONG KONG

明愛專上學院
Caritas Institute of Higher Education

HKUSPACE
香 港 大 學 專 業 進 修 學 院
HKU School of Professional and Continuing Education

Sponsors

SINO-BRITISH FELLOWSHIP TRUST
中英互助會信託基金

Wu Jieh Yee
Charitable Foundation
伍絜宜慈善基金

Table of Contents

Innovations in e-Learning Pedagogy

Open Education and Institution e-Learning Policy

(ii) students' response time in responding to instant messages sent from the
sor concerned. The response time to the first instant message sent from thei
sor concerned over each of the incidents (relating to the dissertation supervi
the whole supervision period. Statistical analysis is then carried out to chara
student engagement data collected. The possible relationship of such stude
ment and the final assessment result achieved by the group of students is inv

2 Relevant Research

The topic of student engagement has been considered by Chickering & C their study of good practice in undergraduate education [3]. They discuss th engagement can be facilitated through student-teacher contact, cooperati students, active learning, prompt feedback, time on task, high expecta respect for diverse talents and ways of learning. In another study of stude ment [4], the following aspects: level of academic challenge, active and c learning, student interaction with faculty members, enrichment with educati riences and supportive campus environment are found to be effective e practice

Jeffries et al. describe flexible learning should suit the needs of individu [5]. Haynes suggests that learners should be given greater flexibility to where they study, what they learn, how they learn and how they are assess considers flexible learning should be unrestricted in terms of timing and l delivery, the pace of study and the entry requirements.

Wolcott [7] and Repman & Logan [8] point out that timely feedback ca interaction between the students and supervisors. Supervisors should be s the learning difference of individual students. Light & Cox consider the ne vide student support, encourage independence and develop interpersonal q students during dissertation/thesis supervision [9]. They also point out tha tion supervision is a form of formative assessment. Martinez-Pons emph supervisors have to monitor the performance during dissertation supervi Phillips & Pugh describe a set of expectations that postgraduate researc have of their supervisors [11]. Two such expectations are that supervisors available when needed and are friendly.

Yue points out that as many IM tools are now available in the market [2] able supervisors to be always "available" (in terms of time) and "friendly" of giving feedback) to students. Dissertation supervision involves a clos relationship between supervisor and student. Yue examines the student reac use of an instant messaging (IM) tool, WhatsApp [12], used by him in supe dissertation students. A survey was administered to a group of seventeen stu have experienced the communication with their supervisor using instant m The survey questionnaire is based on that used by Kovalik & Hosler [13]. tionnaire is divided into three sections. The first part consists of questions teaching and learning. The response to questions is measured on a Likert 5-point scale. Point 5 corresponds to full agreement of the testing statements. Yue concludes that students are very positive with the use of instant messaging communication [2]. According to [2], as shown in the Appendix 1, the Accountancy mean scores for questions 10-21 (except Q11 and Q16) are always lower than the Marketing mean scores. The use of IM communication is more popular with the Marketing students. Also, there is a clear difference between the male respondents' mean scores and those of the female respondents for questions 10-21 (except Q12). The male mean scores are always lower than those of female respondents. The female students are more positive in the use of IM communication.

3 Methodology

The data used in the present study is the same as that of [2]. Further information about the data set is given as follows. There are two groups of undergraduate students who are supervised by the same supervisor over a 26-week period from July till December 2013. The dissertation project lasts for two semesters (26 week in total). There is one group of 10 Marketing students and another group of 7 Accountancy students. All the students are aged 18-25. Eight of the seventeen respondents are male students while the other female. All students need to submit a dissertation outline and a dissertation report at the end of the process. A final overall mark (with a maximum of 100 marks) is awarded to each student on their dissertation. The outline accounts for 25% while the report accounts for 75% of the overall mark.

During the whole 26-week dissertation supervision period, several major types of instant messages (using WhatsApp) were exchanged between the supervisor and students on an individual basis. They are: (1) reminders of coming meeting details (such as date, time and venue); (2) agenda of the coming meetings; (3) confirmation of work required from student for the coming meeting; (4) group announcements made by the supervisor; (5) feedback on queries arising from matters discussed or to be discussed.

The instant messages exchanged between the students and supervisor are classified into two types: (T1) messages initiated by the supervisor; (T2) messages initiated by the student. In this paper, the student engagement in the use of IM communication is measured. This involves the recording of the number of instant messages initiated by the supervisor and sent to the students, as well as the students' first response time to such messages. Each valid issue raised for IM communication can be initiated by either the supervisor and student involves a series of instant messages exchanged them. For each valid issue, the student's response time to the first instant message sent to him/her by their supervisor (T1 message), OR the supervisor's response time to a student's first instant message (T2 message) is recorded. The response time was all measured in terms of minutes. It is usual that students and supervisor exchanges more than one instant message for each valid issue. There can be more one issue discussed between a student and supervisor in a day. The collected data are analyzed using the statistical software SPSS.

6. Haynes, D.: Mentoring – Flexible Approaches to Staff Development: A Case
New Zealand. In: Bell, C., Bowden, M., Trott, A. (eds.) Implementing Flexibl
Kogan Page Limited, London (1997)
7. Wolcott, L.L.: Distant, But Not Distanced: A learner-Centered approach to Di
cation. Techtrends 41(5) (1996)
8. Repman, J., Logan, S.: Interactions at a Distance: Possible Barrieres and Collab
lutions. Techtrends 41(6) (1996)
9. Light, G., Cos, R.: Learning and Teaching in Higher Education: The Reflect
sional. Paul Chapman Publishing, London (2001)
10. Martinez-Pons, M.: The Continuum Guide to Successful Teaching in Higher
Continuum, London (2003)
11. Phillips, E., Pugh, D.: How to Get a PhD: A Handbook for Students and their S
Open University Press, Buckingham (2000)
12. WhatsApp (2014), `http://www.whatsapp.com`
13. Kovalik, C.L., Hosler, K.A.: Text Messaging and the Community of Inquir
Courses. Journal of Online learning and Teaching 6(2) (2010)

Appendix 1

Table 4. Average score values for 12 questions (Q10-Q21) for 17 respondents gro
different areas of study (A=Accountancy, M=Marketing) and sex (M=male, F=fema

Questions	*Mean (by area of study)*
Q10. IM is a good way to communicate with instructor	4.14 (A) 4.40 (M)
Q11. Receive useful information through IM messages	4.29 (A) 4.20 (M)
Q12. Will follow up IM messages using computers if needed	3.43 (A) 3.90 (M)
Q13. IM messages from instructor is good to obtain course information	4.00 (A) 4.30 (M)
Q14. Receiving IM messages from instructor is normal to me	4.14 (A) 4.50 (M)
Q15. Frequently replied to instructor on receiving IM messages	4.00 (A) 4.30 (M)
Q16. Received the right number of IM messages from instructor	3.86 (A) 3.70 (M)
Q17. Initiated instant messages to instructor at least once during 1-2 weeks	4.00 (A) 4.50 (M)
Q18. Receiving IM messages from instructor help me to stay up-to-date with the course	4.14 (A) 4.60 (M)
Q19. Instant messages is useful in an educational setting	3.71 (A) 4.50 (M)
Q20. Receiving instant messages is a positive aspect of this course	3.57 (A) 4.60 (M)
Q21. IM is useful in the teaching and learning process	3.86 (A) [illegible]

Investigating Acceptance towards Mobile Learning in Higher Education Students

Kenneth Wong, Fu Lee Wang, Kwan Keung Ng, and Reggie Kwan

Caritas Institute of Higher Education
{kfwong,pwang,sng,rkwan}@cihe.edu.hk

Abstract. Mobile learning or M-learning brings a new aspect of learning environment. Due to the large amount of available applications in mobile devices, students use their mobile devices for many purposes including entertainment, sharing, communication, video recording, photo shooting and learning. The acceptance toward mobile learning has naturally become a major interest for educators. In this paper, we will present preliminary findings from a small scale study exploring the students' experiences on using mobile devices versus desktop computers, as well as perceptions towards mobile learning. The data are obtained from the quantitative survey. The preliminary findings indicate that students will use mobile devices rather than desktops to access the Internet. Students are willing to use mobile devices to conduct learning activities.

Keywords: Mobile learning, e-learning, mobile technology, motivation, cyber behavior, learning activities.

1 Introduction

We have seen the processing power of mobile technology grown exponentially while becoming more affordable and even ubiquitous. According to a report from CNNMoney [1] on February 28, 2014, Americans used smartphone and tablet apps more than PCs to access the Internet last month. It is obvious that mobile devices have been overtaking desktop computers and will dominate the future Internet. The current 4th-generation mobile technologies are so powerful that making mobile devices can serve as a tablet, notebook, PDA, telephone, or camera, and data transference as well as video and audio files. In this way, the growth and popularity of mobile applications have been profoundly impacting on our daily life, including learning activities. Mobile technology seems to open a big door for a new kind of learning and performance support in teaching and learning. Students not only learn at school, but also learn informally when they are out of school. Students can use their mobile devices to enhance learning anywhere at any time: waiting for bus, travelling on train, dinning at restaurant, etc. Since mobile devices are increasingly used for learning in classrooms, researches on mobile learning have been becoming a major interest for educators [2]. This study is to explore the students' experiences on using mobile devices versus desktop computers, as well as students' perceptions towards mobile learning.

K.C. Li et al. (Eds.): ICTE 2014, CCIS 494, pp. 9–19, 2015.

2 Mobile Learning in Education

Mobile learning or M-learning can be broadly defined as the exploitation c ous handheld technologies, together with wireless and mobile phone ne facilitate, support, enhance and extend the reach of teaching and learning schools recognized that mobile devices are important learning tools for a va classroom application [4]. To enhance learning, mobile devices can provi tional opportunities for students to access course content, as well as intera structors and classmates wherever they are located [5]. A study from the Center for Applied Research [6] indicated that 67% of surveyed undergra dents believed that mobile devices were important to their academic succ would use their mobile devices for academic activities. They are also d adoption of mobile devices, such as smartphones and tablet computers, in h cation. In this way, mobile learning is an expanded form of e-learning for mobile devices that involves connectivity for downloading, uploading a working via Wi-Fi or mobile networks, and linking to institutional e-learnir [7].

3 Research Methodology

In this study, students' experiences and perceptions on mobile learning vers computers were investigated. It used a convenient sampling method to data. It was conducted in the academic year 2013-14, 68 students were invi ticipate in this research. They were enrolled in a course called "Mathemati the core curriculum courses required for all students who are pursuin secondary programme in the Institute. They were invited to complete a qu about their experiences and perceptions on mobile learning on voluntary ba

3.1 Research Questions

This study attempts to answer the following research questions:

- What are general experiences of students in using the mobile devices ve top computer?
- What is students' perception on using the mobile devices for academic a
- What are students' attitudes on using the mobile devices for academic ac

3.2 Data Collection

A questionnaire was developed and distributed to students during the sprin in academic year 2013-14. Participation in the survey was on voluntary ba responses were anonymous. The survey comprised of a combination of Lik

4 Preliminary Findings

68 of the students enrolled in the post-secondary programme took part in this survey. The survey included four broad types of measures: demographic information, daily Internet usage habits using personal computers (PC) and mobile devices, daily e-learning activities, and students' attitudes on using mobile devices for learning. The survey data were analyzed by the "SPSS" software. In our sample, 59% and 41% of the students were male and female respectively. 97% of respondents were below 25 years old, about 77% of them were 18 to 20 and 20% of them were 21 to 24.

From the survey, 49% of the students spent 3 hours or more daily on the Internet through PC. However, 79% of the students spent 3 hours or more daily on the Internet through mobile devices. The distribution of students' Internet daily usage on using PC versus mobile devices was shown in Figure 1. In the usual place to get the Internet access measure, students could choose more than one option in this item. From the result, the most popular place to access the Internet through PC was at home and 55 students chose this item. The most popular place to access the Internet through mobile devices was at campus and 61 students chose this item. The distribution of popular places to access the Internet was shown in Figure 2.

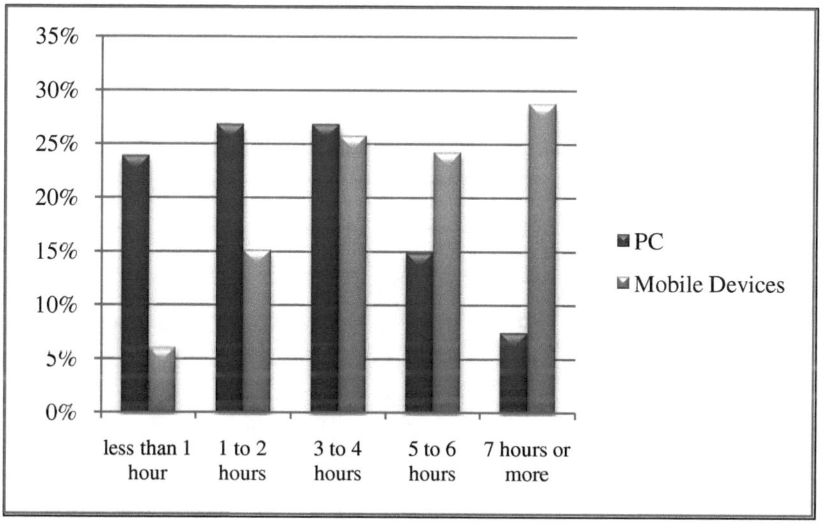

Fig. 1. The distributions of students' Internet daily usage on using PC versus mobile devices

In the e-learning activities measure, most of daily e-learning activities on PCs are searching information and downloading documents. On the other hand, most of daily e-learning activities on mobile devices are searching information and discussing assignments, as shown in Figure 3.

Table 1. The summary of the questions (5-point Likert scale) in the surve

	Questions	Mean Score	S D
1.	In contrast with PC, I will spend more time on using mobile devices for Internet.	3.69	1
2.	In contrast with PC, I prefer to use mobile devices for Internet.	3.46	1
3.	In contrast with PC, I prefer to use mobile devices for learning.	3.55	1
4.	In contrast with PC, I prefer to use mobile devices for discussing assignments with classmates.	3.75	1
5.	In contrast with PC, I prefer to use mobile devices as an e-Learning tool.	3.31	1
6.	In contrast with PC, I prefer to use mobile devices for conducting learning tasks.	3.45	1
7.	In contrast with PC, I prefer to use mobile devices to view learning materials.	3.27	1
8.	In contrast with PC, I prefer to use mobile devices for conducting quiz.	3.13	1
9.	In contrast with PC, I prefer to use mobile devices for watching learning video.	3.31	1
	Average	3.43	1

A total of 9 items were used to measure the students' attitudes on learni mobile devices versus PC, Table 1 shows the summary of findings. T showed average ratings of 3.43 on a five point Likert scale and all items w than the average. The results indicated that students would prefer using mo es for discussing assignments with classmates. The average mean of this it highest score 3.75 out of 5. Regarding the students' attitudes on using inst bile apps, 58% of students agreed or strongly agreed that instructors can d learning activities through mobile apps. 64% of students agreed or stron that our institute should develop more mobile apps for them to enhance thei details as shown in Table 2. Furthermore, it is found that 9 items related to attitudes on learning through mobile devices versus PC" and 2 items relat dents' attitudes on using institute's mobile apps" could be combined into The factor named "M-learning attitude" was formed. The Cronbach's alp items was 0.935, as shown in Table 3. These items were significantly relate

Regarding the students' attitude of using institute's mobile apps, 74% reflected that they were willing to use our institute's mobile apps for re learning. This finding echoes the research results from [6].

Table 2. Students' attitudes on using institute's mobile apps

	Questions	Strongly agree	Agree	Fair	Disagree
1.	wish instructors can design more learning activiti sing mobile apps.	17%	41%	30%	9%
2.	wish our institute can develop more mobile apps	23%	41%	29%	4%

Table 3. The Cronbach's alpha of the 11 items related to students' attitude towards social networking for learning

Cronbach's Alpha	Cronbach's Alpha Based on Standardized Items	No of Items
.935	.935	11

Table 4. The correlation among the items related to students' spending time on mobile devices and perceptions

		Spending time on Internet using mobile devices	Spending Time on learning using mobile devices	Enhance learning effectively
Spending time on Internet using mobile devices	Pearson Correlation	1	.006	.241*
	Sig. (2-tailed)		.963	.049
	N	68	68	67
Spending Time on learning using mobile devices	Pearson Correlation	.006	1	.325**
	Sig. (2-tailed)	.963		.007
	N	68	68	67
Enhance learning effectively	Pearson Correlation	.241*	.325**	1
	Sig. (2-tailed)	.049	.007	
	N	67	67	67

*. Correlation is significant at the 0.05 level (2-tailed).

**. Correlation is significant at the 0.01 level (2-tailed).

5 Discussion

This study provided a useful view of what students are currently doing and of what they can do with mobile devices regarding learning. It has provided valuable insights for the mobile learning. The results of the survey indicate that the majority of the students perfered using mobile devices to conduct learning activities. It is hypothesized that students would benefit from the mobile learning.

For the general experiences of students on using the mobile devices versus desktop computers, the finding seems confirm the trend that people used more mobile devices than PC to access the Internet daily. In contrast with PC, students prefer using mobile devices to perform more activities, including academic activities. The reasons why students like using mobile technology as a learning tool may be simply their habits or daily usual rituals. We may conclude that mobile devices become necessities for our daily life and people are willing to spend more time there. We can forecast that mobile learning will play a dominant role in e-Learning in the near future.

ally use mobile devices which are becoming necessities on daily life. Sec finding has indicated that students' perceptions are towards mobile learnin students' attitudes are also positive towards on mobile learning.

The finding of this study suggests that mobile technologies have the p provide new learning experiences. In this study, students felt that mobile d have great potential to replace desktop computers on conducting learning searchers [9][10][11] have reported positive reactions of students on usi devices for language learning because of the portability and perceived co However, there are also some limitations; for example, students might ha access to mobile devices due to device and service costs. Some students ma with new technology when using it as a learning tool. Moreover, small scr mobile phones may limit the mobile content presented.

The Mobile technologies are perceived as an effective tool in improving cation and learning [12]. As more students make use of mobile learning, th more comfortable with using mobile devices for learning. We can see emp in adopting new technology in their study. Educators should be more lik mobile devices for pedagogical purposes in their future classes. Finall learning is certainly an interesting approach in learning. The world of lea become more mobile, more flexible and more exciting. The mobile learn approaching.

References

1. CNNMoney, `http://money.cnn.com/2014/02/28/technology mobile-apps-Internet/`
2. Meurant, R.C.: iPad Tablet Computing to Foster Korean EFL Digital Literacy. al Journal of u- and e-Service, Science and Technology 3(4), 49–62 (2002)
3. Hashemi, M., Azizinezhad, M., Najafi, V., Nesari, A.J.: What is Mobile Lear lenges and Capabilities, Procedia - Social and Behavioral Sciences 30(2011), (2011)
4. Johnson, L., Adams, S., Cummins, M.: NMC horizon report: 2012 K-12 editio Media Consortium, Austin (2012)
5. Gikas, J., Grant, M.M.: Mobile computing devices in higher education: Stud tives on learning with cellphones, smartphones & social media. The Internet Education 19, 18–26 (2013)
6. ECAR: ECAR Study of Undergraduate Students and Information Technol http://net.educause.edu/ir/library/pdf/ERS1208/ERS1208.pdf
7. Simkova, M., Tomaskova, H., Nemcova, Z.: Mobile Education in Tools. Proc and Behavioral Sciences 47(2012), 10–13 (2012)
8. Wong, K., Ho, W.S., Kwan, R., Wang, F.L., Leung, K., Cheung, I.: The implementation of a mobile app for language learning. In: Proceedings of th International Conference on Open and Flexible Education (2014)
9. Cavus, N., Ibrahim, D.: m-Learning: An experiment in using SMS to support l English language words. British Journal of Educational Technology 40(1), 78–

11. Stockwell, G.: Vocabulary on the move: Investigating an intelligent mobile phone-based vocabulary tutor. Computer Assisted Language Learning 20(4), 365–383 (2007)
12. Al-Fahad, F.N.: Students' attitudes and perceptions towards the effectiveness of mobile learning in King Saud University, Saudi Arabi. The Turkish Online Journal of Educational Technology 8(2), 111–119 (2009)

An Adaptive Mobile Learning Application for Beg to Learn Fundamental Japanese Language

S.C. Ng, Andrew K. Lui, and Y.K. Wong

The Open University of Hong Kong
30 Good Shepherd Street, Ho Man Tin, Kowloon, Hong Kong SAR, Chin
scng@ouhk.edu.hk

Abstract. It is difficult for beginners to learn Japanese by self-learning bec there is no teacher can give any guidance and feedback to them improvement. Besides, most of the beginners may not have any b knowledge of Japanese language, for example, Japanese alphabets phonology, they don't have any idea how to get start with and what shoul learnt at the beginning. This paper introduces an Android mobile applicatio the beginners to acquire fundamental knowledge of Japanese language so a gain the self-learning proficiency in Japanese. This application prov learning materials, auto-generated exercises, handwriting practice tool, v recording and recognition tool for beginners to learn Japanese. Besides, application proposes an adaptive learning system to users, which aim provide different supplementary exercises or learning approaches to lea based on the current performance of an individual learner.

Keywords: mobile learning application, Android apps, learning Japa Language.

1 Introduction

Although many people want to learn Japanese by self-learning, many of the idea how to get started to learn Japanese because there is no teacher to d what kind of topics should be studied or how to study during self-learnin most of the beginners do not have any fundamental Japanese language k like Japanese alphabets or phonology. Without learning the basic Japanes knowledge, beginners may not be able to learn further difficult Japanese cause they do not have the self-learning proficiency in Japanese yet.

Another serious problem beginners may encounter in their self-learning that no one can provide suitable comments or teach them how to impro learners have done some exercises, practiced speaking or written Japanese.

Comparing with using textbook or computers to learn Japanese, mobile a better choice. Mobile learning is a kind of e-learning which learns with vices [1]. It increases the ubiquity and accessibility of e-learning [2] since

bile devices anywhere, anytime with mobile learning [3]. Learning Japanese not only involves reading materials but also involves listening, speaking and writing. Mobile applications can provide interactive activities with using multimedia, like animation or audio, for learner to leaner Japanese in different aspects interactively.

Besides, adaptive mobile learning can be applied in the self-learning process. It adjusts the learning process depending on the learning performance of individual learners by providing different learning materials, exercises or learning approaches in order to create an individual learning style for each learner [4], [5]. With adaptive mobile learning, learners can have a virtual teacher who gives them feedbacks or assign suitable exercises to learners just like what a real teacher does.

2 Current Applications for Learning Japanese

In the current app markets, there are many apps for learning Japanese. However, most of the apps are not suitable for beginners to learn fundamental Japanese topics for several reasons:

- Lack of teaching sessions, only focus on exercising
- Lack of adaptive learning element
- Lack of assessment to measure the learning performance of learners
- Syllabus is not all-rounded. For example, only vocabulary or Japanese character is taught in an applications
- Some applications are exam-oriented, e.g. Japanese-Language Proficiency Test
- Lacks of explanation of the learning material
- The target of the applications is not beginners
- Purpose of some applications is mainly for travelling but not learning

"Learning Japanese Tool" [6] is a pretty good and nearly all-rounded mobile application for learning Japanese. It contains learning tools for learning Japanese alphabet, vocabulary and exercises. However, the application does not have any learning materials and adaptive learning system. It may be difficult for beginners who have never learnt Japanese to use.

Other than learning syllabus and materials, learning tools are also very important for learning Japanese insides a mobile application. For example, many mobile applications for learning Japanese have handwriting practicing tools for learners to learn or practice writing Japanese characters. The mobile application "Japanese Kana by Hand" [7] is one of an example. However, it only recognizes the handwriting of users but not teaching them how to write. Even if learners write the character in a wrong way, the tool still can recognize the handwriting without telling learners whether it is correct or not. Some applications, like the app "Japanese Hiragana Handwriting" [8], do not have any recognition or checking function. It simply allows learners to follow the mold to write Japanese characters, just like writing on a copybook.

3.2 Exercises

According to the content of the learning materials, exercises of related top vided to learners in order to review what they have learnt. There are thre exercises in the application: **kana, vocabulary** and **listening**.

Exercise Generating System

In order to make the exercises more challenging so as to attract users to do exercise generating system is created to generate different questions fo every time. Even if the user does the same exercise for several times, the q the exercise will be different from time to time.

Fig. 5 below shows how the exercise generating system generates diff tions for an exercise. For each exercise, it contains several kinds of quest kind of questions is generated by its own question generator randomly. Th tion of the kinds of questions in each exercise is stored in the Android SC base.

When a user requests to do an exercise, like adjective exercise, the exe rating system will read the exercise data in the database to see which sever questions the exercise contains. As each kind of question type has its ow generator to generate that specify kind of question, the system will call tl question generators to generate the kinds of question the exercise want. All the questions are stored in the SQLite database. The question generator w relevant data to generate a set of question randomly and return it in a list. will group all the questions which are returned from different question together to form an exercise. There are at most ten questions in an exercise.

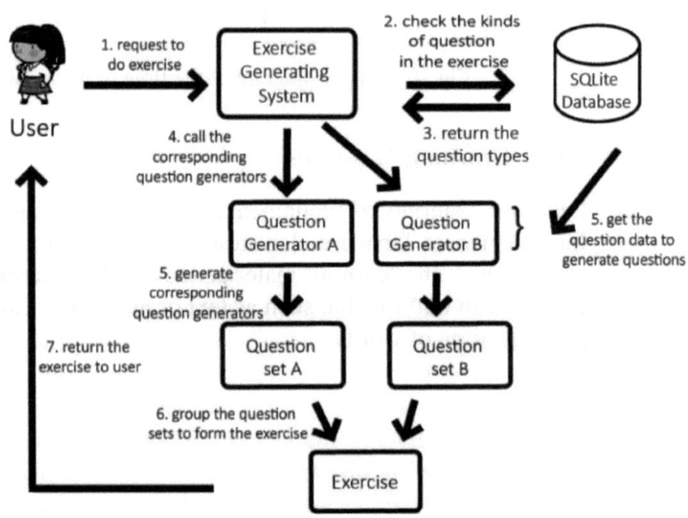

Fig. 5. Diagram of how the exercise generating system generates exercise

Questions Insides the Exercises
Kana and vocabulary exercises are in the form of multiple choice questions. For example, choose the correct pronunciation of the character or choose the correct meaning of the word.

To generate random multiple choice questions, the question generator first reads the related question data in the SQLite database. Then, it selects one question randomly. To make the exercise more challenging, the options of the multiple choice questions will also be generated randomly based on the correct answer of the question in one of the following two ways:

1. Generate Similar Wrong Options Based on Modifying the Correct Answer

The correct answer of the question will be modified in the following ways to form the wrong optional answers:

1. Swap two positions of characters inside a word
2. Change one of the characters of a word
3. Delete one of the characters of a word

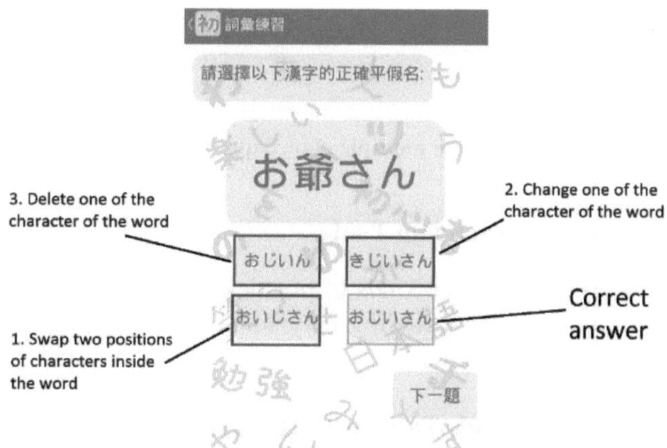

Fig. 6. Generate similar wrong options based on modifying the correct answer

2. Generate Options by Directly Selecting from Database Randomly

For listening exercises, each question is associated with an audio recording. Learners need to listen to the recording and input the answer according to the recording. All the listening questions are also auto-generated. The corresponding question generator will generate a string as the question, for example, "two thousand and three". An external function Google text to speech [9] is applied. The question string generated by question generator will be sent to the Google text to speech for retrieving an audio recording. Learners can listen to that audio recording and answer the question.

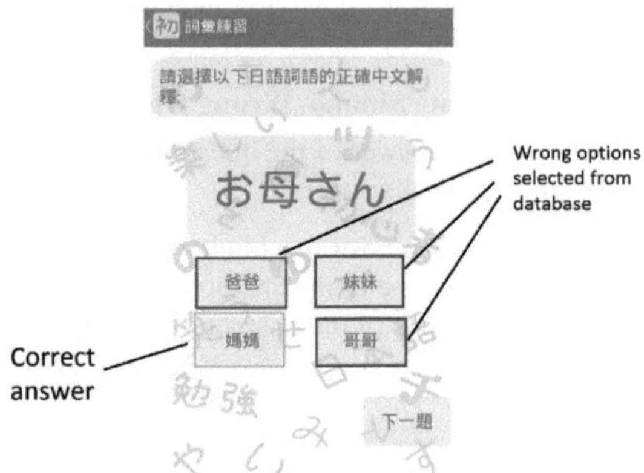

Fig. 7. Generate multiple choice question options by directly selecting from databas

3.3 Practicing Tools

There are three kinds of practicing tools to assist the learners to learn Japa application, including fifty sounds table, vocabulary list and Japanese prc enquiring tool.

Fifty Sounds Table with Handwriting Practicing Tool

The fifty sounds table is a 5×10 table for learners to learn Japanese alphab pronunciation. The table orders the Japanese characters according to their s type. There are two modes for users to select in the table, the pronunciation handwriting practicing mode. If pronunciation mode is selected, users ca pronunciation of the Japanese character they selected when they click on a of the table. If handwriting practicing mode is selected, users can use the h practicing tool to practice handwriting of the selected character. Users can mode by clicking the "寫" button.

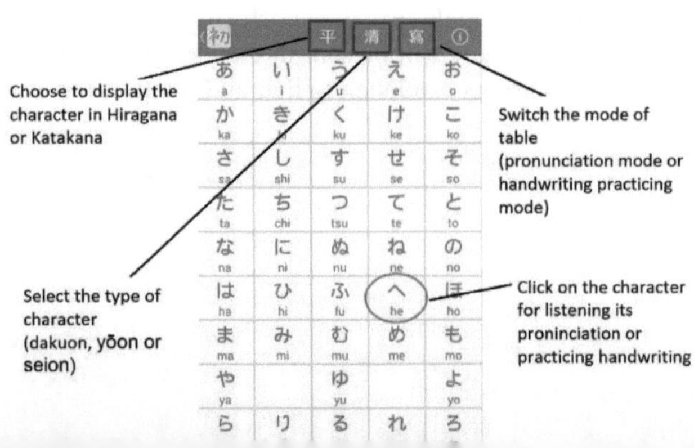

Handwriting Practicing Tool with Recognition Function

The handwriting practicing tool allows learners to practice writing different Japanese characters. A writing box will appear with a mold which displays the strokes of the character. Learners need to follow the mold to write the character. After finishing writing, the tool will check if learner write the character correctly.

To be able to do the recognition and checking on the user written character, some data of the characters must be collected first, including the following things:

1. Number of strokes in a character
2. The stroke order of the character
3. The starting point and ending point of each stroke
4. The turning points in the middle part of each stroke

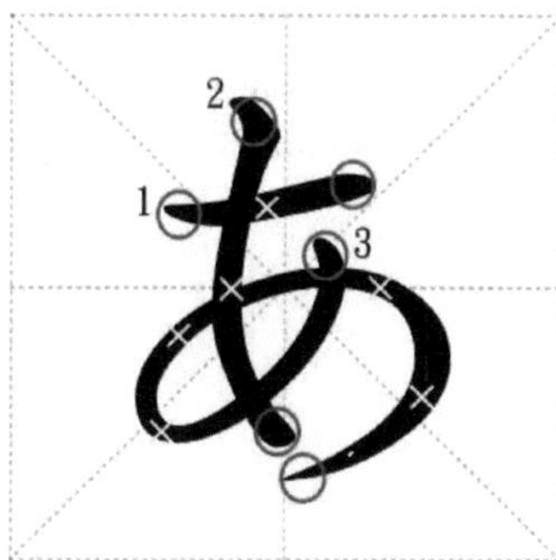

Fig. 9. Data collection points of a Japanese character

In Fig. 9, the number indicates the stroke order of the character and the character "あ" has totally 3 strokes. The circles are the starting point and ending point of each stroke which are needed to be collected. The "X" marks are the turning points in the middle part of each stroke.

When users touches the touch screen, moves and finally puts up their finger, it is considered as inputting a stroke. The tool will save a stroke immediately after the user has inputted so that the input order of strokes of the character can be reserved. Saving a stroke includes saving its starting point, ending point and multiple middle points. A stroke will be saved in a stroke class and a character class contains one or more stroke objects. After user inputting all the strokes and click the finished button, the checking will be started.

The tool will check three things of a user written character to determine whether the inputted character is written correctly:

1. Number of stroke user has inputted
2. The writing direction of each stroke
3. The writing position of each stroke

If the user written strokes are correct, the strokes will become green. Otherwise, the strokes will become red to indicate that the strokes are written wrongly.

Fig. 12 is an activity diagram that shows how the tool determines if a c written correctly. First, the tool will compare the number of stroke user h with the correct one. If the number of inputted stroke is correct, the check progressed to the next stage. Otherwise, the stroke will be considered as wr

Next stage is to check each stroke one by one. The writing direction of e will be checked first. It can be checked by comparing the (x, y) coordi starting point and the ending point of the user written stroke with the correc one of these two points is not matched with the correct stroke, the stroke w sidered as wrong.

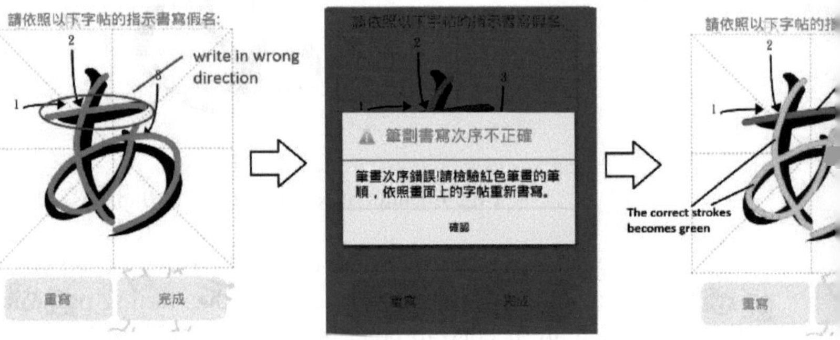

Fig. 10. Write a stroke with wrong direction

The writing position or shape of each stroke can be checked by compa y) coordinate of multiple middle points of the user written stroke with stroke. The correct stroke has a list which contains some (x, y) coordinates turning points of the stroke. If the user written stroke has points which n key turning points of the correct stroke, the stroke will consider as correct. the stroke will be considered as wrong.

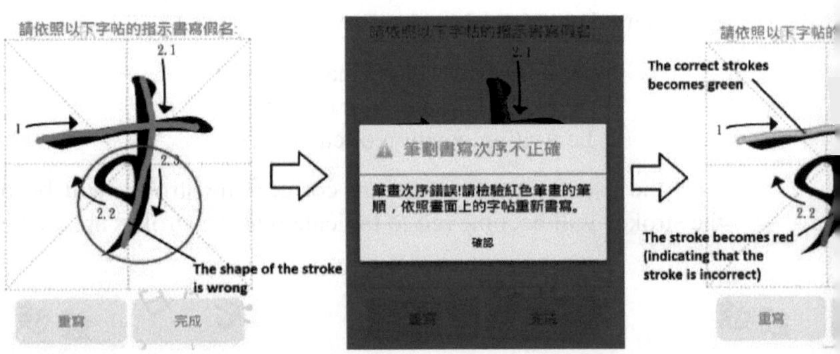

Fig. 11. The shape of the stroke is wrong

Checking of the points by comparing [illegible] (x, y) coordinates directly is n

mold but they do write the character correctly. Therefore, the (x, y) coordinate of the correct position will add and subtract a threshold value to create the threshold for comparing with the position of the user inputted stroke. For example, if the correct starting point of a stroke is (120, 450) and the threshold value is 50, the valid area for the user to write the starting point of the stroke is (70-170, 400-500).

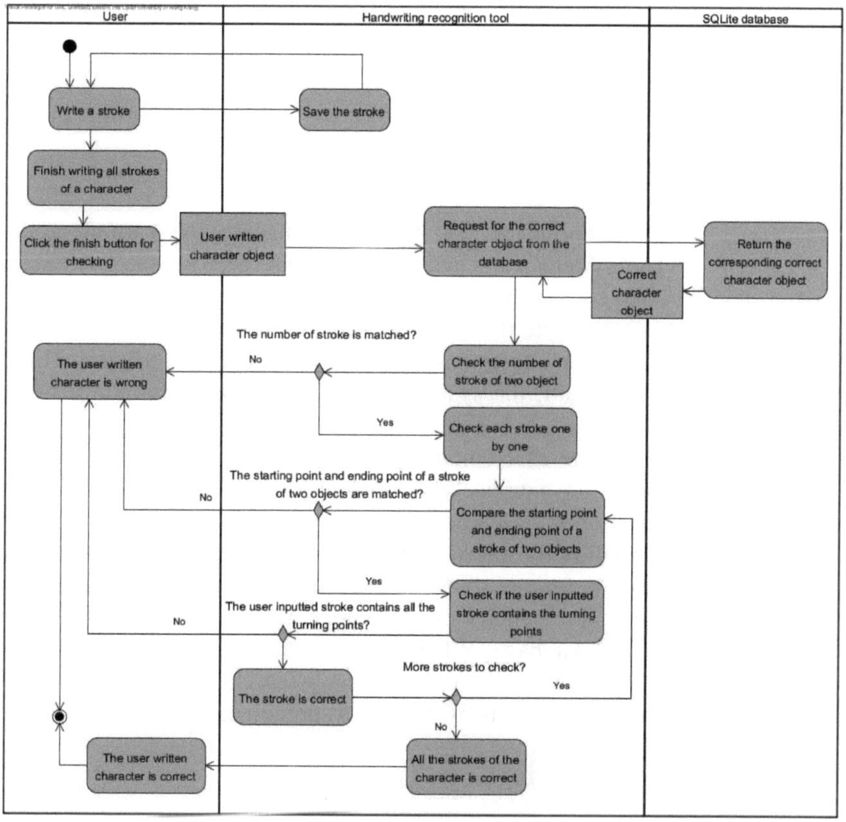

Fig. 12. Activity diagram of how to determine if a character is written correctly

3.4 Assessment System

The assessment system assesses the performance of exercises that the users have done. With the help of question generator of the exercise generating system, different types of questions will be generated for exercises. After the users have answered the questions, the answers will be checked if they are correct. Then, the assessment system will store the result into the SQLite database, which will be used for evaluating users' learning performance later.

All exercises are defined into different types, like vocabulary, listening or kana. The system stores the result of the exercises with their type. When learners want to check their performance, the system will show the result of different kinds of exercise

they have done and generate suitable comments and advices to tell learn
improve.

3.5 Adaptive Learning System

The adaptive learning system personalizes the learning process for individu
The system starts with checking the performance of exercises which lea
done by retrieving data from the SQLite database through the assessment
will calculate the mark of each exercise and check frequency of doing the
there is an exercise which learner has done it for several times but still coul
good result, the system will analysis the performance of each question t
exercise.

As the assessment system has recorded the performance of each que
inside an exercise independently, the adaptive system can spot out wh
question type learner is poor at. Then, the adaptive learning system can
formation for question generator to generate supplementary exercises to le
suitable type of questions according to the weakness of learners. The info
the supplementary exercise generated by the adaptive learning system wil
in the database. When learners visit the exercise page, the system will
learner that the supplementary exercise is ready for them. Learners can
their weak points by doing the supplementary exercise.

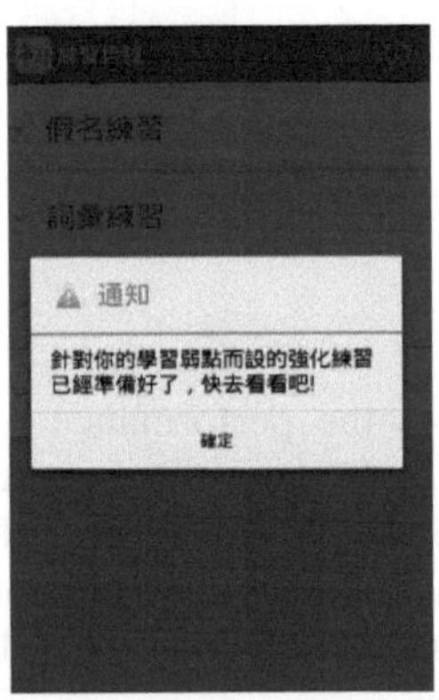

Fig. 13. Dialog box notifies learner for supplementary exercise

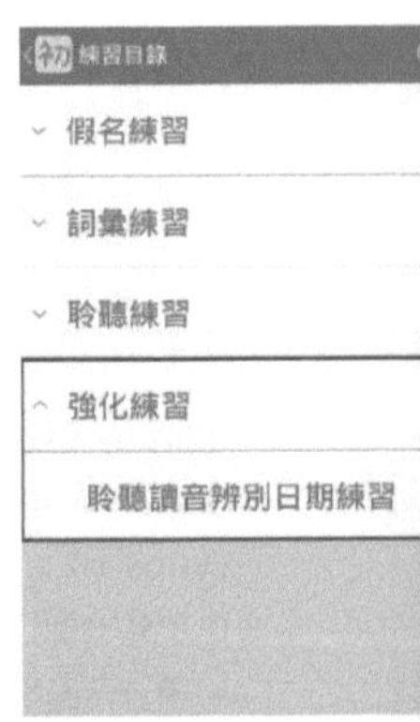

Fig. 14. Supplementary exercise
exercise menu

4 Evaluation

To evaluate whether the learners can acquire the knowledge of fundament
topics and be able to read, write, speak and listen some basic Japanese afte
application, fifteen people were invited to use Hello Japanese application

acquire basic knowledge of Japanese. Besides, a questionnaire was designed to obtain comments and feedbacks from interviewees. 83% of the interviewees have never learnt Japanese before using this application and 13% of interviewees have learnt Japanese at an elementary level.

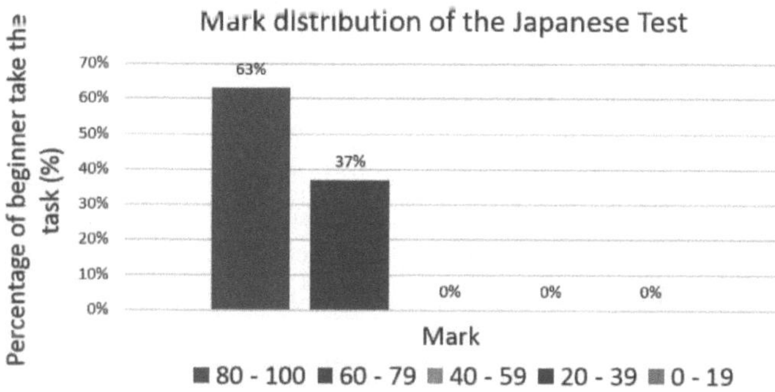

Fig. 15. Mark distribution of the Japanese Test

According to Fig. 15, 63% of the learner got 80-100 marks and 37% of the learner got 60-79 marks in the Japanese test after using the application. No one got fail in the test, which was a very outstanding result.

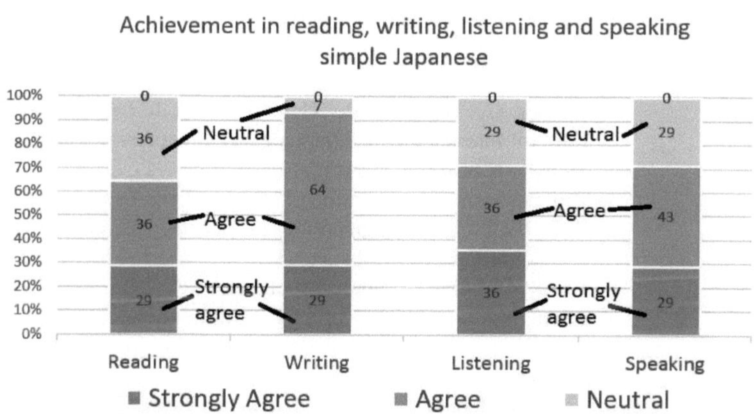

Fig. 16. Achievement in reading, writing, listening and speaking simple Japanese

For the questionnaire part, it asked whether the learners can read, write, listen and speak simple Japanese after using the application. From Fig. 16, over 60% of learners agreed or strongly agreed that they can read, write, listen and speak simple Japanese after using the application and no one chose disagree or strongly disagree option.

5 Conclusion

An adaptive mobile learning application has been developed for beginne fundamental Japanese language. It provides an all-in-one and adaptive lear rience to the learners. Learners can study learning materials, do exercises, u ing tools to practice Japanese handwriting or pronunciation as well as c learning performance and progress. 100% of the learners who had used th tion agree that using "Hello Japanese" was effective in learning Japanese. of them agreed or strongly agreed that they can read, write, listen and sp Japanese after using the application. Many learners commented that the ha practicing tool of the fifty sounds table was the most attractive feature in th tion. More interactive elements should be brought into the application in For example, the voice recognition can be added to check the pronunciatio ers or more multimedia can be added into the learning materials.

References

1. Houser, C., Thornton, P., Kluge, D.: Mobile Learning: Cell Phones and PDAs tion. In: International Conference on Computers in Education, pp. 1149–1150 (2
2. Hockly, N.: Mobile learning. Elt Journal 67(1), 80–84 (2013)
3. Zimmermann, M.: Adaption of multimedia E-Learning services to mobile envir 2011 IEEE Global Engineering Education Conference, pp. 671–678 (2011)
4. Abouelfetouhs, A., El-bakry, H.M.: A Novel Adaptive Mobile E-Learning Mo tional Journal of Computer Applications 63(14), 12–25 (2013)
5. Jones, V., Jo, J.H.: Ubiquitous learning environment: An adaptive teaching s ubiquitous technology. In: Beyond the Comfort zone: Proceedings of the 21st Conference (2004)
6. Learning Japanese Tool - Google Play Store, https://play.google.co apps/details?id=com.sage.ljp
7. Japanese Kana by Hand - Google Play Store, https://play.google.cc apps/details?id=se.tokotoko.android.kanabyhand
8. Japanese Hiragana Handwriting - Google Play Store, https://play.goo store/apps/details?id=com.teachersparadise.japaneseal raganahandwriting&hl=zh_TW
9. Google Text to Speech, http://translate.google.com/tr tts?tl=ja&q

A Mobile Application for Preparing the Driving Tests in Hong Kong

S.C. Ng, Andrew K.F. Lui, and S.W. Ng

The Open University of Hong Kong
scng@ouhk.edu.hk

Abstract. This paper presents an educational mobile application in Android platform called "HK driving tests All-In-One" to help young private automatic car learners prepare for driving tests in Hong Kong. Car learners who are going to take the driving tests may do revision at anytime and anywhere provided that they have an Android device on hand. They can learn in an interesting way and understand the driving techniques more easily with notes, mock tests, animations and games. It will also help in reducing dangerous driving and promoting proper driving skills. The results indicated that developing a mobile application to prepare driving tests in Hong Kong is useful and helpful.

Keywords: mobile learning, driving tests in Hong Kong, Android apps, educational mobile application.

1 Introduction

It is difficult for people who are going to take driving tests in Hong Kong to revise the driving skills and theories themselves because most of the driving schools will not provide many materials or notes although learners have paid ten thousand or more for about fifteen driving lessons.

This paper presents an educational mobile application on the Android platform for preparing both the driving theory test and road test in Hong Kong. It provides guidebooks, mock tests, animations and virtual driving games to help users, especially young private automatic car learners who are going to take the driving tests, to do revision and pass the driving tests in Hong Kong easily.

1.1 Impact and Value of this Mobile Application

Car learners who are going to take the driving tests in Hong Kong may practice and revise the main points of driving anywhere at any time provided that they have a mobile device in their hands. They can have most of the driving materials in one application without bringing a lot of notes or heavy books. Also, those materials inside the application would definitely clam them down and bring back the memory before taking the tests, thus having a better performance.

K.C. Li et al. (Eds.): ICTE 2014, CCIS 494, pp. 33–44, 2015.

Also, there are animations and virtual game-based driving practice fc driving tests so the users can learn in an interesting way and understanc niques more easily. Learners can experience driving a car with a first-persoı similar physical settings in real life to get familiar with driving a car. Thos with graphics and games which contextualize the learning may help users long term memory and a better performance in revision. [1-2]

It is free of charge so everyone who is interested in driving may know driving in Hong Kong and pre-learners can understand some basic drivin before learning driving without paying. Therefore, this application does no learners to pass the driving tests, but also helps in increasing road safety an dangerous driving.

1.2 Hong Kong Driving Tests

There are three parts of the tests which are written test (Part A), Comp (Part B) and the on-the-road test (Part C). The learners have to pass the before learning to drive and the two driving test parts can be tested separate bined to test at the same time.

In the written test, candidates have to answer twenty multiple-choice about driving theories in twenty minutes. Competence test is the basic d parking techniques test including parking the car, making a U-turn on a n and stop on the steep road. Candidates will be asked to drive for around nutes on the real road in the city in the on-the-road test (Part C) where th skills and responses in real situation can be tested.

1.3 Review of Existing Solutions

There are about five driving applications for Hong Kong driving theory te are listed to compare with the other two applications from the United Ki Mainland China respectively [3-6]. Table 1 below compares those applicat have been downloaded more than 10,000 times in Google play store. It shc the applications focus on the driving theory part only by providing practice test but there is no handbook for users to study the theories before doing mock test. There is no application that provides lessons on the road test par

Table 1. Comparison of Existing Applications

Function\App	Driving Theory Test(UK) [3]	HK Driving Written Mock Exam[4]	Hong Kong Driving Test[5]
1.Theory Handbook	✘	✘	✘
2.Theory Test practice	✔	✘	✔
3.Theory Mock Test	✔	✔	✔
4.Driving animation	✘	✘	✘
5.Virtual driving test	✘	✘	✘

2 Methodology

The application platform will be Android OS which is written in the Java language with Eclipse. Android OS is preferred because it is an open-source mobile phone operating system where its application market is popular and has less restriction so it is easier for beginners to develop mobile applications [7-8].

A game engine called Unity will be used to develop all the animations and games contained in the application. JavaScript and C++ language are used for coding and the libraries of Unity are widely used to get the best quality of the graphics and object design. Most of the animations and games are drawn in 3D if possible [9].

For the simple 2D graphics in the application, Adobe Photoshop or some simple graphics applications such as Paint are used. All of the graphics will be designed and drawn by myself, except some special logos which have been permitted [10].

All the questions, answers, theories and other text-based contents inside the application are mostly stored in a rational database using a popular free relational database management system called SQLite because it is a reliable embedded database which is fast, powerful and simple to use [11].

2.1 Design of the Application

There are two main sections in the application which are the theory test and road test. The overview of the application is shown in Fig. 1.

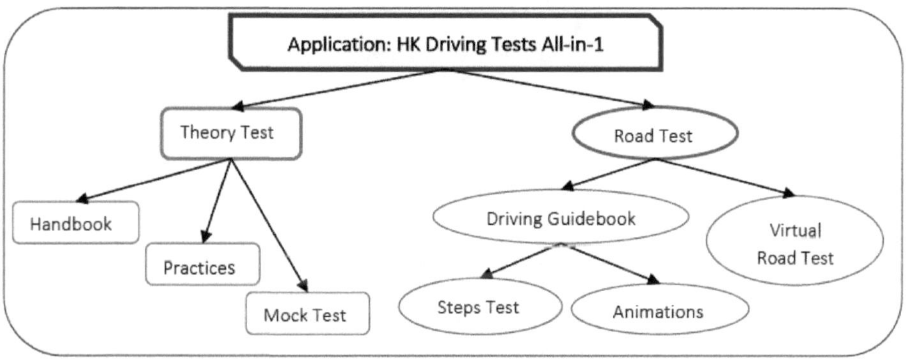

Fig. 1. Overview of the application

Fig. 1 shows the structure of the application. In the theory test section, there are three parts including a theory handbook, theory test practice and theory mock test. There are driving guidebooks with animations, driving step test and virtual road test games inside the road test section.

All materials in the application are sorted by topics so users can follow the flow to revise step by step. Also, the format of the mock tests is similar to the real driving tests so users can get familiar with it.

3 Implementation

The starting page of the mobile application is shown in Fig. 2. Fig. 3 show menu which is entered by clicking the rotating red car in the animation on page.

Fig. 2. Starting page of the application

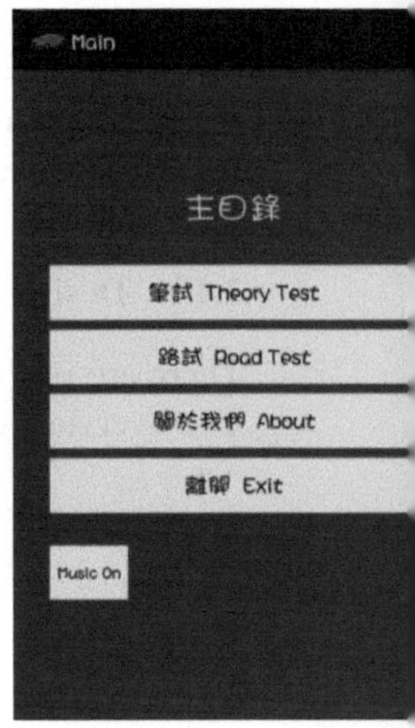

Fig. 3. Main menu of the appl

3.1 Theory Test Part

In theory test section, there are three parts including a theory handbook, practice and theory mock test.

3.1.1 Theory Handbook

The handbook shows all the theories from the Road Users' Code sorted Sliding layout is used to have a multi-plane layout on top of the UI and ea of the handbook will be displayed in a slider which is designed to look like Users can turn the page by swiping the slider to left or right or clicking th the top right corner in the action menu bar. The content will be interprete ranged into essential notes so learners can study the theories easily and Also, fewer activities will be created so the structure of the program will b the performance of the application will be improved [12-14].

3.1.2 Theory Test Practice

There are practices for the theory test sorted by topics without time limit u

question and the options will also be randomly generated to prevent users from memorizing the correct option instead of the answer. After answering a question by choosing and submit the option, the answer chosen will be compared to the correct answer from the database. The result will then be shown right after answering each question like the one in Fig. 4 and the correct answer will be given if the answer is wrong. Fig. 5 shows the final score after answering all the questions in that topic so users may revise the topic if the score of the topic is low. Users may keep doing the practices of the same topic until getting full mark or they may stop at any point by closing the slider. The practices may help users to get used to the question format and to know which topic should be strengthened.

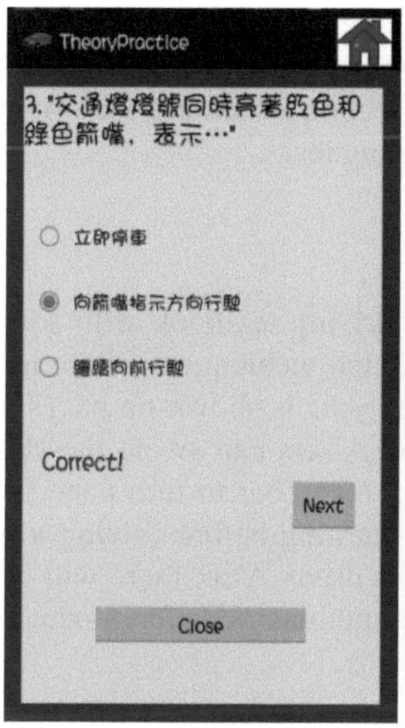

Fig. 4. Answer correctly in the Theory Practice

Fig. 5. Last Question in Theory Practice Slider

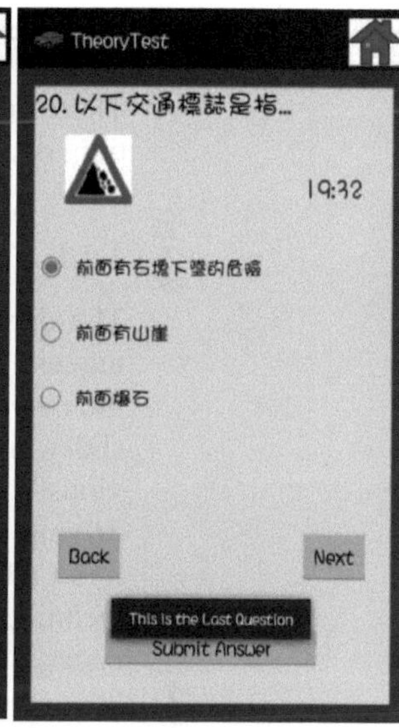

Fig. 6. Last Question in Mock Test

3.1.3 Theory Mock Test

The theory mock test can help learners to check if they are ready for the real written theory test or not. The format is the same as the real test where candidates have to answer twenty multiple-choice questions within twenty minutes. When the test is started, the timer will start and is always on the right hand side in blue which is shown in Fig. 6. The questions will be randomly chosen from all topics in the database. The options selected by the user will be saved into the database after user answering the question. If the user does not select any option in a question, that question will be marked as incorrect.

During the test, all answers can be checked and modified by clicking "Back" and "Next" buttons unless the answers are submitted or time is up. The result and correct answers will be shown after the end of test by comparing the correct answer and options user selected which are stored in the database. Users will pass the test if they

answered 16 or more questions (out of 20 questions) correctly and the user
the solution after receiving the result.

3.2 Road Test Part

There are four parts in the road test section which are the driving guidebo
tion, driving steps test and virtual driving test.

3.2.1 Driving Guidebook

The driving guidebook is kind of a driving textbook with some basic dr
niques. There are some driving skills and techniques written in texts whic
the resource file. The content of each topic is shown on pages with the us
slider similar to the theory handbook. Users can swipe the slider or clic
vious" or "Next" button in the action menu bar to turn page. Learners ca
driving steps and skills to have pre-learning before driving a real car or
mind when there is no car for users to drive. Also, there will be some rem
techniques of driving, such as some solutions in different situations, for u
ences.

3.2.2 Driving Steps Test

After studying the driving guidebook, there are some mini game-based test
driving steps sorted by topic. The driving steps of the same topic will be s
arraylist in correct order. After selecting the test topic from menu and en
there are buttons with different driving steps assigned randomly and use
select the step buttons in the correct order. If correct step button is chosen,
driving step on the corresponding button will disappear; else, nothing w
Fig. 7 shows a partially completed test. The timer will start at once the ste
clicked and the time used to finish the test will be shown after all the drivir
selected correctly. All the driving steps will be reassigned randomly and t
be reset if users clicked the restart button. The more the user study, the
time may be used.

3.2.3 Driving Animations

For further demonstration, users can watch the driving animations to und
driving skills shown in the guidebook more clearly which is especially
those who have not driven before to have the fundamental images in m
animations are recorded with Unity player which are the game scenes in
driving tests.

There are three animations including S-shape parking, L-shape parking
the-road driving which are stored in the raw file in resource and one of th

through the whole driving test and there are narrations in Chinese telling the actions that the driver is doing so users can understand the driving steps easily. Also, the animations can be the demonstration of the virtual road tests so the users can know what to do in the virtual road tests with these instructions showing in animations.

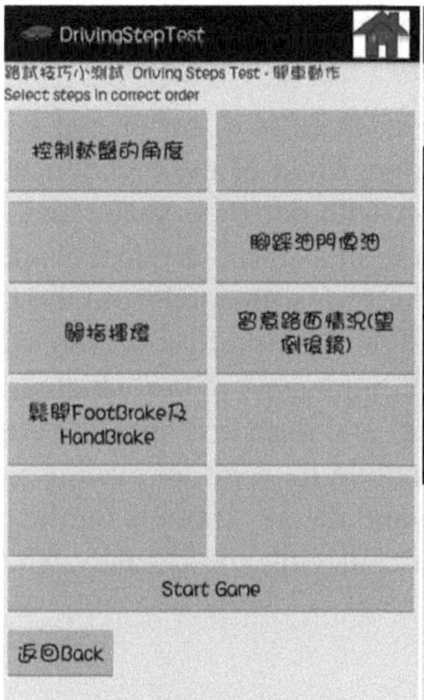

Fig. 7. Half-completed Driving Steps Test

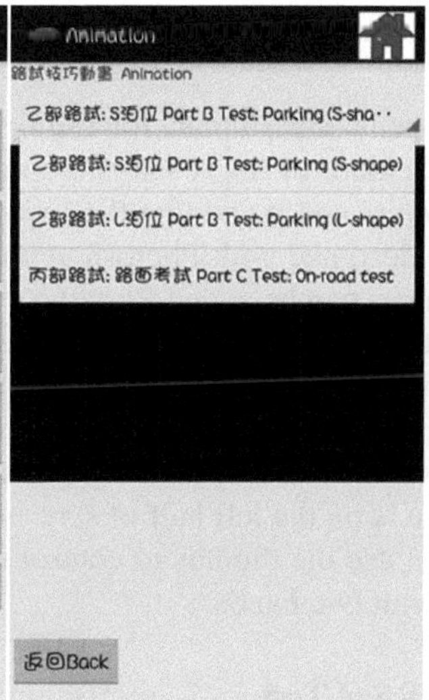

Fig. 8. Driving Animation Dropdown Menu

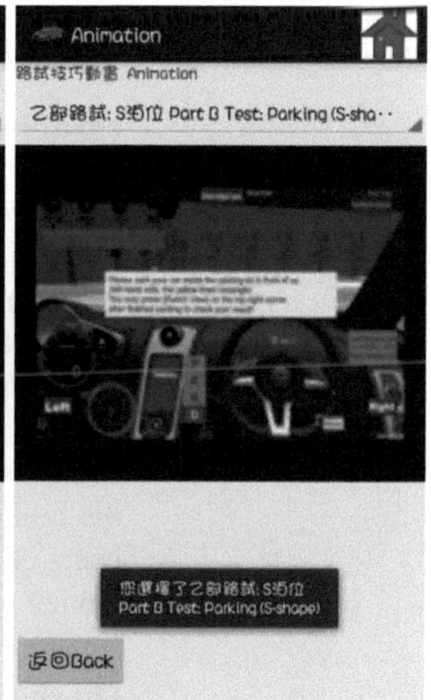

Fig. 9. S-shape parking Animation

3.2.4 Virtual Road Tests

Learners can take the virtual road tests after watching the animations to see if they have studied the guidebook well enough. There are three virtual driving tests which are the L-shape parking test, S-shape parking test and on-the-road test developed with the game engine Unity.

The car used in these tests is not powerful with an automatic transmission although it is designed like a sport car. The car is created by putting different components together such as car engine, glasses, brake and indication lights. Then, adding the accessories to decorate the interior of the car like the steering wheel, rear mirror and dash and speedometer board. Different cameras have to be used for different views like the driver view, rear mirrors view and map view so they have to put in different positions with specific angles of view. A C-sharp (C#) script will be written for each component to handle user input, update the states and do different actions under specific conditions. Finally, the physical settings of the car have to be adjusted and the painting and artwork can be added to make the car look better.

There are two parts in the virtual road tests similar to the real tests, which are the parking test and on-the-road test. Therefore, the settings of the tests are not the same where the parking tests are held in a car park with parking lots and the on-the-road test is held in a city with traffic lights, buildings and street light poles. However, their environments are similar, for example, there is a sun on top with the sam and the texture of the roads is the same. Most of the components in the te ment are created by adding the object with deciding shape and size, and th textures designed with Photoshop on it and set its physical properties. Som components can be added from the assets downloaded from the Unity Asset

The test scenes in all tests are designed as the first-person view which i of the driver and there are the major components of car which are required such as the rear mirror, steering wheel and dash and speedometer board. T wheel is controlled by rotating the mobile device like turning the steering the brake is on the left half of screen and the gas input is on the right half o users can use the thumbs to control the driving speed easily when holding device with two hands.

On-the-Road Test

Users have to follow the driving steps to drive like having driving lessons real car with an instructor so there are instructions and warning given in fo voice and text. During the test, users have to choose the actions in the corre do the right things in different situations. The scripts of each component whether the user is doing correctly. For example, the left indicator light turned on before turning left by turning the steering wheel so there is a indicator light script to check if the correct indicator light is turned on ceived the turning angle from the function of the steering wheel script.

Users will be asked to drive according to the instructor's commands soundtracks will only be played once with text version shown in the scen car is detected in a specific position.

When the mistakes that users have made are detected from all the scripts, they will be sent to the result script and the records will be saved warning voice message will be played like what the examiners or instructo real world and there will be a text box on the scene showing the warning. be reminder when minor mistake is made where Fig. 10 shows as an ex users forget to turn off the indicator light.

If there is any big serious mistake, such as car crash and driving 90km/h, the test will immediately stop and a special menu will show the s take that the user has just made and users may choose to restart or exit th that menu. This mechanism is designed for preventing users misusing this as a car racing game instead of an educational virtual driving practice.

The marking scheme will be similar to the real one where the users there is no big mistake or there are no more than three minor mistakes. script collects all the mistakes detected by different component and integra a clear mark sheet. The final mark sheet will be shown after finishing th showing the numbers of different mistakes have been made during the wh the result of passing the test or not.

Users can get used to the driving test environment and format with a

careful of those mistakes they have made and can practice more on those aspects in real driving lessons.

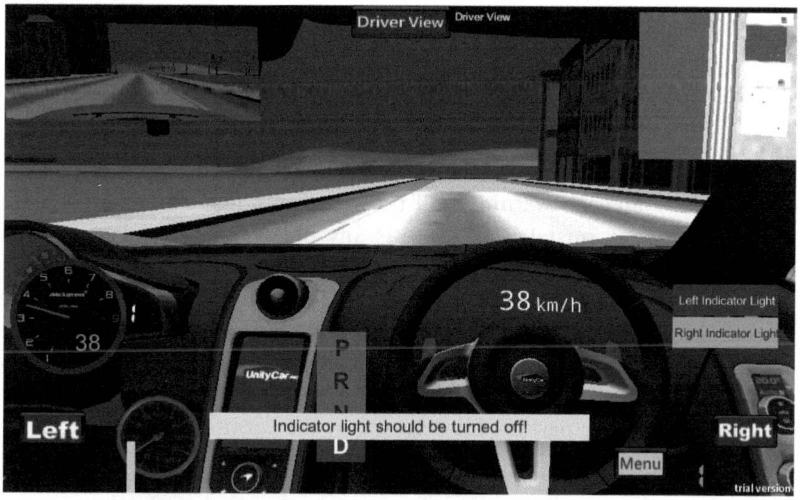

Fig. 10. Examiner's reminder in On-the-road test

Parking Tests

There are two parking tests, L-shape and S-shape parking where Fig. 11 and Fig. 12 show the overview of the car park, for users to choose as different style of parking will be tested in random in the real competence test where Different position of the parking lots need different way to park the car but the control of the car and driving skills are the same.

Fig. 11. S-shape parking test

Fig. 12. L-shape parking test

The target car park lot is always on the left hand side of the users' car and users can make use of the three rear mirrors to help checking the parking position. The driving steps and the control of the car in this test are the same as the virtual on-the-road test where it is similar to the real driving. For example, the car cannot move backwards without gear R and the car should be parked with gear P where those are controlled in the car controller script.

Similar to the virtual on-the-road test, the warning voice message will and the warning will be shown in a text box on the scene when the users any mistakes. If there is any big serious mistake like crashing other car d collision detection, the test will immediately end.

After finishing parking, users can click the "Switch View" button on th corner to get the test result and see if the car is parked correctly by switchin era to the a top view which allows users to overlook the car. Users will pas there is no big mistake and the car is parked inside the lot without touchin of the parking lot detected by the car tires where Fig. 13 shows as an examp

Fig. 13. Passed in the L-shape parking test

4 Evaluation Results and Findings

The purpose of the evaluation is to check the effectiveness of the mobile whether it can help car learners to prepare the driving tests in Hong Kor participants are invited to evaluate the application. There are three kinds of data including the results of tests in the application done by the participants questionnaires and comments from interview. The overall results tend to but there is still room for improvement.

4.1 Evaluation Data

- 90% and 100% of the participants in (Group A) get a better result in Th Test and the Virtual on-the-road Test respectively after revision with t tion for five days.

- The average overall score of the application is 4 out of 5 (80/100).
- Fig. 14 shows that 100%, 50% and 70% of participants agree that the application help in preparing written test, competence test (Part B) and on-the-road (Part C) test in Hong Kong respectively.
- 100% of participants agree that the application helps in preparing the driving tests in Hong Kong and gives basic driving concepts.
- 100%, 75% and 80% of participants believe that the attractiveness of this application is free of charge, multi-purpose (helps in preparing all parts of driving tests) and the multimedia (helps in memorizing) respectively.

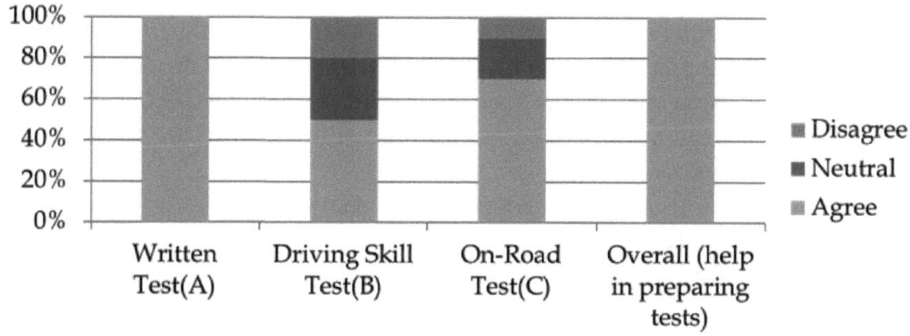

Fig. 14. Participants' attitude toward the help of the application in preparing driving tests in Hong Kong

4.2 Interpretation

The mobile application helps in preparing both the driving theory test and road test in Hong Kong and gives basic driving concepts to learners. Users are quite satisfied with the application with score of 4 out of 5 in average.

This application provides enough materials for car learners to do revision themselves and they may pass the driving tests in Hong Kong easily with better result. The virtual road tests provide a contextual learning which may help learners to learn driving effectively in an interesting way. It is believed that the multimedia in the application can help learners to have long term memory which is in favor of preparing driving tests.

5 Conclusion

In this paper, an Android educational application for car learners to prepare driving tests in Hong Kong is developed. The virtual examiner and the function of detecting driving mistake in virtual road tests is one of the big successes to make the road test practice more useful and realistic. Also, the use of slider layout in the theory practice and handbook greatly reduces the number of activities used and the memory usage because of the decrease of the activities in the stack. It also helps with the file size due to the reduction of coding. The design will be optimized and the application can become more user-friendly.

However, there are some limitations in the virtual road test because tl setting of Unity is slightly different from the real world. For example, th mirrors cannot be shown together in the scene without clicking the button l number of cameras shown in one scene is limited. Also, the road test part v available for the learners who want to learn driving a car with an automati sion due to the lack of driving techniques of the manual one. However driving skills and theories are still useful to all private car learner drivers motorbike learners.

It is suggested that more scenario cases can be added to test the users' re increase their experience for future work. For example, someone runs unde strian red-light or the driving test is held under a special environment or w dition. Also, the results of all the tests and exercises can be saved and s charts so the users may know their weaknesses and practice more on th which can have a better learning outcome and efficiency.

References

1. Ally, M.: Foundations of educational theory for online learning. Theory and Online Learning 2, 15–44 (2004)
2. Imel, S.: Contextual Learning in Adult Education. Practice Application B (2000)
3. Deep River Development LTD. Driving Theory Test(UK) (version 1.3.2) 2013), https://play.google.com/store/apps/details?id=co deepriverdev.carlite
4. Studenttwok HKDrivingWrittenMockExam (version1.0) (2012), https://play.google.com/store/apps/details?id=net.hkl DrivingWrittenMockExam
5. Party Shop Studio: Hong Kong Driving Test (version 2.0.0) (2012), https://play.google.com/store/apps/details?id=air.com .writtentest
6. 易點時空：考駕照 (version 2.1.0) (2013), https://play.goo store/apps/details?id=cn.eclicks.drivingtest
7. Rogers, R., et al.: Android application development: Programming with the G O'Reilly Media, Inc. (2009)
8. Mednieks, Z., et al.: Programming Android: Java Programming for the New G Mobile Devices. O'Reilly (2012)
9. Unity Technologies: Unity (version 4.2.2) (2013), http://unity3d.com/
10. Adobe Systems: Photoshop CS6 (version 13.1.2) (2013), http://www.ad mena_en/products/photoshop.html
11. Owens, M.: The definitive guide to SQLite. Apress (2006)
12. Government of HKSAR: Road Users' Code (2000), http://www.td.go road_safety/road_users_code/index.html
13. Morris, J.: Android User Interface Development: Beginner's Guide; Quickly Develop Compelling User Interfaces for Your Android Applications. Packt Pul (2011)

A Case Study on the Students' Attitude and Acceptance of Mobile Learning

Simon K.S. Cheung

The Open University of Hong Kong
Good Shepherd Street, Homantin, Kowloon, Hong Kong
kscheung@ouhk.edu.hk

Abstract. Transcending the time and geographical constraints of traditional classroom-based learning, mobile learning allows students to study anywhere and at any time. Learning is facilitated, and students generally welcome this flexible mode of learning. According to a study recently conducted by the Open University of Hong Kong, mobile learning is effective for enhancing language proficiency. This paper reports the results of this case study. In brief, it is found that students generally show a positive attitude towards mobile learning and its effectiveness in learning languages. There is a significant acceptance among students towards mobile learning, especially on the usefulness, efficiency, interactivity and convenience. The results further affirm that mobile learning can be an effective means to delivering language proficiency courses, not only for its accessibility from virtually anywhere and allowing the students to learn at any time, but also for enriching learning experience and arousing learning interest by making good use of multimedia components and features.

Keywords: mobile learning, e-learning, online learning, students' acceptance, learning effectiveness, learning experience.

1 Introduction

Evolved as a new mode of learning, mobile learning is usually regarded as a logical extension or a variety of e-learning or online learning that possesses the potentials to further expand and make learning available anywhere and anytime through mobile or portable devices [1][2]. In the past decade, with the advent of new mobile devices (mobile phones, smart phones, tablets, etc.) offering sophisticated functional features, students become adapted to mobile learning.

Mobile learning essentially transforms the learning process and changes the ways of learning. A number of unique advantages and pedagogical outcomes are identified, as reported in the literature [3][4][5][6][7]. In summary, mobile learning creates learning opportunities beyond the traditional classrooms, offers flexibility and mobility in learning, expands learning experience in terms of time and space, facilitates the communications and interactions among teachers and students, and encourages collaborative learning and group learning.

K.C. Li et al. (Eds.): ICTE 2014, CCIS 494, pp. 45–54, 2015.

According to Cheung et al., there are three factors for successful adopt bile learning, namely, technological feasibility of mobile learning, learner flexible learning, and pedagogical benefits [8]. Similarly, Poon and Koo the students' behaviour, technology or system, and interactive application a factors influencing the readiness of mobile learning [9]. Also, according mides, the students' learning needs and learning quality are important con for mobile learning [10].

In Hong Kong, the advent of telecommunication, broadband and wirele infrastructure has provided the opportunities for mobile learning. Accor Census and Statistics, in November 2013, 81.9% households had personal at home [11]. For those households with personal computers at home, connections to the Internet. 59.3% had portable or notebook computers w had tablet devices. As revealed in a survey conducted in the Open Universi Kong, mobile devices are popular among its students, no matter pursuin studies or distance-learning studies [12][13]. Nearly all the students own devices, and about half of them owned more than one device. The high rates, especially on students, imply the readiness of mobile learning in Hon

In the past two years, the Open University of Hong Kong has develope of mobile learning modules with an aim to enhance the Chinese and Englis efficicncy of students. Target for the first-year students of the University, bile learning modules essentially cover a wide range of language eleme vocabulary, grammar rules, sentence structure, advanced level syntax a conversation techniques, and the basic language skills. Combined with s made practices and scenario-based contents, each module is designed t students' individual language learning needs. All the modules are presente format, allowing students to learn in a mobile environment. They are co with multimedia and interactive materials. Students' learning progress is e a continuous assessment.

The mobile learning modules were deployed in 2013, and trial used by 159 students of the University. An evaluative survey comprising questio interview was conducted, immediately after the deployment of the mobi modules. Among the first batch of 159 students taking the modules, a tota dents agreed to participate in the survey. One purpose of the survey is to the students' attitude and acceptance of mobile learning for language lea survey results clearly show the students' positive attitude towards mobile le its effectiveness in language learning. The results also show a significant among students towards mobile learning, especially on the usefulness, interactivity and convenience. This paper reports the survey results and s findings on the students' attitude and acceptance of mobile learning fo learning.

The rest of this paper is structured as follows. Section 2 gives the bac the four mobile learning modules in the study. Section 3 describes the eva vey and reports the survey results with a discussion of the findings. Sectic

2 Mobile Learning Modules for Language Learning

This section provides a background on the four mobile learning modules developed by the Open University of Hong Kong for enhancing language efficiency of students. The functional components of these language modules are described, with a highlight on the design features.

In 2011, the Open University of Hong Kong successfully secured a grant from the Government for developing four mobile learning modules for enhancing the language proficiency of students [14]. Primarily targeted for the first-year students of the University, these languages modules are in the areas of English for communication, the use of Chinese and English, and the command of Putonghua, as highlighted below.

- *English for Effective Communication.* This module aims to enhance the students' understanding of advanced level grammar rules and sentence structures, and provide practice to improve their listening and writing skills for effective communication in English.
- *Business Communication for Executives.* This module aims to develop the students' basic and advanced level Business English. Practical workplace topics are included to prepare students for their careers, such as handling electronic mails, preparing meeting notes, writing proposals and giving presentations.
- *Use of Chinese.* This module aims to sharpen the students' reading and writing skills in formal Chinese language. Some advanced level syntax and idioms are also covered in the module to improve sentence composition and reading comprehension.
- *Use of Putonghua.* This module aims to enhance students' understanding of advanced sentence structures and vocabulary in Putonghua. Scenario-based content is included for effective communication in travel, dining, job interview and shopping.

The mobile learning modules are presented in e-book format, readily readable in Apple devices such as iPhone and iPad. They can be downloaded through the Apple iTunesU [15]. The modules use context-based contents and adopt an interactive approach to learning languages. Multimedia materials are incorporated to enrich the students' learning experience. Intended for mobile learning, students can study at their own pace without time and space constraints. The modules encourage collaborative learning among students. A virtual environment (including an online discussion forum and an online platform for interactive communications among teachers and students) conducive to collaborative learning and group learning is provided to enhance the students' learning efficiency.

The design features of these modules are summarized as follows.

- Use of context-based contents, together with multimedia, animations and graphical elements;
- Provision of interactive and game-based learning activities, and recording exercise and interaction summary;
- Continuous assessments for monitoring learning progress;
- Provision of a discussion forum for students to discuss and share useful learning experience.

3 Evaluative Survey

The mobile learning modules were deployed in 2013, and trial used by 1
of the University. The students were invited to participate a survey on co
study. A total of 61 students agreed to participate by completing a questic
attending an interview. In this section, the questions of the survey are repor
findings are discussed.

3.1 Survey Questions and Responses

There are 16 questions relevant to the study on students' attitude and acc
mobile learning. These questions and the responses are listed below.

Q1. How often did you study the modules?

Frequency	% of respondents
Every day	5%
Once to twice a week	79%
Three to four times a week	16%
Five to six times a week	0%
More than six times a week	0%

Q2. Where did you usually study the modules?

Location	% of respondents
Classroom	2%
Library	3%
Other School settings (e.g. canteen)	8%
On the move	13%
Home and other settings (e.g. dinning place)	74%

Q3. Which part(s) of the modules do you like the most (select all that a

Parts or components	% of respondents
Audio component	36%
Case scenario	44%
Online discussion forum	0%
Practice activity	44%
Vocabulary section	41%
Interactive summary	25%
Other features (recording, dictionary, etc.)	31%

Q4. I think it is convenient to learn a language by using mobile device(s).

Responses	% of respondents
Strongly agree	25%
Agree	62%
Neutral	11%
Disagree	2%
Strongly disagree	0%

Q5. I think it is effective to learn a language by using mobile device(s).

Responses	% of respondents
Strongly agree	13%
Agree	52%
Neutral	31%
Disagree	3%
Strongly disagree	0%

Q6. I think the mobile learning module is interactive.

Responses	% of respondents
Strongly agree	15%
Agree	46%
Neutral	31%
Disagree	8%
Strongly disagree	0%

Q7. I think the interactive exercises are effective to help learn the concepts.

Responses	% of respondents
Strongly agree	13%
Agree	70%
Neutral	15%
Disagree	2%
Strongly disagree	0%

Q8. I think the scenario-based learning is effective to help learn the concepts.

Responses	% of respondents
Strongly agree	13%
Agree	66%
Neutral	20%
Disagree	2%
Strongly disagree	0%

Q9. I think the design features (e.g. note-taking, bookmark, audio re
the mobile learning module are useful to assist learning.

Responses	% of respondents
Strongly agree	8%
Agree	64%
Neutral	25%
Disagree	3%
Strongly disagree	0%

Q10. I think mobile learning can enhance my overall academic perfor

Responses	% of respondents
Strongly agree	2%
Agree	43%
Neutral	49%
Disagree	7%
Strongly disagree	0%

Q11. I think using the mobile learning module(s) for study enhanc
guage proficiency.

Responses	% of respondents
Strongly agree	0%
Agree	70%
Neutral	26%
Disagree	3%
Strongly disagree	0%

Q12. I think the mobile learning module arouses my interest and m
self-study.

Responses	% of respondents
Strongly agree	11%
Agree	56%
Neutral	23%
Disagree	10%
Strongly disagree	0%

Q13. I think my level of engagement using the mobile learning module for language learning was high.

Responses	% of respondents
Strongly agree	3%
Agree	48%
Neutral	41%
Disagree	8%
Strongly disagree	0%

Q14. I think my level of satisfaction using the mobile learning module for language learning is high.

Responses	% of respondents
Strongly agree	7%
Agree	59%
Neutral	33%
Disagree	2%
Strongly disagree	0%

Q15. I enjoy self-paced learning by using the mobile learning module.

Responses	% of respondents
Strongly agree	18%
Agree	64%
Neutral	16%
Disagree	2%
Strongly disagree	0%

Q16. I think this learning experience with the mobile learning modules adds value to my overall school performance.

Responses	% of respondents
Strongly agree	3%
Agree	51%
Neutral	43%
Disagree	3%
Strongly disagree	0%

3.2 Findings from the Survey Results

(a) Most of the respondents study the modules once or twice a week
in Q1. According to Q2, they usually study at home and other fix
such as a dining place. Only 13% of the respondents usually st
move, and 5% of the respondents usually study in a place for se
such as a classroom and library. These show that mobile learning i
in a fixed setting but not a place for serious study.

(b) According to Q3, respondents mostly like audio components and
activities as well as case scenario and practice activities. Howev
not interested in the online discussion forum. This reflects that cc
learning and group learning are not adopted.

(c) Most of the respondents considered that mobile learning made lea
convenient and effective, as shown in Q4 and Q5. According to (
they generally agreed that mobile learning is interactive and that
activities are effective for learning. They considered scenario-bas
and other features (such as note-taking, bookmark and dictionary)
understanding the concepts, as shown in Q8 and Q9.

(d) When asked whether the mobile learning modules could enhanc
performance in Q10, about half of the respondents (49%) respon
while another 45% strongly agreed or agreed. However, more r
(70%) agreed that the mobile learning modules could enhance the
proficiency, as shown in Q11. This implies a discrepancy in th
views on the learning effectiveness between academic performan
guage proficiency enhancement.

(e) According to Q12, more than half of the respondents strongly
agreed that the mobile learning modules could arouse their interes
tivate self-study. When asking on the learning engagement in Q13
of the respondents (51%) strongly agreed or agreed that the level
ment in mobile learning was high while another 41% consider
These show that mobile learning can arouse learning interest an
self-study and help engage learning.

(f) Based on Q14 and Q15, the respondents generally agreed that t
satisfaction was high in learning language through the mobile lea
ules. They also consider the mobile learning modules added posi
to their overall learning experience, as indicated in Q16. These d
that mobile learning can raise learning satisfaction and enrich
learning experience.

4 Conclusion

Mobile learning has become a reality that makes learning available any
anytime. As claimed in many researchers and practitioners, mobile learn

tiveness of mobile learning for enhancing the language proficiency of students. This paper reported some results of this study, which is on the students' attitude and acceptance of mobile learning in language learning.

It is found that the students generally show a positive attitude towards mobile learning and its effectiveness in language learning. Most of them considered mobile learning made learning convenient and effective, and agreed that mobile learning could arouse learning interest and motivate self-study and help engage learning. Mobile learning could also raise the students' learning satisfaction and enrich or expand their learning experience.

While the findings are mostly positive, it is also revealed that the students prefer mobile learning to take place at home or a fixed setting but other than a place for serious study. They do not usually study on the move, such as walking on street, or riding on transportation. Besides, some features designed for collaborative learning or group learning, such as the online discussion forum, are not popular as compared to other online interactive features, such as multimedia elements, interactive summary, case scenario and practice activities.

The findings further affirm that mobile learning can be an effective means to delivering language proficiency courses, not only for its flexibility to learn anywhere and at any time but also for enriching the learning experience and arousing learning interests by making good use of interactive and multimedia components. However, it is not clear whether mobile learning can encourage collaborative learning or group learning. These findings would provide a reference for researchers and practitioners in designing and deploying mobile learning modules.

Acknowledgement. The author would like to acknowledge the support of the Education Bureau of the Government of Hong Kong SAR in offering a grant of HK$1.5 million under the Quality Enhancement Grant Scheme for the project "Development of Four Mobile Learning Modules to Enhance the Language Proficiency of Students" in 2011. This paper reports the findings of an evaluation study based on the project. It is noted that the author is one of the Principal Investigators of the project.

References

1. Ellis, K.: Moving into M-Learning. Training Journal 40(10), 56 (2003)
2. Winters, N.: What is Mobile Learning? In: Sharples, M. (ed.) Big Issues in Mobile Learning, Report of a Workshop by the Kaleidoscope Network of Excellence Mobile Learning Initiative, University of Nottingham, pp. 7–11 (2007)
3. Lam, J., Yau, J., Cheung, S.K.S.: A Review of Mobile Learning in the Mobile Age. In: Tsang, P., Cheung, S.K.S., Lee, V.S.K., Huang, R. (eds.) ICHL 2010. LNCS, vol. 6248, pp. 306–315. Springer, Heidelberg (2010)
4. Muyinda, P.B., Lubega, J.T., Lynch, K.: Unleashing Mobile Phones for Research Supervision Support at Makerere University, Uganda: The Lessons Learned. International Journal of innovation and Learning 7(1), 14–34 (2010)
5. Peng, H., et al.: Ubiquitous Knowledge Construction: Mobile Learning Re-defined and a Conceptual Framework. Innovations in Education and Teaching 46(2), 171–183 (2009)

6. Sharples, M., Taylor, J., Vavoula, G.: A Theory of Learning for the Mobi
Andrews, R., Haythornthwaite, C. (eds.) The Sage Handbook of e-Learnin
pp. 221–247. Springer (2007)
7. Traxler, J.: Defining, Discussing and Evaluating Mobile Learning: The Mo
Writes and Have Writ... The International Review of Research in Open a
Learning 8(2), 17–28 (2007)
8. Cheung, S.K.S., Yuen, K.S., Tsang, E.: A Study on the Readiness of Mobile
Open Education. In: Proceedings of the IEEE International Symposium on IT
and Education, pp. 133–136. IEEE Press (2011)
9. Poon, W.C., Koo, A.C.: Mobile Learning: The Economics Perspective. I
Journal of Innovation and Learning 7(4), 412–429 (2010)
10. Economides, A.A.: Requirements of Mobile Learning Applications. Internati
of Innovation and Learning 5(5), 457-49 (2008)
11. Census and Statistics: Thematic Household Survey on Personal Computer
Penetration, Report No. 53, Census and Statistics Department, The Governm
Kong SAR (November 2013)
12. Cheung, S.K.S.: A Study on the Use of Mobile Devices for Distance L
Cheung, S.K.S., Fong, J., Kwok, L.-F., Li, K., Kwan, R. (eds.) ICHL 2
vol. 7411, pp. 89–98. Springer, Heidelberg (2012)
13. Cheung, S.K.S.: A Survey on the Use of Mobile Devices for Learning Purpo
tional Journal of Innovation and Learning 16(2), 192–202 (2014)
14. Yuen, K.S., Cheung, S.K.S.: Development of Four Mobile Learning Modules
the Language Proficiency of Students, Funded Project, Quality Enhance
Scheme, Education Bureau of the Government of Hong Kong SAR (2011),
http://www.ipass.gov.hk/eng/55A2011.pdf
15. iTunes U: Website of Apple's iPad in Education – the iTuneU Courses (2014),
http://www.apple.com/education/ipad/itunes-u/

Wearable Technology in Education: From Handheld to Hands-Free Learning

Daniyar Sapargaliyev

Almaty Management University
227, Rozybakiyev Str., Almaty, Kazakhstan
dsapargalieff@gmail.com

Abstract. The use of wearable computers in education can significantly help teachers and students in the near future. Last years we can observe the appearance of new wearable devices such as bracelets, clothing, watches, and glasses. One of the most popular wearable computers is Google Glass. In our article we will try to analyse a number of quantitative and qualitative researches on the use of wearable devices in teaching and learning. We found that Google Glass successfully using in pharmacology and healthcare. The Google Glass allows the teacher to demonstrate the practical skills (such as a doctor performs surgery) for the students in real time from any places. In spite of the fact that Google Glass has some technological limitations, any learner needs only a short adaptation period for comfortable usage. The Google Glass helps to create seamless interaction between educators and learners.

Keywords: wearable technology, Google Glass, handheld devices, hands-free devices.

1 Introduction

It is becoming increasingly difficult to ignore the wide dissemination wearable technology in everyday life. First wearable computer was invented and tested in the early 1960s of the twentieth century. Then this cigarette pack sized analog device was used for predictions in the roulette game [1]. Today, various types of wearable computers (such as bracelets, clothing, watches, and glasses) are used in medical centers, libraries and universities.

One of the most significant current discussions in mobile or handheld learning is the use of wearable technology in education. As Kukulska-Hulme argues: 'mobile learning is taking on new qualities and characteristics as devices become ever more integrated with everyday life and wearables intensify the increasingly close relationship between people and technology' [2].

In fact, one of the most popular wearable devices is Google Glass. This computer displays information in a smartphone-like hands-free format that can interact with the Internet via natural language voice commands [3].

K.C. Li et al. (Eds.): ICTE 2014, CCIS 494, pp. 55–60, 2015.

Nowadays, a wearable device such as Google Glass allowing people to flow of everyday life and link these experiences to resources such as we information sources [4].

The purpose of this paper is to review recent researches into the use c technology in medicine and higher education.

2 Literature Review

More recently, literature has emerged that offers some findings about usin devices in different areas (Table 1). A number of studies have found tha computers help to seamlessly integrate consumers' bodies into network inf and virtual world [5][6][7]. Moreover, Pedersen argues that wearable strives to change human-centric interaction with computers [8]. Starner i how to create interfaces for technology which are designed for creating "mi tions" to fit a user's lifestyle [9].

Table 1. Possibilities of wearable technology

Wearables allows…	Authors	Key words and ideas
To integrate consumers' bodies into network infrastructure	Gates, 2013	Wearable technology is designed to literal bodies more seamlessly with devices.
	Pace, 2013	Wearable devices will empower users or them from reality.
	Norman, 2013	Paradox of wearable technologies and myt tasking.
To change human-centric interaction	Pedersen, 2013	Dehumanizing representations and hu interaction with wearable computers.
To create interactions to fit a user's lifestyle	Starner, 2013	Design principles for creating "microir with wearable devices.
To use it in augmented reality games and services	Ackerman, 2013	Wearable technology could lead to an unp loss of control over personal information.
	Campbell, 2013	It was designed a game that puts a Go wearer in the role of an ant in a colony.
	Furlan, 2013	The use of wearable technology will enab a wide range of augmented cognition appli
	Wang *et al.*, 2013	Wearable devices could be effectively us enabling humancentric augmented reality.
To explain the expectations of society in privacy issues	Hong, 2013	Gap in the community's understanding in wearable computers.

to explain the expectations of society in privacy issues of using Google Glass and other wearable computers [14]. However, the practical using of wearable technology (such as Google Glass) can be found in two main areas: medicine and higher education.

2.1 Wearable Devices in Medicine

Medicine is one of the most successful areas where wearable technology can be used. Many medical centers have already tested Google Glass in its daily practice. For example, Fox & Felkey described their experiences with Google Glass in a medical center and suggested ways how it can be used in the hospital pharmacy setting [15]. The another researcher, Marks studied the ways of using Google Glass in healthcare, such as helping to predict glucose levels in the food of diabetics [16].

Some researchers consider the functionality of Google Glass to create a new medical applications and software. For example, Wiltz analysed the medical application for Google Glass that allows doctors and nurses to look up patient records through voice command or by taking a picture of the patient's face [17]. The author argues that face recognition is the most efficient way to bring up data relevant to helping the wearer in many use cases. Jonas *et al.* propose a novel concept of system for supporting everyday clinical pathways with Google Glass [18]. The system supports clinical staff as a documenting observer and has the capability to boost clinical care.

2.2 Using Google Glass in Medical Education

Medical faculties of the universities are the most frequent places where Google Glass is using in teaching and learning. A professor of medicine can use wearable technology for training students with real time video. For example, Vallurupalli *et al.* conducted the experiment with the use of live video stream from the professor's Google Glass which was transmitted to the mobile devices of students [19]. The authors concluded that wearable technology has great potential to enhance medical education in the near future. Another scientist, Glauser points out how students watched medical procedure in real time from Google Glass video camera [20]. The physicians are excited about how Glass could revolutionize medical education. The wearable camera is also a helpful educational tool when it puts on a patient or mannequin. Because the camera allowing residents to view the bedside manner from the patient's perspective. In same time, Wu *et al.* found that Google Glass is successfully integrated into simulation-based training exercises without disrupting the medical students' experience [21].

2.3 Hands-Free Learning

Wearable technology allows teacher and student to better collaborate between each other by using hands-free devices. Llorente & Morant highlight the need to use interconnected devices such as Google Glass in higher education [22]. The authors suggested that professors can communicate with a large computing infrastructure, which can be data-mined to monitor the knowledge-building process. Additionally, wearable computers have unique research and information discovery potential in u universities' libraries [23].

Nevertheless, Penny & Schugar had claimed that Google Glass has spa of curiosity and skepticism in education [24]. The authors consider th should understand how to use wearable devices in the classroom and pron digital citizenship and responsibility. However, Buchem & Pérez-Sanagu that the type of educational transmission from an eye-level perspective a educators and learners to capture the surrounding environment and particip time activities [25]. The learners can link physical and virtual learning participate in global learning activities.

3 Discussion

This study set out with the aim of assessing the importance of using weara in education. Wearable technologies can bring into our lives a number of involve matters of network security, privacy and health. However, the larg can occur in methods of communication between users of wearable devices ly it will be noticeable in the learning and teaching.

How will the emergence of Google Glass impact on the learning proc work in the classroom? Perhaps the teacher can easily get instant inform any student just looking at him through augmented reality glasses. Thes features of wearable technology can greatly simplify the process of getting information at any time. But probably such devices violate personal spac demic freedom of students.

We think that wearable technology is allowing the opportunities that sho improve the relationship between students and a teacher. We should pay tion to changes in the daily lives of the students who will use Google C university. Some features of the Google Glass (such as video recording and be used in a secretive mode. Thus, the using of these devices will entail a violation of privacy and increase mistrust among students to each other.

Wearable device (such as Google Glass) can become a "Trojan horse" in which will destroy the atmosphere of academic freedom at the universiti the constant presence of a teacher or a student in the information flow v their attention on learning and teaching.

On the other hand, thoughtful actions and rules of using Google Glass environment can significantly improve the process of getting knowledge. ple, using Google Glass will free the hands of the professor for demon practical skills by broadcasting live video to surgical students around the dents can interact with each other in different locations (a library, an au concert hall, a stadium and other places) by using hands-free devices and i understanding in practical exercises.

In general, therefore, it seems that we need to further study the implica Google Glass in education. This technology is just starting to penetrate at sities and this paper has examined the role of Google Glass as a new lear

4 Conclusion

The emergence of new technologies in the classroom is almost always associated with high expectations of its effective implementation. But very often, new technologies do not immediately show their advantages and disadvantages. In the case of wearable technology, the expectations of teachers and students will be matched. Wearable devices provide unrestricted access to information, together with the hands-free use voice control and the possibility of changing the position of the bodies anytime. This freedom allows professors and students to interact in a more seamless mode and at the same time creates the illusion of easy access to the knowledge and practical skills. The permanent interaction and teaching support can significantly improve the academic achievements, but at the same time can reduce the ability for independent learning. Here is the problem of the correct use of wearable technology that should justify many positive expectations of professors and students in the classroom and everywhere.

References

1. Thorp, E.O.: The Invention of the First Wearable Computer. In: Proceedings of the 2nd IEEE International Symposium on Wearable Computers, pp. 4–8 (1998)
2. Kukulska-Hulme, A.: Mobile, Wearable, Companionable: Emerging technological challenges and incentives for learning. Encontro sobre Jogos e Mobile Learning, pp. 12–15. CIEd, Braga (2014)
3. Google: Google Glass (2014), `https://www.google.com/glass/start/what-it-does/`
4. Sharples, M., McAndrew, P., Weller, M., Ferguson, R., FitzGerald, E., Hirst, T., Gaved, M.: Innovating Pedagogy. Open University (2013)
5. Gates, K.: Key Questions for Communication and Critical-Cultural Studies: Posthumanism, Network Infrastructures, and Sustainability. Communication and Critical/ Cultural Studies 10(2-3), 242–247 (2013)
6. Norman, D.: The paradox of wearable technologies. Technology Review 116(5), 101–103 (2013)
7. Pace, S.: Looking at innovation through CCT glasses: Consumer culture theory and Google glass innovation. Journal of Innovation Management 1(1), 38–54 (2013)
8. Pedersen, I.: Ready to wear (or not): Examining the rhetorical impact of proposed wearable devices. In: International Symposium on Technology and Society Proceedings, Toronto, pp. 201–202 (2013)
9. Starner, T.: Wearable computing: through the looking glass. In: Proceedings of the 17th Annual International Symposium on International Symposium on Wearable Computers, pp. 125–126. ACM (2013)
10. Ackerman, E.: Google gets in your face: Google Glass offers a slightly augmented version of reality. IEEE Spectrum 50(1), 26–29 (2013)
11. Campbell, M.: Hive-mind solves tasks using Google Glass ant game. New Scientist 219(2928), 20 (2013)
12. Furlan, R.: Google Glass this wearable computer augments the self, not reality. IEEE Spectrum 50(10), 24 (2013)

13. Wang, H., Bao, X., Choudhury, R.R., Nelakuditi, S.: InSight: Recognizing hun face recognition. In: ACM HotMobile 2013: The 14th Workshop on Mobile Systems and Applications (2013)
14. Hong, J.: Considering privacy issues in the context of Google Glass. Commu the ACM 56(11), 10–11 (2013)
15. Fox, B., Felkey, B.: Potential uses of Google Glass in the pharmacy. Hospit 48(9), 783–784 (2013)
16. Marks, P.: A healthy dose of Google Glass. New Scientist 219(2936), 22–23 (2
17. Wiltz, C.: Google glass bans facial recognition, sets medical apps back. Me and Diagnostic Industry 35(6) (2013)
18. Jonas, S., Hannig, A., Spreckelsen, C., Deserno, T.M.: Wearable technology of clinical care. In: Medical Imaging 2014: PACS and Imaging Informatics: N tion and Innovations (2014)
19. Vallurupalli, S., Paydak, H., Agarwal, S.K., Agrawal, M., Assad-Kottner, C technology to improve education and patient outcomes in a cardiology fellows - A feasibility study. Health and Technology 3(4), 267–270 (2013)
20. Glauser, W.: Doctors among early adopters of Google Glass. Canadian Medi tion Journal 109 (2013)
21. Wu, T., Dameff, C., Tully, J.: Integrating Google Glass into simulation-ba experiences and future directions. Journal of Biomedical Graphics and Con 49–54 (2014)
22. Llorente, R., Morant, M.: Wearable Computers and Big Data: Interaction Pa Knowledge Building in Higher Education. Innovation and Teaching Techno Directions in Research, Practice and Policy, 127–137 (2014)
23. Booth, C., Brecher, D.: Ok, library. Implications and opportunities for Go College & Research Libraries News 75(5), 234–239 (2014)
24. Penny, C., Schugar, J.: Ok Class...Google Glass in Education. In: Searson, M. (eds.) Proceedings of Society for Information Technology & Teacher Educa tional Conference, pp. 2059–2060. AACE, Chesapeake (2014)
25. Buchem, I., Pérez-Sanagustín, M.: Personal Learning Environments in S Current Approaches and Future Scenarios

A Parse Tree Based Computation Technique for Generating Comprehension Style Questions from Chinese Text

Andrew Kwok-Fai Lui, Sin-Chun Ng, and Yin-Chun Fung

School of Science and Technology, The Open University of Hong Kong
30 Good Shepherd Street, Ho Man Tin, Kowloon, Hong Kong SAR, China
alui@ouhk.edu.hk

Abstract. This paper describes our research and development work on a computational method that takes a piece of Chinese unstructured text and generates a set of questions and answers as the output. Our method is largely based on Heilman & Smith's over-generation approach [1] and is included with techniques specific for handling Chinese text. Using the syntactic and semantic features identified in a sentence, various question types can be generated with answers also available. Automatic question generation is potentially a key component in future intelligent e-learning systems, but it is also a very challenging problem. A major objective of this work is to investigate technical issues and limitations that would provide direction of future research.

Keywords: question generation, question taxonomy, online learning.

1 Introduction

Text reading remains a main activity in many types of learning scenarios, despite the widespread adoption of multimedia learning where pictures, animations, and videos providing learners with other dimensions of learning experience. Education psychologies have recognized that text content and visual content have difference uses for different purposes, and texts as descriptive representations have higher representation power than visual materials [2]. However, effective text comprehension depends on a number of readers' characteristics such as vocabulary identification, background knowledge, and structural awareness [3]. An active and effective reader knows how to make connection with text, but many second school students and even university students are not capable readers. To help students comprehend their text-based learning materials, teachers should develop strategies to increase student-text interaction [4][5].

Asking readers relevant questions can promote intrinsic reading motivation and reading engagement [6]. It can also prepare readers with a focus to search for core information as they read. The *Do You Know* feature in the online encyclopedia Wikipedia is a prime example of attracting visitors to read selected articles. This paper describes our research and development work on computational question generation methods that take a piece of text as an input and generate a set of questions as the output. Computational question generation is a relatively new research area that aims

K.C. Li et al. (Eds.): ICTE 2014, CCIS 494, pp. 61–73, 2015.

at reducing or eliminating human effort in creating questions for variou scenarios. Our work focuses on generating questions from good quality u Chinese text, thus in the long run we aim at providing tools for future e-le tems enhanced with question-guided learning.

1.1 Background

Computational question generation is becoming a crucial component in online learning delivery modes for its ability to generate large amount o with reduced or no human effort. It can potentially generate various ques such as factual or discussion questions, on different topics found in the t different difficulty levels. A teacher can then choose and refine the questio sion or assessment. In fully automated mode, computational question gen provide assessment questions needed in intelligent tutoring systems, adap systems, and even Massively Open Online Courses (MOOCS) platform potential application is for vicarious learning, where observing a dialogue ered to be beneficial to learning [7][8]. Converting a piece of plain text of discourse into a question and answer format is one useful way of produ logue between two avatars.

The focus of this work is in generating questions from unstructured te already literature on generating questions from structured data in databas tionaries. On the other hand, papers on generating questions from English t and began to appear only recently. In the following we briefly describe existing approaches: article-based definitional question generation and sent factoid question generation based on over-generation approach.

Kalady, Elikkottil, & Das proposed a method to generate definitiona (see Figure 1) [9]. Definitional questions challenge people to answer the d a concept. The main approach is to look for keywords (called up-keys), used to determine the corresponding question-word for the generation of There are a number of statistical based methods to discover suitable keywo

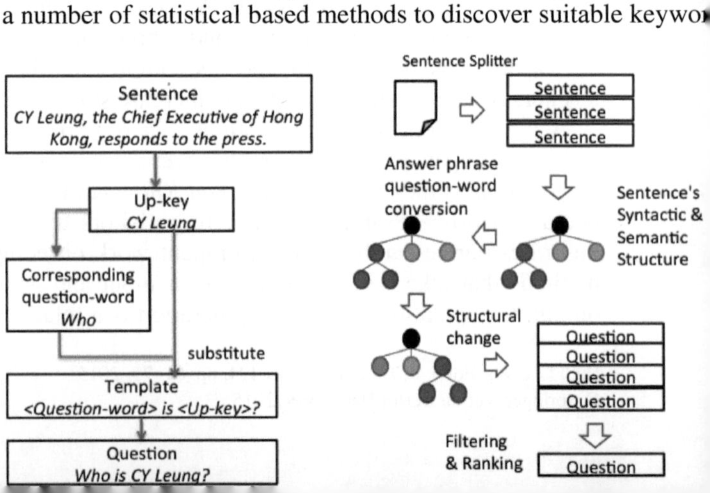

Heilman & Smith proposed a sentence-based approach that generates questions asking for facts [1]. The generation of question begins with replacing answer phrases with appropriate question-word in every sentences and then reordering the sentence parts to form a question. This is called an over-generation method, because there are some valid and many invalid questions generated, and a ranker or filter at is needed at the end to select the valid questions. Generating high-level questions and open ended questions is less likely but this method is more consistent and stable than then the first method.

2 Question Generation from Chinese Text

This section describes our method of automatic question generation from Chinese unstructured text. The method is largely based on the over-generation approach proposed by Heilman & Smith [1] and in our research work we have investigated how the various stages in Heilman & Smith's approach can be adapted for processing Chinese text. Results and discussions can be found in Section 4.

2.1 Overview

Our method works on the structure and semantics at the sentence level to identify potential features that characterizes seven types of questions. Five of them belong to the description (concept completion) question type and the other two are explanation question types as defined in the question taxonomy by Nielsen et al. [10]. Each Chinese sentence is turned into a tree structure called a parse tree, which describes the superordinate-subordinate relation between terms and phrases. Potential questions are identified based on specific patterns of the parse tree or its parts. The generation of explanation question types also exploits the existence of keyword markers such as因為 (*because*) 所以 (*therefore*).

2.2 System Architecture

Figure 2 shows the architecture of a prototype system based on the automatic question generation method.

Our method begins with refining source text into a form suitable for question generation. The source text should be in plain Unicode format made up of traditional or simplified Chinese characters and punctuations. The *Sentence Splitter* converts the source text into a set of sentences based on punctuations, and each sentence will become the unit of processing in the later stages. The *Parser* then analyses each sentence and produces a parse tree, which depicts the semantic relation between phrases and terms, as well as the part-of-speech (i.e. noun, verb, preposition, etc.) and the entity type (i.e. person, organization, etc.) of each term. These recognized semantic features inform the two *Question Generators* the potential questions and the question type, but because it could happen, the *Sentence Pre-processor* attempts to prune the parse tree to remove irrelevant parts, and to extract independent sub-parts of a sentence. The two *Question Generators* are designed to *over-generate* questions, which produce a lot of poorly structured questions as well as some good ones. Th *Filter* selects the good questions from the poor ones based on rules and patt

Figure 3 illustrates the function of the Parser and an example of a parse represents this Chinese sentence "在室町時代，兵庫津作為日明貿易的據點 際港口。" from Chinese Wikipedia article titled "神户市".

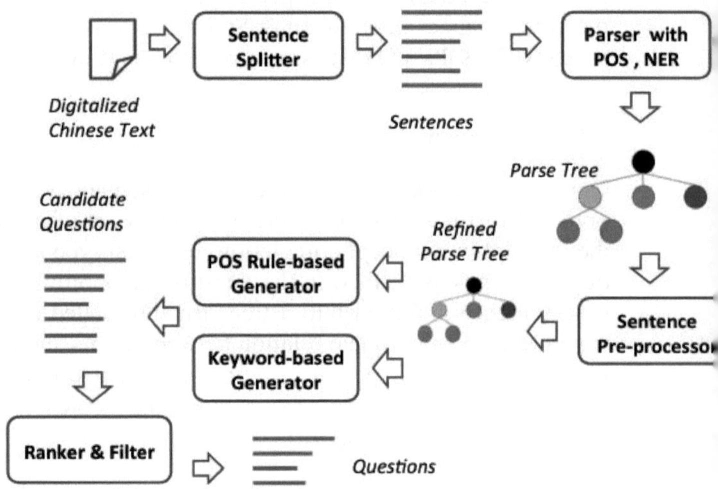

Fig. 2. System architecture of our Chinese automatic question generato

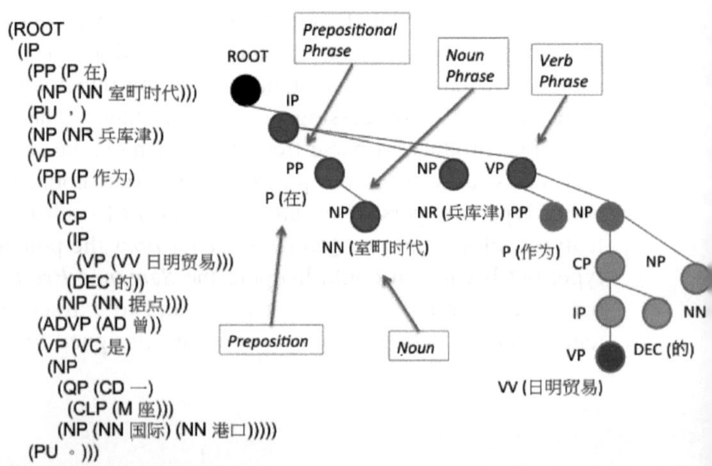

Fig. 3. The parse tree on the left is displayed with nodes in brackets and the depth

The above Chinese sentence, terminated by a full stop, consists of two sub-sentences separated by a comma. The parse tree carries key relational information between terms, such as室町时代 (i.e. an era in Japanese history) is a noun that is a child of a pre-positional phrase with the head term 在 (*during*). Such relational information is to be exploited in the question generation stage of our method.

Our Chinese automatic question generator is implemented with Stanford CoreNLP[1]. In natural language processing research and development work, it is common to rely upon available natural language programming tools. Stanford CoreNLP provides the following set of tools that work in a pipeline of input text processing:

1. Sentence splitter: It splits a piece of text into sentences according to a set of defined delimiters. We used full stop, question mark and exclamation mark in our method.
2. Segmenter: It segments a sentence into terms based on a pre-trained model and a dictionary or acceptable terms.
3. Part-of-speech tagger: It annotates terms with their part-of-speech according to a pre-trained model.
4. Name entity recognizer: It annotates nouns with an entity type such as person, location, or organization. It is crucial for generating the appropriate question stem for a noun-based question (e.g. a *where* question for location type of nonu). Figure 4 shows an example of how this tool could help in question generation.
5. Parser: It converts a sentence into a parse tree based on a pre-trained model.

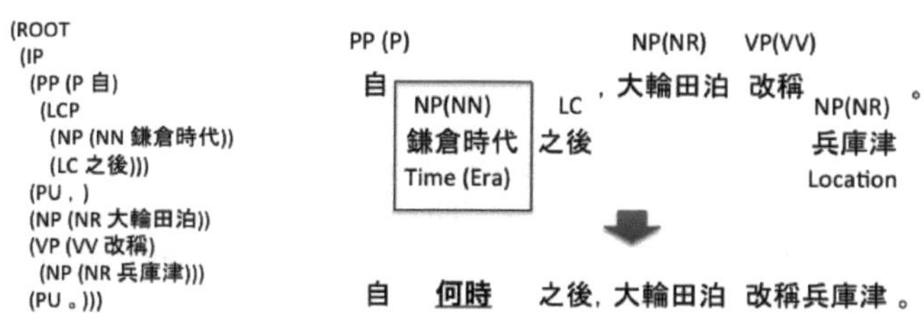

Fig. 4. The role of the name entity recognizer is to determine the question stem. For example, the noun 鎌倉時代 is recognized as a time (era), and the question term何時 (where) can be used accordingly.

Finally, our implementation work also depends on parse tree query and manipulation tools *Tregex* and *Tsurgeon* [11]. The former allows identification of specific patterns in a parse tree with rules based on part-of-speech, keywords, and parse tree structure. For examples, a dot means immediately follow and a left shaped arrow means an immediate sub-tree relation. So "`A.B`" means phrase A is immediately followed by phrase B, and "`A<B`" means A is the parent of B. A and B can be part-of-speech or actual keywords.

[1] http://nlp.stanford.edu/software/corenlp.shtml

2.3 Qualities and Pre-processing of Source Chinese Text

Source text must be syntactically correct for the *Parser* to have any chance ing a parse tree. Parsing Chinese text is known to be difficult due to semant ity of often multiple ways of segmenting a sentence into terms and of terms [12]. It is found that formal academic text sources, including Wikipe are generally acceptable by common parsers such as the Stanford CoreNL from Hong Kong newspaper are found to be problematic due to colloqu style and inclusion of novel terms.

We attempted to improve the accuracy by helping the parser to reco words. Most parsers, including Stanford CoreNLP, allow adding new wor tionary. We also added a pre-processing stage that segment a sentence i terms before putting it to the parser [13].

We also dealt with the issue of source text that is made up of either tra simplified Chinese characters. We converted all text into simplified chara on a character conversion map. The choice of using simplified characters match the better performing lexicon resources available for Stanford CoreN

2.4 Pruning of Parse Trees

Heilmen and Smith's work emphasizes pruning of parse trees before th generation stage [1]. The target is to identify auxiliary phrases in a comple that could be removed without affecting the main clause. The remove phrases may also be considered as a new sentence for generating que Figure 5).

However, in our Chinese question generation method, we only defined (1) marking out prepositional phrases, (2) marking out phrases that end considering the phrase as appositive, and (3) marking out adjective phra noun modifier. After marking out the phrases, we used *Tsurgeon* to prune th

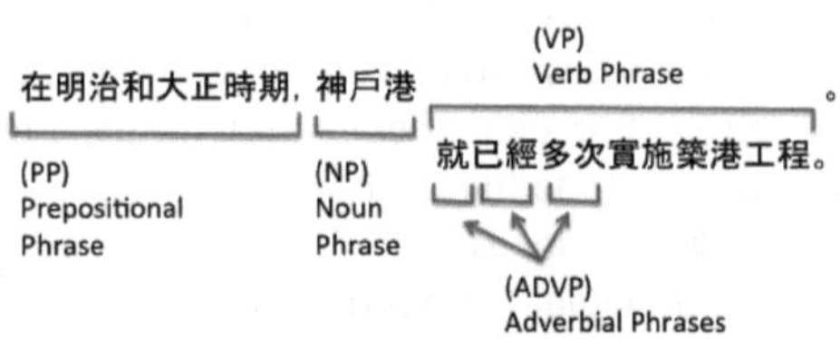

Fig. 5. Marking out a prepositional phrase for pruning or further processi

2.5 Part-of-Speech-Based Question Generation

The part-of-speech based question generation method first identifies possi phrases or terms, works out the entity type, and replaces it with a suitab stem. This method is capable of generating the concept completion type of

1. Numeric questions (`QP < CD=number < CLP`)
   This rule looks for a quantifier phrase with a number and a classifier phrase.
2. Rank questions (`QP < OD=number`)
   This rule looks for a quantifier phrase with an ordinal number (e.g. 第六).
   Source sentence: 它是薩克森第六大城市。
   Question: 它是薩克森第幾大城市？
   Answer: 第六
3. Time questions (`NP=time < NT`)
   This rule looks for a temporal noun within a noun phrase.
   Source sentence: 神戶港在1868年開港之後再次發展為國際港口。
   Question: 神戶港在何時開港之後再次發展為國際港口？
   Answer: 1868年
4. Positional and relational questions (`LCP < (NP | IP=place) < LC`)
   This rule looks for any phrase followed by a localizer such as中or外.
   Source sentence: 1919年時 日本的貿易額中有34%的都是經由神戶港進行。
   Question: 1919年時，那裡中有34%的都是經由神戶港進行？
   Answer: 日本的貿易額
5. Noun questions (`NP=noun !> LCP !< NT !<< PN`)
   This general rule looks for all noun phrases and depends on the name entity recognizer for the question type and suitable question stem. The recognition of a pronoun is essential for questions with meaningful answers.
   Source sentence: 在明治和大正時期，神戶港就已經多次實施築港工程。
   Question: 在明治和大正時期，神戶港就已經多次實施甚麼？
   Answer: 築港工程

2.6 Keyword-Based Question Generation

The keyword based question generation method makes use of keywords such as因為 and所以to generate explanation type questions. We defined two keyword-based rules as described below.

6. Cause and effect questions (`ROOT [<< (((IP|PP=reason << 由于|因为)) .. (IP|PP|VP))| << (IP|PP=reason [(PU . (IP|PP|VP << 所以|于事|如此)) |. (IP|PP|VP << 所以|于事|如此)]))]`)
   This rule looks for sentences stating cause and effect and identifies the reason part as the answer and generates a question asking what causes the result. The answer should be the remaining part of the sentence.
   Source sentence: 然而由於日本在江戶時代實施鎖國政策，兵庫津轉變為國內港口，但仍然擁有重要的地位。
   Question: 日本在江戶時代實施鎖國政策，導致甚麼？
7. Argumentative questions (`ROOT [<< ((IP|PP=front << 虽然|尽管|虽|虽说|即使) [. IP=however| . (PU . IP=however)]) | << (IP|PP=front [ . (PU . (IP|PP|VP=however << (但|但是|可是|不过|可惜|竟然|居然|然而|而|却|然|只|只是`

))) | .(IP|PP|VP=however << (但|但是|可是|不过|可
居然|然而|而|却|然|只|只是))])])

This rule looks for sentences changing the narrative or argument fl
tifies the phrase before and after the change, and generates a questi
the effect of the change.

Source sentence: 戰後神戶港雖然很快就開始復興，然其日本第
地位在1960年代被橫濱港取代。

Question: 戰後神戶港雖然很快就開始復興，但怎樣了？

2.7 Name Entity Recognition and Pronoun Resolution

Table 1 describes the mapping between the question stems and the enti
noun questions.

Table 1. Entity type and question stem

Entity types	Question stems	Examples
Organization	甚麼	神戶港不僅是甚麼，也是日本重要的
Location	哪裡	神戶港亦開通有前往哪裡的定期客船
Person	誰	誰是當時的神戶市長？
Time	何時	神戶港在何時開港之後再次發展為國

A good performance name entity recognizer is important for generat
question stem. We constructed a name entity recognizer based on the
Wikipedia articles. Proper nouns such as 大正時期and神戶港 are often titl
Wikipedia and their category information can be exploited. This technique
very slow and not used in this implementation.

Pronouns are often used for concise writing, but their original noun
found in previous sentences. In our sentence-as-an-unit approach, their r
must be resolved before a question with a proper answer can be gen
adopted a simple approach of replacing the pronoun with the nearest nou
pervious sentence.

2.8 Filtering and Ranking

The over-generation approach leads to generation of some good question
poor questions. A filtering and ranking stage is essential to weed out thos
questions. If a question satisfies any one of the rules below, it is remove
question set.

1. Duplicated questions.
2. Length of answers is rather long with respect to the length of questi
3. Number of commas in a question is 2 or more.

3 Results

We successfully implemented the prototype system with Java, Stanford CoreNLP, Tregex and Tsurgeon. There were two focal points in the system evaluation: question generation and filtering of valid questions.

3.1 Evaluation on Chinese Question Generation

We used five excerpted Wikipedia articles as our source text in the evaluation:

1. 哥利茲: describing Goerlitz, a city in Germany.
2. 樹熊: describing Koalas, with some long sentences.
3. 日本料理: describing Japanese cuisine with a poor writing style.
4. 神戸港: describing the Kobe Port.
5. 大時代: describing a soap drama with a story-telling tone.

We applied the seven rules of question generation and the number of times each rule was applicable are summarized in Table 2. The noun rule has been applied the most, which is not surprising given that noun is the most common part-of-speech type. We noted that the cause-effect rule has been applied more in the two articles,樹熊 (*koala*) and日本料理 (*Japanese cuisine*). These two articles contain many long sentences with conjunctions to connect the ideas. Although a number of reasoning questions are generated but most of them do not have a very strong relation between the marked causes and effects. The article 大時代 (a HK TV drama) produces the most argumentative questions. It introduces a TV drama with a story-telling tone and narrative change is common.

Table 2. Number of times each of the question generation rules is applied in the evaluation

Rule types	哥利茲	樹熊	日本料理	神戸港	大時代	*Total*
Numeric	1	4	0	0	0	*5*
Rank	3	0	0	1	2	*6*
Time	5	0	2	8	3	*18*
Position	4	7	2	4	14	*31*
Noun	58	163	119	151	184	*675*
Cause-Effect	0	30	10	2	6	*48*
Argumentative	0	6	1	3	17	*27*
Total	*71*	*210*	*134*	*169*	*226*	*810*
Length (Char)	*250*	*967*	*518*	*664*	*961*	
Sentences	*17*	*88*	*43*	*43*	*107*	

3.2 Analysis of Deficiencies of Generated Questions

Analysing the deficiencies of generated questions is a major objective of this research because this area is at a very preliminary stage. Tables 3 and 4 show the distribution of deficiency types, and the results of manual evaluation of question quality. Two

coders carried out the manual evaluation with reliable inter-coder reliabil
types of deficiencies are found in the generated questions, which are listed i

Table 3. Summary of number of poor and valid questions generated from each

Articles	Total	Deficient	Valid	% of valid
哥利兹	71	43	28	39.4%
神戸港	169	77	92	54.4%
日本料理	134	104	30	22.3%
樹熊	210	113	97	46.2%
大時代	226	128	98	43.4%

Table 4. Number of questions with deficiency generated from each artic

Deficiency types	*哥利兹*	*神戸港*	*日本料理*	*樹熊*	*大時代*
1	16	29	10	19	63
2	5	7	29	6	22
3	5	1	14	7	10
4	0	12	10	58	1
5	0	13	17	17	6
6	4	1	2	0	0
7	1	2	0	0	3
8	8	9	6	2	10
9	4	2	2	1	4
10	0	0	6	0	6
11	0	1	8	3	3
Total	*43*	*77*	*104*	*113*	*128*

3.3 Discussion

The percentage of valid questions is apparently very low, ranging from 22
We argue that this is a baseline performance that could be drastically imp
better filtering and ranking methods. The over-generation approach de
Heilman and Smith for English text relies on a machine-learning based ra
lect only a small percentage of questions. Similar techniques have not yet
oped in this work.

The deficiencies found in the evaluation may be categorized into 3 cause

1. Poor quality source text: causing the generation of a wrong parse tre
2. Error in pre-processing: causing irreversible problems such as se noun subject from its related text, and separation of cause and effec statement.
3. Error in part-of-speech and entity type annotations: causing erro trees.

Table 5. Common deficiency types found in generated questions

Deficiency types	*Causes*	*Examples (Answer in brackets)*
1. Wrong question word	Annotation problem – wrong NER analysis	丁蟹母親為方家的家佣，丁蟹自小與甚麼相識？(方家少爺方進新)
2. Missing subject	Effect after sentence splitting	所以不論是高湯、調味、刀工、烹調方式都是以甚麼為前提？(保留食物的自然原味)
3. Ambiguous question	Original sentence too short	耳有甚麼？(茸毛)
4. Long question	Original sentence is written poorly	甚麼貼合自然風物，並且被認為能體現四季的分明、地理多樣性以及日本人尊重自然的精神，營養均衡，也與正月、插秧等傳統節慶密切相關，代表了日本獨有的價值觀、生活樣式和社會傳統？(裝盤)
5. Missing preface	Effect after sentence splitting	所以當地人稱它甚麼？(克瓦勒)
6. Ungrammatical	Annotation problem – POS tagger wrongly identify a verb as a noun	以桉樹葉和嫩枝為食，幾乎從不下地甚麼？(飲水)
7. Ungrammatical	Annotation problem – wrong parsing	哪裡的發展有着密不可分的關係？(神戶的歷史和神戶港)
8. Ungrammatical	Annotation problem – wrong segmentation	丁蟹母親甚麼家的家佣，丁蟹自小與方家少爺方進新相識？(為方)
9. Vague	The answer phrase is a low information content	她何時是一名中學生？(當時)
10. Does not make sense	Keyword is matched but it does not change the narrative flow	二弟益蟹是黑社會的打手，但怎樣了？(性格衝動而殘忍)
11. Does not make sense	Wrong clause captured	是劇中完全的反派人物，但怎樣了？(但丁蟹這自以為是仁義)

Annotation of Chinese terms is found to be difficult because, first, Chinese is a delimiter-free language, second, many Chinese terms can be both a noun and a verb, and, third, proper nouns are not lexicographically distinguishable from other nouns.

Table 5 shows that wrong question word is the most frequent deficiency type. The correctness could be improved if we would adopt a better algorithm that better determine name entity of a noun.

4 Conclusion

A computational Chinese question generation method was developed and Automatic question generation from unstructured text is a very difficult pr this study found out that Chinese language would pose much more challeng number of language specific reasons. Chinese sentences are formed by lo mar rule and there are often a variety of ways of parsing a Chinese staten are far fewer prepositions in Chinese sentences so that relations between te as clear as in English. Process like appositive removal and prepositic removal in English question generation algorithm cannot be performed sentences.

Despite the apparent unsatisfactory rate of generating good questions generation approach should be highly promising. Future work should be two aspects: a more accurate noun phrase and entity recognition method, a precision ranking method. The former aspect requires advances in lexica for Chinese or more intelligent methods of using existing resources such Wordnet and Wikipedia. The latter aspect requires more understanding ab tic and semantic characteristics of proper question in Chinese.

References

1. Heilman, M., Smith, N.A.: Question generation via overgenerating transfor ranking. Carnegie Mellon University, Pittsburgh (2009)
2. Schnotz, W.: Commentary: Towards an integrated view of learning from tex displays. Educational Psychology Review 14(1), 101–120 (2002)
3. Eason, S.H., Goldberg, L.F., Young, K.M., Geist, M.C., Cutting, L.E.: interactions: How differential text and question types influence cognitive skil reading comprehension. Journal of Educational Psychology 104(3), 515 (2012)
4. Tierney, R.J., Readence, J.E.: Expository reading-writing think-sheets. In: T Readence, J.E. (eds.) Reading Strategies and Practices, 5th edn., pp. 278–2 Bacon, Boston (2000)
5. Collins, J.L., Madigan, T.P.: Using writing to develop struggling learners' reading comprehension. Building Struggling Students' Higher Level Litera Ideas, Powerful Solutions, 103–124 (2010)
6. Guthrie, J.T., Wigfield, A., Barbosa, P., Perencevich, K.C., Taboada, A., I Tonks, S.: Increasing Reading Comprehension and Engagement Throug Oriented Reading Instruction. Journal of Educational Psychology 96(3), 403 (2
7. McKendree, J., Stenning, K., Mayes, T., Lee, J., Cox, R.: Why observing a di fit learning. Journal of Computer Assisted Learning 14(2), 110–119 (1998)
8. Craig, S.D., Gholson, B., Brittingham, J.K., Williams, J.L., Shubeck, K.T. vicarious learning of physics using deep questions with explanations. Comput tion 58(4), 1042–1048 (2012)
9. Kalady, S., Elikkottil, A., Das, R.: Natural language question generation usin keywords. In Proceedings of QG 2010: The Third Workshop on Question

10. Nielsen, R., Buckingham, J., Knoll, G., Marsh, B., Palen, L.: A Taxonomy of Question for Question Generation. In: Proceedings of the Workshop on the Question Generation Shared Task and Evaluation Challenge (2008)
11. Levy, R., Andrew, G.: Tregex and Tsurgeon: tools for querying and manipulating tree data structures. In: Proceedings of the fifth International Conference on Language Resources and Evaluation, pp. 2231–2234 (2006)
12. Levy, R., Manning, C.: Is it harder to parse Chinese, or the Chinese Treebank? In: Proceedings of the 41st Annual Meeting on Association for Computational Linguistics, vol. 1, pp. 439–446. Association for Computational Linguistics (2003)
13. Xia, F.: The segmentation guidelines for the Penn Chinese Treebank (3.0). IRCS Technical Reports Series (2000)

A Web-Based Computer-Aided Assessment Creation and Invigilation System

Jeff K.T. Tang[1], Hei-Chun Yeung[2], Yat-Fai Man[2], Kwok-Kwan Li
Tak-Lam Wong[3], Wai-Man Pang[1], and Wai-Shing Ho[1]

[1] Department of Computer Science, Caritas Institute of Higher Educatio
18 Chui Ling Road, Tseung Kwan O, New Territories, Hong Kong
[2] The Open University of Hong Kong
Good Shepherd Street, Ho Man Tin, Kowloon, Hong Kong
[3] The Hong Kong Institute of Education
10 Lo Ping Road, Tai Po, N.T., Hong Kong
jtang@cihe.edu.hk

Abstract. Computer-Aided Assessment (CAA) is more than managing co materials and assignment submissions. In recent years, automated assess has become more popular. Public examinations such as the Internet-Based (iBT) of TOEFL and IT Certificate Examinations are computerized assessm with multiple-choice questions (MCQ) and the answers are automati scored. This is an efficient way of assessing students and especially usefu self-financing degree awarding institutes in Hong Kong that are lackin resources such as time and manpower. In this paper, we propose a web-b computer-aided assessment creation and invigilation system that promot paper-free electronic assessment and it is environmental friendly. The sy provides a user interface for the teachers to input questions to the database, generate a computerized assessment paper by the teacher inputting the desi topics and difficulty levels. In addition, the system allows the examine customize assessment rules and regulations in a in-class examinatio automatically saves the data over time to prevent accidental crashes. cheating is prevented by software measures. We have invited some users education sector to try out our system and evaluated their satisfaction, an overall result is positive.

Keywords: assessment creation, question bank, online examination, onlin vigilation.

1 Introduction

Assessments are necessary for teachers to evaluate the learning performa students. According to Hurst, a good assessments should show what t actually have learned [1]. However, preparing good assessment materials (

degree awarding institutes as they have limited resources and supports. If less time to be spent in such tedious and repetitive assessment preparation works, teachers can spare more time to improve their teaching skills and materials, and discuss and communicate with students.

Computer-Aided Assessment (CAA) has been widely used in managing course materials and assignment submissions in the last decade. In recent years, automated assessment is becoming more popular. For example, IT certificate examinations are computer-based, which are consisting of Multiple-choice questions (MCQ) automatically retrieved from a *question bank* (a database that contains a vase amount of questions of different topics). The answers input by the participants are automatically scored at the end of the examination. However, existing computerized examinations are simple and not flexible. In fact at higher education institutes, different courses or assessments (e.g. short quiz and final examination) may have different styles such as *sectioning*, *question type*, *topics* and the *distribution of difficulty levels*. Existing CAA systems cannot satisfy the needs of teachers.

In this paper, we propose a web-based computerized assessment and invigilation system that reduces the teachers' workload in preparation of different types of assessments, and also promotes an environmental friendly paper-free electronic assessment. The system consists of two parts: the *assessment creation tool*, and the *computer-based invigilation tool*. The former tool provides a user interface for the teachers to input questions to enrich the *question bank*. And then, by inputting the desired *sectioning*, *question types*, *topics* and their *difficulty levels*, the tool can generate an assessment paper in XML format, which can be outputted to PDF version for traditional paper-based examination and/or directly used in computer-based examination. The *computer-based invigilation tool* provides a platform that able to conduct an online computer-based examination, such that both invigilator and students are required to login to the system. The students' activities and status are monitored by the invigilator in real-time. In order to make sure the examination is fair for every participant, accidental crashes are handled and cheating are prevented by software methods.

2 Related Work

In the last two decades, *Learning Management Systems* (LMS) such as Blackboard [2] and Moodle developed by Dougiamas and Taylor [3] have widely been used in high schools and universities. These systems are mainly for managing course materials and assignment submissions. In comparing with Blackboard, which is a commercial product, Moodle is an open source platform that provides a large amount of plugins for system administrators to customize according to their colleges' needs, for example, some useful reporting and statistic tools are available.

In recent years, *Computer-Aided Assessment* (CAA) is getting more popular. The majority of them are web/Internet-based, so we called them *online assessment*. The TOEFL Internet-Based Test [4] and Cisco Certification Examination [5] are online assessments consist of Multiple-choice questions (MCQs) that are automatically retrieved from a *question bank*. The answers input by the participants are a ly scored at the end of the examination.

Traditional LMS (such as Moodle) also provide the capability for crea online assessments with MCQs too. The plugins found in the "Quiz" c Moodle's official website provide a great variety of question types and fo used in Moodle system. *Testmoz* [6] is a free web-based platform that allo create online tests and it supports True/false, MCQs, multiple response, an blank questions. Valentín et al. used the *Google Forms* to implement onl ments in an IMS Learning Design course [7]. The above systems cou automated scoring by exact-matching with the given model answers. How could not maintain a question bank (i.e. every time the user has to input tions). In fact, teachers are desired to keep a record of questions created and reuse/update them in future [8].

To maintain the fairness, invigilation is also an important issue in onl ments. NetSupport School shows the current status of every student during [9]. It can be applied in invigilation such as the invigilator can monitor an the control of the student's computer for emergence. Besides, according knowledge there seems no existing system available for in-class invigilatio

3 Proposed System

Our proposed system consists of two major components: the *Assessment creation* *Computer-based assessment invigilation tool*. The login interface and the main m ferent roles are shown in Fig. 1.

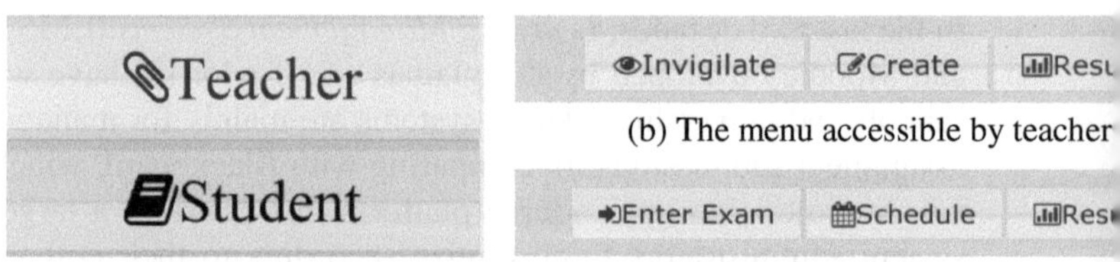

(a) The login roles. (b) The menu accessible by teacher (c) The menu accessible by student

Fig. 1. The teachers and students can see different menu after logging in our s

After logging in, the user will see an icon that specifies his/her role a Fig. 1(a). The two major user roles *teacher* and *student* access to distinct m that contain different functions as shown in Fig. 1(b) and Fig. 1(c) respec teacher can create/edit questions and assessments, conduct invigilation ar result; while the student can check the assessment schedule, take the asse view his/her own result. We will describe these components and functions lowing sub-sections.

3.1 Assessment Creation Tool

The assessment creation tool is only accessible by teachers. There are two steps to generate an examination paper and its flow is shown in Fig. 2.

Firstly, the teachers should *build the question bank* by creating new questions with the provided interface. Our system maintains a *question bank* (a database of questions). The teachers are required to input the questions along with model answers over time. The questions stored in the database can be reused or updated in future. In this prototype, we support close-ended questions such as MCQs, True/False, Fill in the blanks, as well as Open-ended questions.

The second step is to *create the structure of an assessment*. Provided there has a significant amount of questions, the teachers could design the structure of a assessment (e.g. an examination paper) including how many parts, and the topics to be covered in the assessment. Finally, the system could automatically generate the assessment by retrieving the questions from the question bank and arrange them into the right sections according to the requirements.

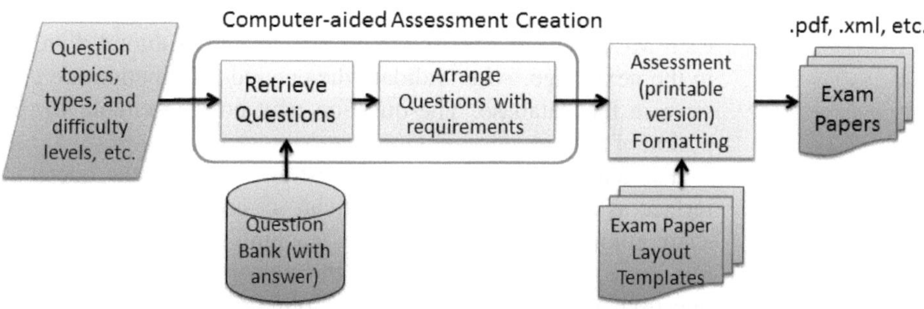

Fig. 2. The flow of the assessment creation tool

Build the Question Bank. An interface as shown in Fig. 3 is provided for teachers to create a new question that to be stored in the question bank. S/he should input the

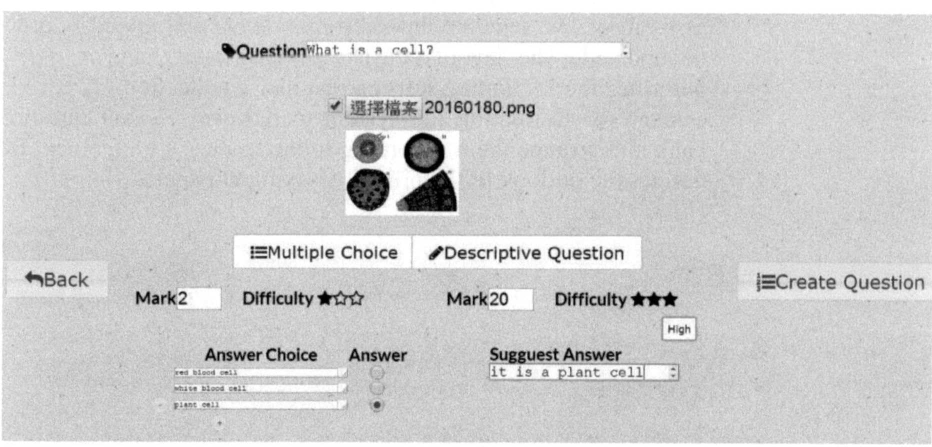

Fig. 3. The teacher can create a question and save into the question bank through this interface

mandatory information such as the *content*, *question type*, the *marks* it ca cultly level, and *model answer*. If it is a MCQ, the teacher should provide choices and specify which one is the correct option; otherwise, the teache needed to input the textual answer for open questions.

Note that, our system only capable to score the MCQs, the open que need to be marked by the teachers themselves. Each question can be attache optional image. It is necessary to specify the difficulty level, in terms of t of stars. The marks input here is mainly use for open question type. In pr MCQs in the same section are always carrying the same mark. Hence, th each MCQ will be overridden by the sectional subtotal divided by numbe in the next stage. After validate the entered information are correct, the qu store in the database. The question may not be suitable for the examina period of time.

The teachers can review the questions stored in the question bank thro terface as shown in Fig. 4. They can set each question either private, pub share among the teachers who are teaching the same course. The teacher w (i.e. owns) the question reserves the rights to change the access rights or question from the database if s/he found a particular question is no longe outdated. As the database could grow to huge size, the questions are browsed by their course codes and disciplines.

Create the Structure of an Assessment. We provide another user interface fo ers to create an assessment by retrieving the questions from the inventory assessment, we separate the *question content* and *layout* in order to make be updated. The layout consists of a *structure* and a *style sheet*. Th describes the sectioning information and a collection of requirements, wh cessary for instructing the system to retrieve relevant questions from th bank and arrange them according to the teacher's preference. Besides, the defines the outlook of the printed assessment papers.

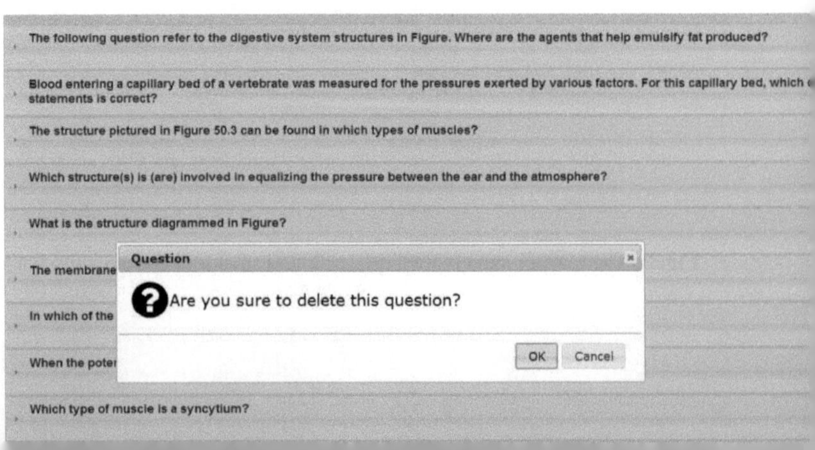

Fig. 5 shows a sample structure defined by a teacher, who has to input required information such as *course code*, *question type*, *topic*, *difficulty level*, and *ratio*, etc. The *ratio* is the proportion of a particular topic to be appeared in an assessment. In this prototype, we assumed each assessment only for a single course. We restrict the structure to have one single type of questions per section. After entering the above information, an examination structure is created and saved in XML format, and its local path is added into the database.

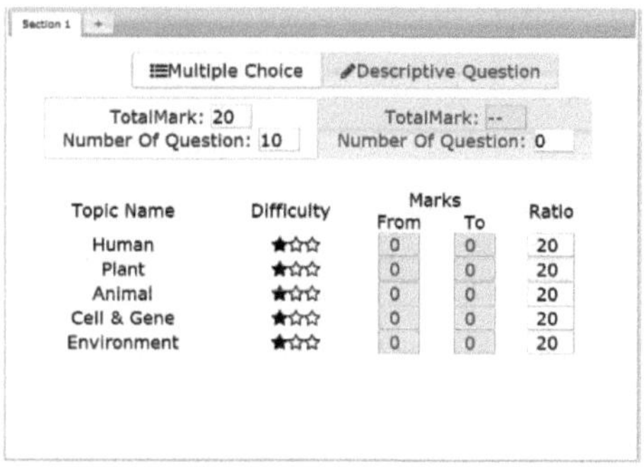

(a) Section 1 with MCQs

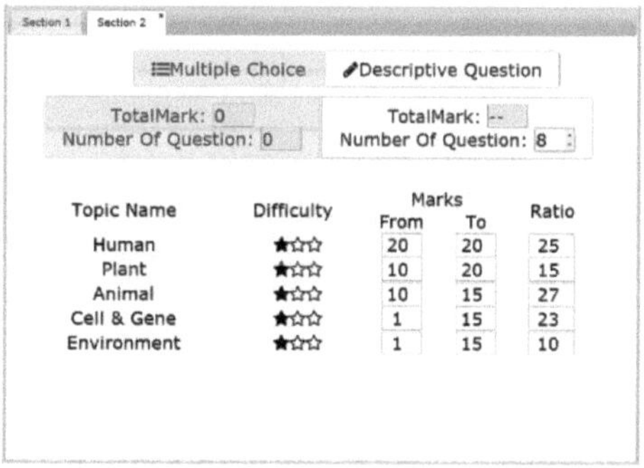

(b) Section 2 with open questions

Fig. 5. The teacher defines the structure (e.g. the sectioning and topics) of an assessment

Finally, the teacher can review and pick any one of the created assessments with the user interface as shown in Fig. 6. The teacher loads a structure template for generating a new assessment. The system retrieves questions randomly from the question bank that satisfy the given requirements. The teacher can either output the assessment in printable format, or set an online examination by inputting the examination details such as the date/time as shown in Fig. 7. The examiner can tailor made the examination rules with the existing options as shown in Fig. 8.

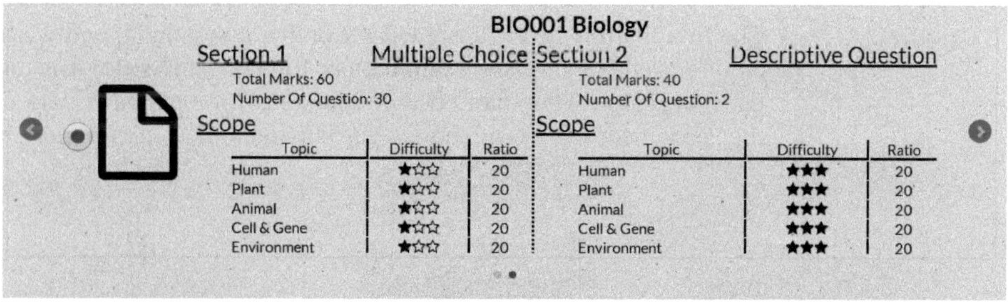

Fig. 6. The teacher loads a structure template for generating a new assessment

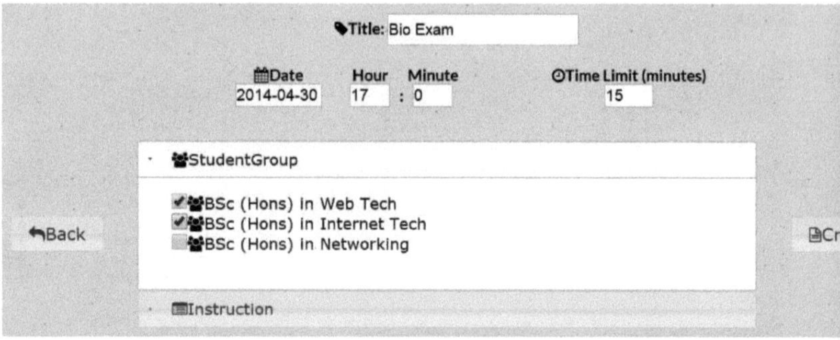

Fig. 7. The teacher can set an online examination with the generated assessment (i

The electronic version of examination paper can be exported to a PDF sion, which can be saved to hard-disk and printed out as hard copies in examination sessions. We used the *PDF Toolkit* developed by Alfresco [1(a software add-on that capable for generating the file to be a PDF format. user to insert the PDF file on some specific page, PDF Encryption, etc. Acc information, our system focus on generate the examination paper in PDF f database only without encryption and inserting pages. Fig. 9(a) and 9(b) *cover* and *content* pages of the exported PDF file respectively.

3.2 Computer-Based Invigilation Tool

The invigilation tool is designed for online assessment, and we highlight h can be used for in-class examination. Fig. 10 shows the user interface to the invigilator. They can observe the status of each candidate on the scre the presence of examination participants. The invigilator has the a

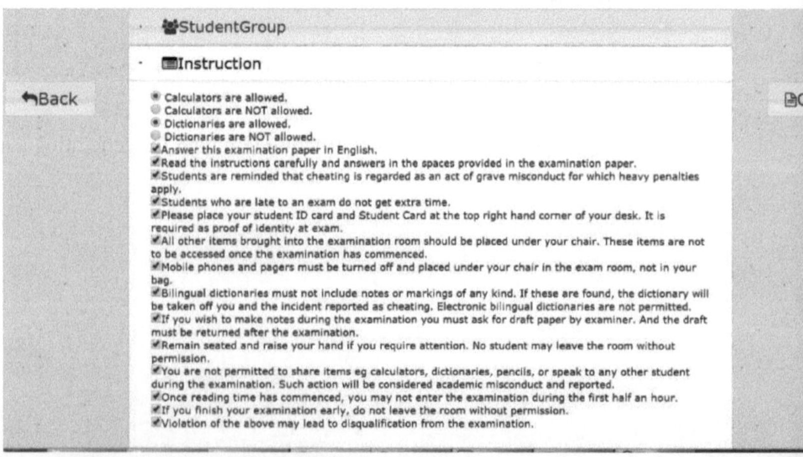

Fig. 8. The examiner can tailor made the assessment rules with the existing

end/pause the examination session of any suspicious students at any time. The students (i.e. the examination participants) can see another user interface as shown in Fig. 11. The questions are shown on the left hand side, while the assessment rules and remaining time are shown on the right hand side. The students have to answer the questions within the given time. The tool will automatically save the input text of open questions per minute, and every time the student click-select a radio box. When the time is up, the examination will be closed and the answer will be saved and submit to the system automatically.

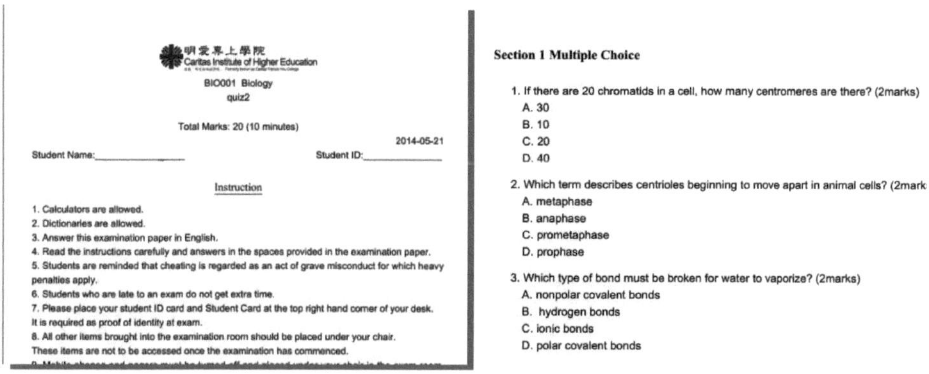

(a) The generated examination paper cover after formatting

(b) The generated content after formatting

Fig. 9. An example of the generated (a) cover, and (b) content formatted with a style sheet

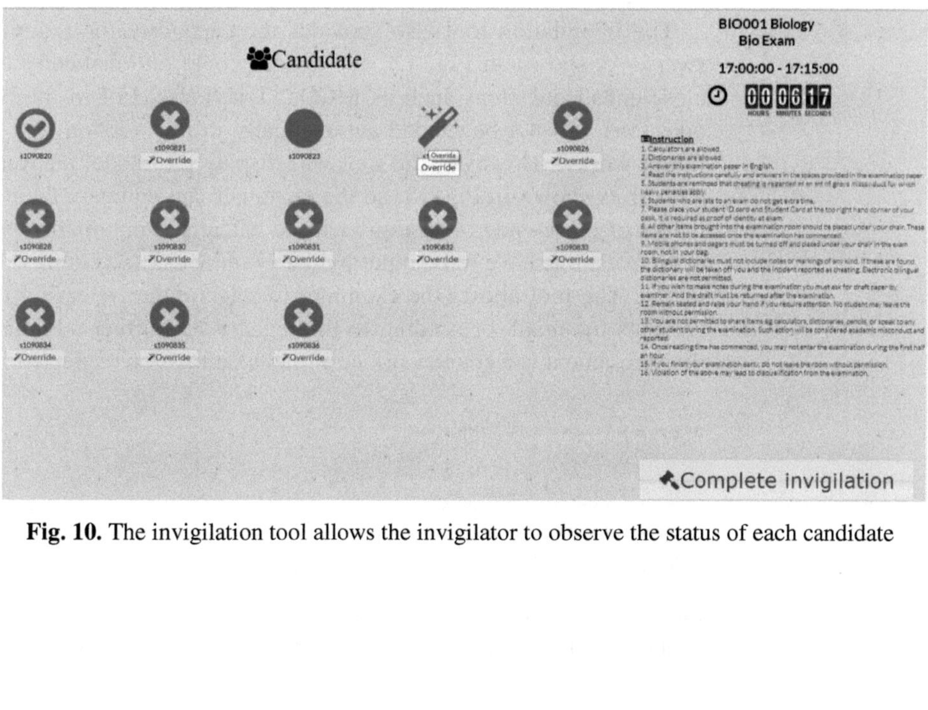

Fig. 10. The invigilation tool allows the invigilator to observe the status of each candidate

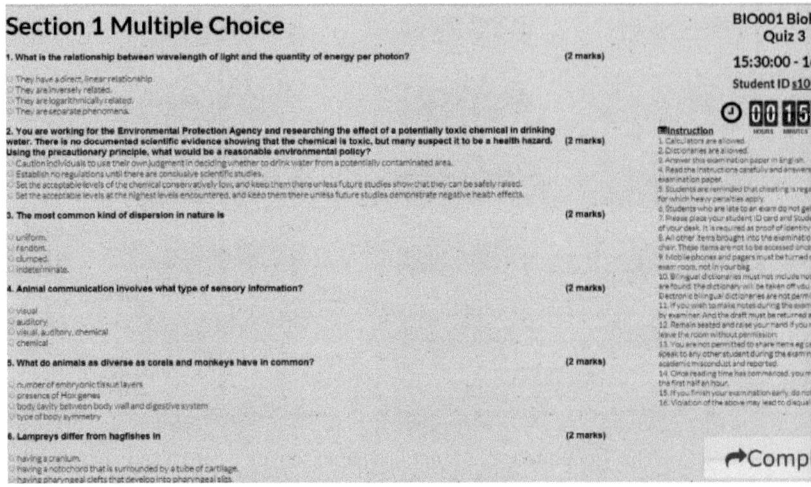

Fig. 11. What a student would see of s/he is taking the online examination. The click the "Complete" button to submit the answer script within the allowed time.

The invigilation tool also provides the capability for examiners to gr swers. As shown in Fig. 12, our system could automatically check the close-ended questions such as MCQs, True/False, Fill in the blanks, etc questions will not be graded automatically in this version (but it will be future works). However, the tool will display the model answer below th answer as shown in Fig. 13, so the examiner can compare them easier. Th marks of close-ended questions will be calculated automatically, while th open questions have to be input by the examiner. The system will add up a marks. The tool allows the examiner to select either releasing the total m students by email, or sending to the registry for further administration pr the assessment is a coursework or a final examination respectively.

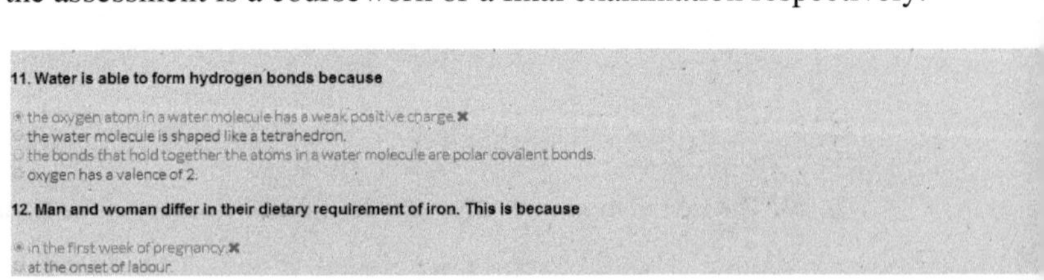

Fig. 12. The close-ended questions are checked by our system automatically. The wrong answers are highlighted in green and red colors respectively.

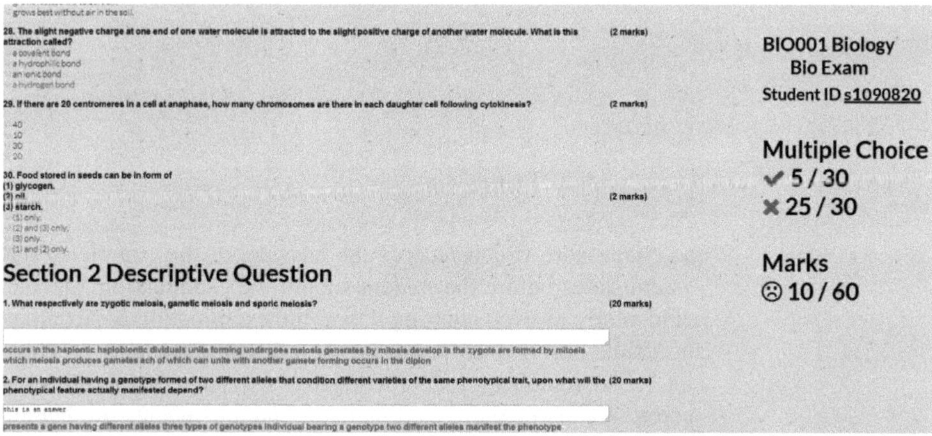

Fig. 13. The model answer is shown below the student's answer, which helps examiner to check them more efficiently

4 Evaluation and Discussion

We have conducted a preliminary system evaluation. We have invited 18 subjects to try out our system and answer a post-test questionnaire. All these subjects are belonging to the education sector (they are either teachers or students from education institutes). The subjects are told to do some tasks focus on the assessment creation part, such as create new questions, create a new structure, and generate a new assessment. We also show them the usage of the user interfaces of our invigilation tool. In the post-test questionnaire, their feelings and comments are collected.

Table 1. The result regarding the usability and usefulness of the assessment creation tool

Score	1	2	3	4	5	6	7	8	9	10
Count	0	0	0	0	1	4	6	5	2	0
Percentage	0%	0%	0%	0%	6%	22%	33%	28%	11%	0%

Firstly, there are over 80% (15/18) subjects agreed that the system save their time and effort for creating new assessments. Secondly, the subjects scored the usability and usefulness of the assessment creation tool in a 10-point scale (the higher the score, the better the subject feels), and the result is shown in Table 1. The average score is 7.16 that implied that the education professionals felt our system is easy to use and useful to them. In which, the majority of subjects have given score higher than the average, and 94% of the subjects felt positive to our system (>5 marks). Besides, according to their written feedback, the assessment creation tool is easy to learn and they can master the assessment creation process shortly.

There are two potential risks of our system: the *accidental crashes* and *cheating* by students. In order to prevent accidental crashes during the online examination, after the students login the examination system the web server generates a temporal file on

the client side, which records the answers of the completed questions as
system status before the student submit the examination. Once the system
accidentally or even shutting down, the examination environment can be r
short time that tries to minimize the affect the students continue to answe
can be prevented by randomizing the sequence of the questions to be di
screen. We also require an invigilator and all students present at the venue
time, and their system clock are needed to be synchronized.

5 Conclusion and Future Work

In this paper, we proposed the web-based computer aided system that hel
to create, invigilate, and grade assessments. The assessment creation tool
teachers to input questions to the question bank for future reuse/update. It
the teachers to customize the assessment structures by setting requireme
sectioning, topics, difficulty levels. An electronic assessment can be gene
wards, and it can be outputted into printable (PDF) format by giving an e
paper style sheet. With this tool, the teachers can reduce their time spen
assessment preparation tasks. Besides, the online invigilation tool allows
conduct in-class examination. The close-ended questions can be checked a
ly while the open questions are still needed to be marked by teachers.

As future work, we propose to apply Natural Language Processing (
niques to extract and highlight the topics and concepts in both the questi
swers, which help the teachers to mark the open questions. Moreover, ope
could be evaluated in a semi-automated way.

References

1. Hurst, M.: Qualities of Good Assessments: Standardization, Practicality, Relia
lidity. Psychology 102: Educational Psychology (2014), http://ed
portal.com/academy/topic/assessments-of-learning.html
May 31, 2014)
2. Blackboard: Blackboard Inc. (1997), http://www.blackboard.com (re
31, 2014)
3. Dougiamas, M., Taylor, P.C.: Moodle: Using learning communities to cre
source course management system. In: Proceedings of the EDMEDIA 2003
Honolulu, HI (2003)
4. TOEFL iBT: About the Test. ETS, http://www.ets.org/toefl/ibt/
trieved May 31, 2014)
5. Cisco Certification: Pearson Vue, http://www.pearsonvue.com/c
treived)
6. Johnson, M.: Testmoz, http://testmoz.com (retrieved May 31, 2014)
7. de la Fuente Valentín, L., Pardo, A., Delgado Kloos, C.: Using Third Party
Adapt Learning Material: A Case Study with Google Forms. In: Cress, U., D

8. Aldridge, J.: Why and how to create a question bank (2013), http://www.testshop.com/blog/bid/94628/Why-and-How-to-Create-a-Question-Bank (retrieved May 31, 2014)
9. NetSupport School: NetSupport (2014), http://www.netsupportschool.com/ (retrieved May 31, 2014)
10. Alfresco: Alfresco PDF Toolkit, Alfresco add-ons (2013), http://addons.alfresco.com/addons/alfresco-pdf-toolkit (retrieved May 31, 2014)

The Development of a Final Year Project Manag
System for Information Technology Programm

Chun-Hang Leung[1], Chung-Lun Lai[1], Tsun-Kit Yuan[1], Wai-Man Pa
Jeff K.T. Tang[1], Wai-Shing Ho[1], and Tak-Lam Wong[2]

[1] Department of Computer Science, Caritas Institute of Higher Educatio
Hong Kong SAR, China
wmpang@cihe.edu.hk
[2] Department of Mathematics and Information Technology,
The Hong Kong Institute of Education

Abstract. This project tries to develop an online platform which facilitate final year projects (FYP) process implemented by our information techno programme. The whole FYP is a year-long process involving groups of stuc and their supervisors to accomplish a theme based project. It is very neces to employ the latest technologies in order to allow different parties to contri and communicate more efficiently. Therefore, we have designed and devel a comprehensive web-based system to better support the three kinds of u they are the FYP programme organizer (PO), project supervisors and the pr group members.

Before the academic year starts, PO will have to assign project topic cording to the preferences and academic record of the formed project grc This is a tedious and error prone task to manually complete the allocatic projects. The system is therefore useful to help PO to arrange project sele and allocation procedure, as well as helping the students to submit their p rences and group member information. During the academic year, the sy would provide different functionalities for the PO to collect student's as ments and markers' scores via the submission and grading module.

Project supervisors will also be able to employ the system for keep trac the progress of the projects with the use of the project management tools, online chat function. Both the students and supervisors will be benefited these functionalities and allow the project to run more smoothly even fac face meetings are not held very frequently.

Project group members themselves are provided with similarly effe communication tools to allow easy of discussion on project issues among n bers. Moreover, they can share resources about the project including sc code and data files using our online repository

Keywords: project management, online communication, team work, pr supervision, final year project.

1 Introduction

In most of the curriculums in information technology (IT) undergraduate programmes, it is common that students are expected to complete a comprehensive software development project in their final year studies. That is also why it is usually known as final year project (FYP). This project based study aims to provide an integrated training on their team working skill, technical knowledge learnt from different courses, and project management skill.

In the IT degree programme offered in Caritas Institute of Higher Education, this project based course is delivered throughout 2 semesters in the fourth year of the study. Students are grouped to work on a project under the supervision of a professor. Before the semester starts, students are required to form groups of three, and involve in a project allocation process. The project allocation process is trying to match the interest of student to expertise of the professor. Each group of the students can choose their favorite project topics which are proposed by professors, and the allocation will help to resolve any conflict in the choices between groups based on their academic records in last year. Therefore, each project group will be assigned with a theme to work when the semester starts. Apart from prototyping the software according to the project theme, students are required to have meetings with supervisor, hand in project proposals, progress report and carry out presentation of their completed works throughout the whole academic year. As a result, both the supervisor and the students have to work closely, face challenges and deadlines when finishing the project.

As the first implementation of the FYP in Caritas began two years before this paper is written, many of the processes are carried manually and highly rely on traditional ways for communication and assessment submission. For example, in project selection and allocation, students have to form group and choose their favorite project topics by filling in forms on paper. Programme Organizer (PO) will collect all these hardcopy forms and start the project allocation manually. It can become a tedious and time consuming task when the number of groups arrived 20 or more. Moreover, the assignment of projects requires sorting out the priorities of groups based on their average GPA, and this sorting must be done very careful in order to have a fair result, as conflict of choices between groups will always occur and priority do affect the final assignment. Apart from the project allocation, many of the deliverables from the project are submitted via hardcopy or email. Although the FYP is supported by a course management system similar to other courses delivered in the institute, it is not very well suited for a project or group based works submission.

To keep track of students' progress, supervisors usually meet students in a weekly or biweekly basis. However, as supervisors commonly have to mentor three or more groups in a year, a face-to-face meeting has to be limited to as short as an hour or half, or even lesser. Students will just have enough time to report their progress and setup goals for the coming weeks during the meeting. It does not allow students and supervisors to discuss or solve challenges when the project encounters problems. It is kind of hard for students to communicate with their supervisor out of the meeting time purely by email, as the feedback time is prolonged, and progress of the project will be significantly affected. In addition, students usually found it difficult for them to keep up the original planned progress after the project starts. This can due to the

lack of project management knowledge and tools, their busy schedule
semester, and poor management of their prototype's source code and files.

To overcome the various problems encountered during the implement
FYP in the previous years, we decided to develop our own final year p
agement system to serve the whole process. Figure 1 lists a number of pr
the FYP and the corresponding system module to facilitate that procedure.
the project allocation module provides a web-based interface for stude
groups and select favourite topics, supervisors to promote their project the
to automatically complete the project assignments. As all the selections are
online database, PO can easily manage the information without keepin
forms. In addition, the project allocation is performed by the system; this
chance of mistakes in the assignment.

Our system also consists of modules for assessment submission, proje
ment, members' communications and sharing. Deliverables of the proje
posal, reports and presentation slides can be uploaded to the system in a
per group manner. Instant chat module helps students and supervisors to cc
and discuss problems faced in any time and places. A task management
vided for students to record tasks to be completed and keep track of finis
the next meeting. Finally, the management and sharing of deliverables
codes among group members can be done effectively with the file sharing
tory module. All of these modules in the system facilitate the whole FYP
smoothly and efficiently, reduce miscommunication and mistakes to happe

In the following of this paper, we will give a short review of similar sy
other institutes or parties, and then we will focus on the introduction of ev
in our system in detail. Finally, we will present a preliminary evaluation of
through a small scale user study about the current prototype system.

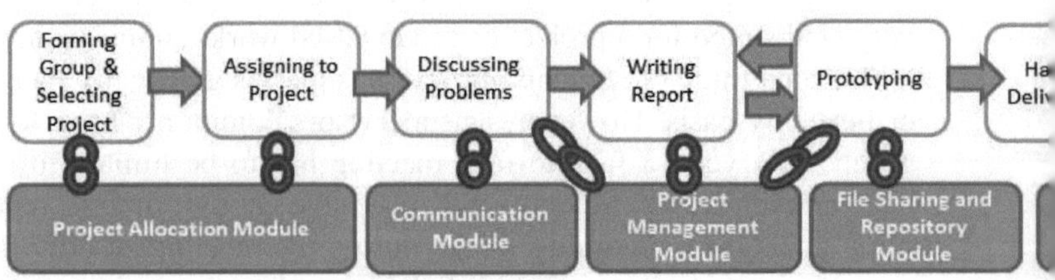

Fig. 1. Overview of the FYP procedures and related system functionalities from
view of students

2 Related Works

Our FYP management system is similar to a typical course managem
(CMS), or a project management system. The comprehensive compariso
had been made by various parties like [1] and [2], especially the two

function like task management with priority assignment to tasks, so that project manager can better arrange manpower and plan the schedule of project. Moreover, it has chat function and forum for ease of communication, while at the same time, it provides share folders for user to access documents and source code simultaneously. This system also included some advanced functions like Gantt chart generator which is a standard tool for project scheduling.

Clement and Bounds shared similar goal as our system in facilitating the management of FYP [6]. While, their focus was to better connect students with potential supervisors before the project allocation starts. Their system also included tools for assessment submission and collection which are normal functions in a CMS. Bakar et. al. had reported their experience in developing and using an FYP management system at Universiti Kebangsaan Malaysia [7]. Their system consists of three major modules including user profile, project monitoring and appointment setting modules. Our system also contains similar functional modules as Barkar's, while we have additional modules like project allocation, file repository and online communication. The HKU CS Project Management System is a project management system that developed in the University of Hong Kong, Department of Computer Science [8]. The system can show project information, news, schedules and project allocation. In the main page of this system, it includes functions like blogs, calendar and forms downloading. Also, there is a list of projects and related information, as well as some advanced function like providing a virtual machine for students as servers for their FYP.

3 System Overview

Our system is divided into five modules based on their functionalities; they are project allocation module, communication module, project management module, file sharing & repository, and submission & grading module. These modules are useful for different parties involved in the FYP, they are the Programme Organizers (PO) or Administrator, Supervisor/Marker and Students.

Before the beginning of a year, PO will use the project allocation module to create all users' accounts and make it ready for supervisors to input their proposed project themes. Later, students can form groups and select project topic through the project allocation module. Before the start of the first semester, PO will allocate projects to each group of students by the automatic allocation function provided, and students will be informed via the system.

When the semester starts, students and supervisors are supported by the system with functions like task management, file sharing, and instant chat and discussion. Finally, students have to submit deliverables like proposals or reports by uploading to the submission and grading module. Marker and supervisors will be notified and insert their score to each project after review.

In the following of the paper, we will have more detail discussions on these five modules individually.

4 System Functionalities and Implementation

4.1 Project Allocation Module

Group formation and project selection are the first two steps the systen students as shown in Figure 1. These processes are done manually before ting paper forms to the PO. Students can use their accounts on the systen invitation to peers to form a group, as shown in Figure 2a. When the invit confirmed the group formation, the system will automatically recognize th as a group and allow the group to select their preferred project themes. In F group can choose three favorite projects from the list of available themes a the interface in Figure 2c. These project themes are prepared and input bef the supervisors to the systems as in Figure 2d. As a result, PO is not neces lect all the project themes from supervisors and announce them to the before. The system leverages the workload to PO and significantly reduce works involved.

An important feature provided by the project allocation module is the au signment of projects according to the academic records of students and the from students and supervisors. The mechanism of assigning project theme project group is illustrated in Figure 3. Project group with a higher averag record in the past years, only GPA is considered in our current implemen have a higher priority in selecting a project theme. As a result, by looping the available groups from the highest to lowest GPA, then assign project tl group based on their preference list will solve the problem of assignment.

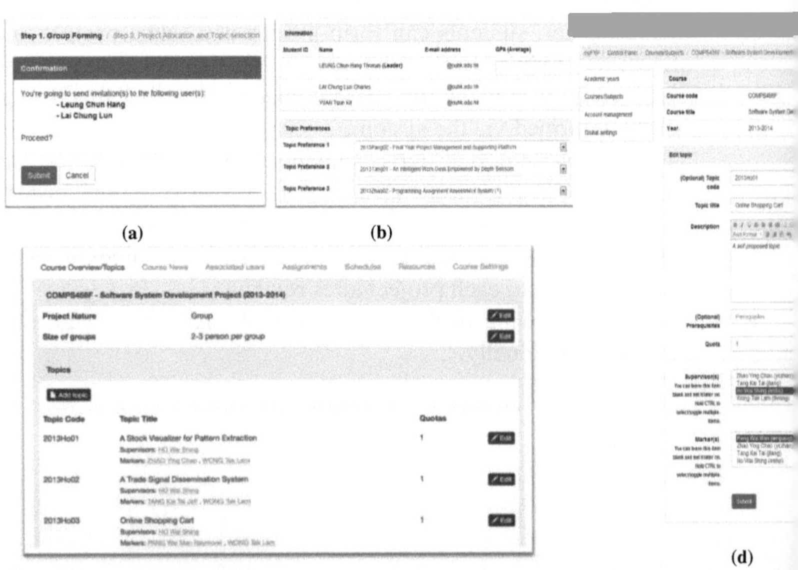

(a) (b) (c) (d)

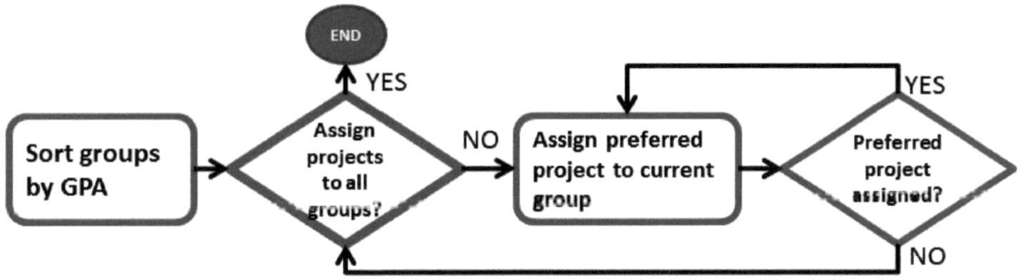

Fig. 3. Mechanism in processing the group assignment

However, when a group has all three preferred projects occupied by other groups already, this creates a problem in deciding which project should be assigned to this group. Our current implementation will try not to resolve this problem and leave these groups unassigned with a project theme in this stage. Groups without any project assigned in the first stage will have a chance for project selection in the second stage of assignment.

There may appear groups with the same GPA, and compete on the same project theme. This kind of conflict is problematic, as a random assignment to a specific group may create cascading effects to the assignments afterwards. For example, we have 3 groups A, B and C with their preferred projects P1 to P4 as shown in Figure 4a.

We see that as Group A and B have higher GPA than Group C, they can match for favorite projects first. However, as both Group A and B have chosen P1 as their first preference, and they have same GPA 3.5. This will cause a conflict between them. A simple random assignment of P1 to either one of them can cause very different overall assignment result due to the cascading effect as shown in Figure 4b and 4c. It is because each assignment is not always independent.

As in our example, if P1 is assigned to Group A, Group B surely has to match with its second preference P3, Group C is left unaffected in this case, and can be assigned with its first preference P2. However, the result can be totally different if P1 is assigned to Group B instead. We can see that Group A is now assigned to P2 which is the first preference of Group C. In this case, Group C can only match to its second preference P3 as shown in Figure 4c.

To avoid similar unexpected effect on the assignments, our system will prompt PO about this kind of tie situations, and stop further processing more assignments. We will rely on PO to resolve the conflict first before further processing, but it is rare to have groups with same average GPA and it should not cause much workload to PO.

Our system provides user-friendly interface for the PO to perform the mentioned assignment. In Figure 5a, PO can perform the assignment at any time he/she wants by just press a single button, and view the result immediately. When conflict occurs, the system will raise the problem as shown in Figure 5b to PO and ask for resolution from PO.

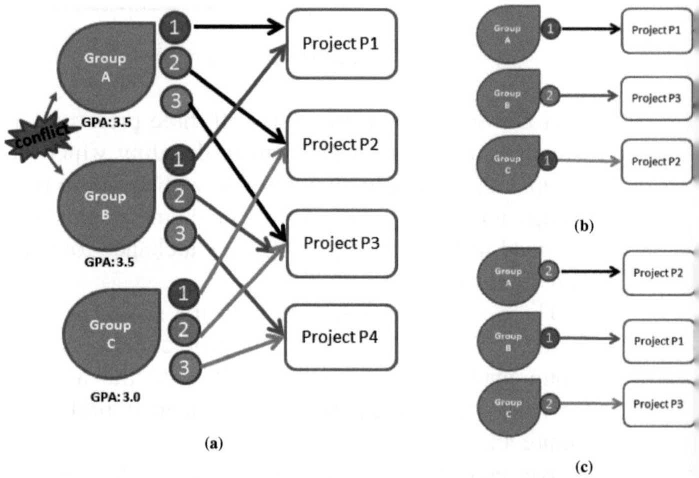

Fig. 4. (a) A sample scenario of final project assignment with three groups (A-
projects (P1 – P4), each group have 3 preferences labeled and pointing to the pro
scenario, conflict occurs because Group A and B have same GPA. **(b)** Result of
conflict by assigning P1 to Group A. **(c)** Result of resolving the conflict by ass
Group B instead. We find that the result of (b) and (c) are different and even affecti

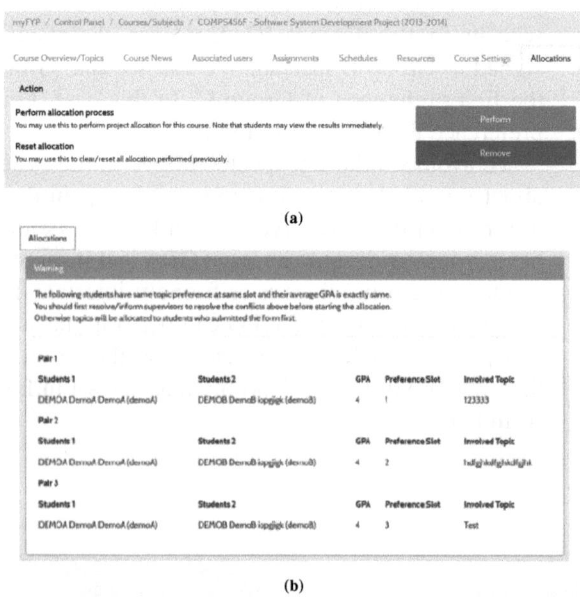

Fig. 5. (a) Administrators can start the allocation process manually through the pag
Conflicts have to be solved when two groups are having the same priority in choos
project.

4.2 Communication Module

Since our final year project is a group based one, communication between members and supervisor is an important issue for the success of the project. Our current channel of communication between supervisor and students mainly relies on the weekly or biweekly regular face-to-face meeting. However, as supervisor usually has limited time spending on the meeting, students are usually difficult to learn or discuss problem with their supervisor when working on the project. This can affect both the progress of FYP and the efficiency of the students in learning new technologies.

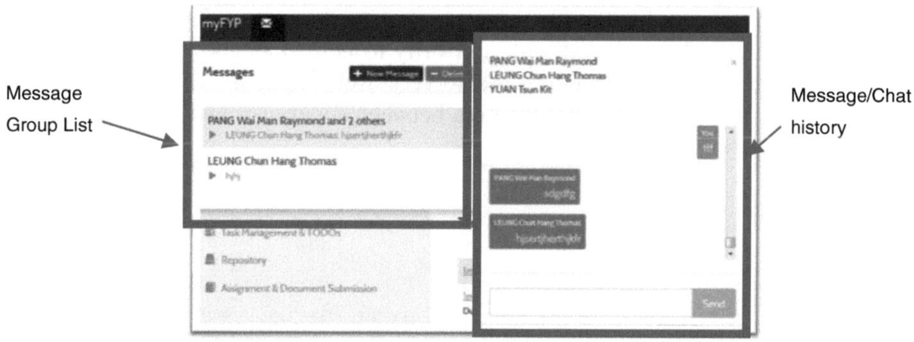

Fig. 6. Chat and messaging functions provide to group members and supervisors to communicate online

As a result, the communication module provides a new and convenient channel for meeting and discussion between project members and supervisors. Figure 6 shows the chat and messaging functionalities which are provided for students to discuss among themselves or ask questions to their supervisor. As message will be left on the system, either party can reply at any time or anywhere. It can provide extra time for discussion and reduce the time for finding each other.

Comparing to e-mail, messages on the system are much clearly organized and will not be overwhelmed by their already cluttered mailbox. It is because messages history can be referenced easily, and only group members can see the discussion.

Moreover, the real-time chat allows meeting to be held flexibly at any time that is convenient for all members and skip traveling time. Supervisor can also hold meetings at the same time with multiple groups and interleaving to response to questions from different groups at the same period of time, this can save time in meeting and become more efficient in communication.

4.3 Project Management Module

Apart from the communication issues, it is essential for all members to have a clear target or goal to accomplish during the development of the project. As both students and supervisors are always busy on the course works, teaching and learning during the semester, in order to keep up the momentum of working on the project, project management tool is useful.

Our current project management module includes a task management t students in keeping their schedule. Students can create and edit tasks on th ler by directly selecting the deadlines as in Figure 7. Each task in this TO be assigned with a priority to help students sorting out the completion or tasks in hand. It is also very useful in facilitating the discussion and progre in the regular meeting between supervisor and students.

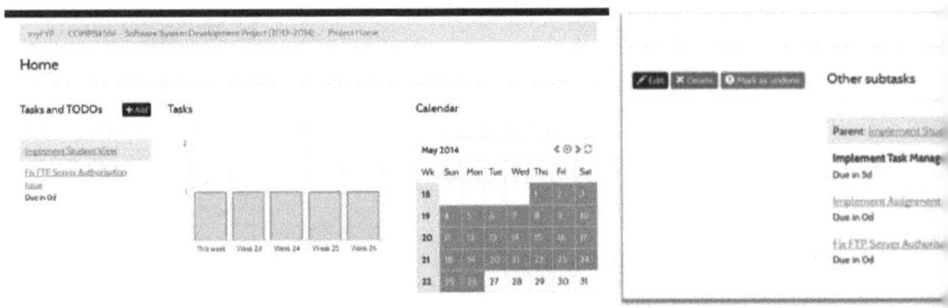

Fig. 7. Student can create tasks on the scheduler and plan for a reasonable compl project milestones. Therefore, students can keep track of their progress more easily.

4.4 File Sharing and Repository Module

During the development of a final year project, it is required that group divide workload among themselves, so that each of them will be respons plement only part of the prototype. Therefore, it is very necessary for the source code, documents and other important resources related to the proje rent students will rely on some cloud resources in public domain or their c device to exchange these important data among themselves.

As a result, our system was designed to provide file sharing function for groups to share source code or other resources among group mates and th sor. This file repository provides a more secure and centralized place for th their produced works. Supervisor can easily access students' work and ke the progress by directly viewing the shared deliverable of the project. Fi played the web interface when accessing the repository, only member of will be able to access the files in the repository and share among themselve

4.5 Submission and Grading Module

At the end of the semesters, our FYP programme will require students to results of the project by preparing the system prototypes and reports. Th submit the assessments to the system (see Figure 9a), instead of sending by email before. PO can easily check all the submission status of the Figure 9b), and obtain all the deliverables by simply download from the sy

Apart from relieving the workload of PO in collecting the assessmen

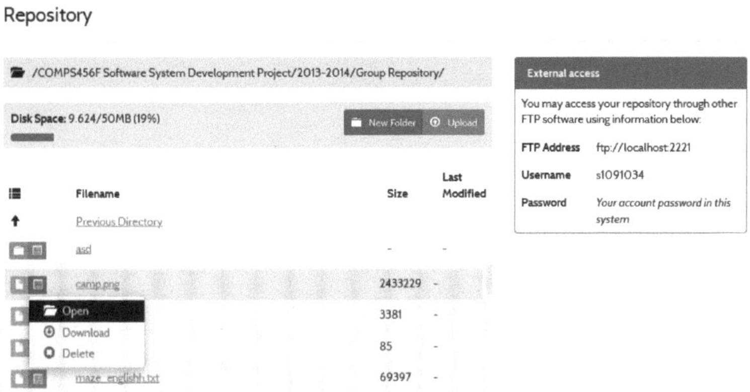

Fig. 8. File sharing and repository module provides a web interface for uploading, storing and sharing of project related resources like source code, documents, images and etc

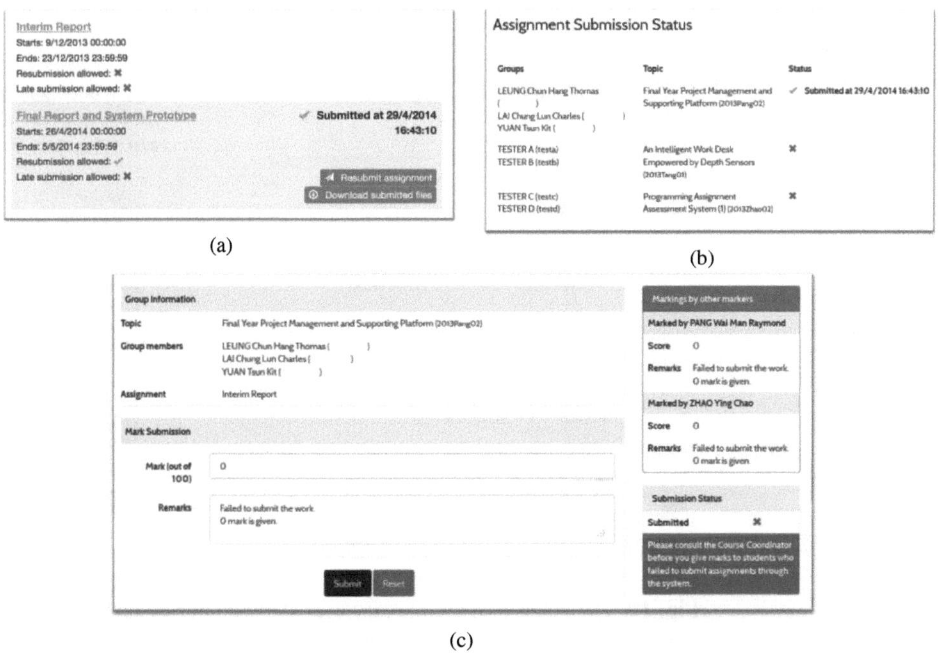

Fig. 9. User interfaces of the Submission and Grading Module. (a) Student can submit assessment. (b) PO can instantly check the submission status of all groups. (c) Markers can grade each assessment online.

5 Preliminary User Study and Evaluation of the System

To better understand the strength and weakness of our system, we have p preliminary study by interviewing thirteen students who are in their thir year's study. They are asked to try using all modules of the system, and the a questionnaire after the trial. The 10 questions are all yes or no question these questions and the response are shown in Figure 10.

Most of the responses are positive to our system, including the ease-o system and certain functions. Also, over 70 percent of the users think th convenient and willing to switch to the system.

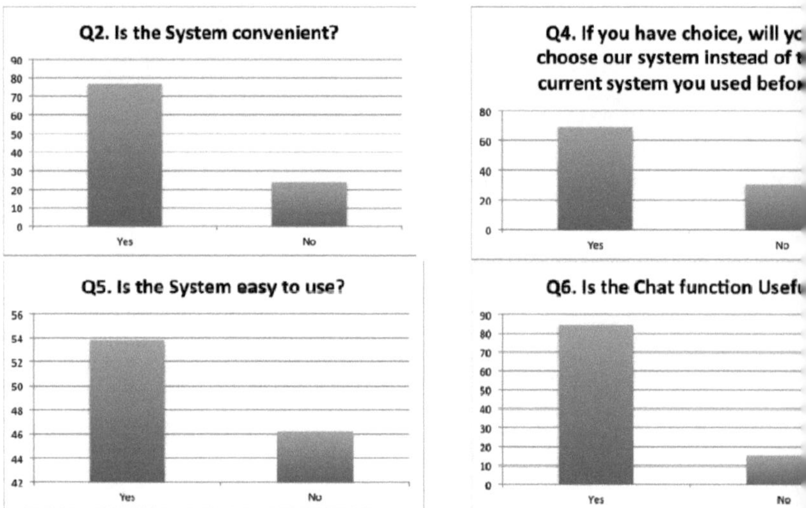

Fig. 10. The result of a preliminary user study on our system by interviewing thirt Results are presented in percentage.

6 Conclusion

We presented a specific system tailor to facilitate the implementation of th project in our IT programme. The FYP management system can significa the workload of programme organizer. Lots of arrangement, announcem sessment collection tasks can be done automatically in the system. At the our system provides convenience for supervisor and students throughout of FYP. First, supervisors and students can better communicate via the ch saging tools in the system. Supervisor can also easily keep track of the students with the project management module and file sharing functio supervisors and markers can quickly manage to obtain the deliverables of and provide grades on the system.

References

1. Unal, Z., Unal, A.: Evaluating and comparing the usability of web-based course management systems. Journal of Information Technology Education 10, 19–38 (2011)
2. Bremer, D., Bryant, R.: A Comparison of two learning management Systems: Moodle vs Blackboard. In: Proceedings of the 18th Annual Conference of the National Advisory Committee on Computing Qualifications, NACCQ, New Zealand, pp. 135–140 (2005)
3. Dougiamas, M., Taylor, P.C.: Moodle: Using learning communities to create an open source course management system. In: Proceedings of the EDMEDIA 2003 Conference, Honolulu, Hawaii (2003)
4. Blackboard Inc.: Blackboard (2013), http://www.blackboard.com/
5. ClockingIT.com: ClockingIT free time-tracking hosting (2008), http://www.clockingit.com/
6. Clement, R., Bounds, P.: Making Connections between Final Year Students and Potential Project Supervisors. In: Proceedings of the HEA STEM Learning and Teaching Conference (2013)
7. Bakar, M.A., Jailani, N., Shukur, Z., Yatim, N.F.M.: Final Year Supervision Management System as a Tool for Monitoring Computer Science Projects. Procedia Social and Behavioral Sciences 18, 273–281 (2011)
8. HKU CS: Hong Kong University Project Management System (2014), https://community.cs.hku.hk/web/csis0801/

Design and Implementation of a Teacher-Guic Semi-automatic Assessment Feedback Genera

Wai-Shing Ho[1], Tak-Lam Wong[2], Wai-Man Pang[1], and Jeff K. T. T

[1] Caritas Institute of Higher Education,
18 Chui Ling Road, Hong Kong
[2] The Hong Kong Institute of Education
10 Lo Ping Road, Tai Po, Hong Kong
{wsho,wmpang,jtang}@cihe.edu.hk
tlwong@ied.edu.hk

Abstract. Detailed feedback to assessments is an integral part of stud learning experience. Students can learn from their mistakes through the te ers' feedback. However, with the increasing workload, teachers may not enough time to write detailed and meaningful comments to every stude every assessment. This paper aims to share our experience in designing anc plementing a teacher-guided semi-automatic assessment feedback gener We observed that students' mistakes are repeating in nature. Instead of wr repeated comments for individual students, teachers may use our syste manage feedback templates and prepare individualized comments. Our sy provides the interface for teachers to record common mistakes and commer student assessments, and it lets teacher assign different comments to stu easily. This approach does not only greatly enhance the consistency in teac marking and comment generation, it also frees the teachers from repeated ing. The challenges faced in the design and implementation in our systen discussed in this paper.

Keywords: automatic feedback generation, case study, teacher support.

1 Introduction

Many studies have shown that feedback is one of the most powerful in learning and achievement [1][2]. Assessments help students locate mistak conceptions in the subject matters, and detailed feedback on incorrectly a sessment items helps students identify where they are actually wrong and h avoid making the same mistakes again. However, giving detailed feedbac assessment item to every student is a very time consuming task. With the workload of teachers in local higher institutions, teachers may not have eno give assessment feedback and the students' learning quality may suffer.

We observe that many teachers use a large portion of time in managing

Blackboard[1] or Moodle[2] to manage online courses. Student enrolments and course materials can be easily manipulated on the platform. Assessment setup and submission can also be managed. However, those platforms do not provide convenient means for teachers to record and disseminate detailed feedback to each assessment item. Teachers may still need to mark their feedbacks on the assessments and return the feedbacks together with the assessments to the students. When the class size is large, marking such assessments is time consuming and tedious.

In order to save teachers time in providing detailed assessment feedback to students, we designed a teacher-guided semi-automatic assessment feedback generation system. This system helps teacher in three aspects. First, it communicates with the e-learning platform (Moodle in our case) to retrieve course, enrolment, and assessment information. The system provides a convenient interface for teachers to record detailed feedback on each assessment item. Second, we observed that most of the students' mistakes in assessments are repeating in nature. i.e., a lot of students share the same mistakes. If the feedbacks are written, the teacher needs to write the same detailed feedback to a large number of students' work. This is inefficient, and it is prone to inconsistency in marking. The system provides a convenient interface for a feedback knowledge base, and teachers may select the most suitable feedback from a list instead of typing them from scratch. This saves a large portion of typing time and enhance the consistency in marking. Third, the system constructs the detailed feedback to every student and disseminates this individual, personalized feedback to the student. With such a personalized feedback, we believe that students will get a sense of being cared and their learning experience is much improved.

This paper is structured as follows. Work related to automatic assessment and feedback will be discussed in Section 2. Section 3 discusses the design of our teacher-guided semi-automatic assessment feedback generation system. A discussion on issues in implementing the system and evaluation plan will appear in Section 4.

2 Related Work

Feedback is one of the most powerful influences on learning and achievement [1]. Timely and detailed feedback is essential in effective delivery of knowledge in classrooms. As shown in many studies [2][3], feedback from teachers (or peers) greatly enhances the learning process of the students. Higgins, Hartley, & Skelton reported that formative assessment feedback is essential to encourage the kind of "deep" learning desired by teachers [4]. Instead of giving grades to the students, teachers' high-quality written feedback can help students engage with the subject in a deep way. Thus, it is important to help teachers to prepare high quality assessment feedbacks to the students under the limited time.

One attempt to helping teachers create timely feedback is to mark the assessments automatically. Such research usually focused at identifying whether the students have

[1] http://www.blackboard.com/
[2] http://www.moodle.org/

found the correct answers or not for the assessment and whether the stu mastered the corresponding course content. For example, a framework different types of automated assessment tools is proposed in a study [5]. proposed can use a wide range of different assessment formats to check students can master the module content. Edwards also proposed the use mated grading approach to assess students' code in a software engineering However, such automated marking systems usually have limited usage correctness is not well-defined in certain types of assessments (e.g., essay ments). The correctness cannot be objectively determined by the system ar intervention is required in generating proper feedbacks. Thus, a sem approach which can incorporate teachers' flexible feedbacks is required.

Learning management systems such as Blackboard and Moodle provi for managing the courses and setting up assessment items. They can au mark whether the students answered the assessment items correctly and pr for teachers to give comments to the students for each assessment item. H comments are limited to be textual, and the comments to different stude pendent. Thus, teachers have to spend a large amount of time typing i comments if many students are having the same mistake. Therefore, a that can manage the comments and avoid repetition is essential in reducin ers' workload.

3 System Design

Our assessment feedback system is a web-based system. It commun Moodle to get the course and enrolment information. After getting that i teachers can create assessments in our system, and then use our interface the detailed feedbacks to the students. When the marking finishes, the sy bines the feedback to each individual student and sends personalized feedb students.

3.1 Course/Enrolment/Assessment Management

This module helps teachers in retrieving the course and enrolment inform Moodle. Teachers can use their accounts to connect to the institutional M retrieve the courses they teach and the enrolment in each course. When a are created in a course, the enrolment information can be used in ma students who need the feedback.

When an assessment is being created, the teacher can choose how much m located to each assessment item. Later, when the teacher marks the assessm student, he/she can give the marks and select the comments for each assessm

3.2 Assessment Feedback Records

When a teacher selects an assessment for marking, he/she gets a list of students as shown in Fig. 1. This is the basis for the teacher to record the detailed feedback to the students. The teacher can access the submitted files through the links; and then he/she can select the student he/she is marking. A new page similar to Fig. 2 will be shown. The teacher can input the marks and select the appropriate comments applicable to the student. If the teacher finds that there is a new situation where previous comments are not applicable, he/she can click on the "add new feedback entry" button to create a new feedback for that assessment item. Then, he/she can select this new entry, together with other applicable entries, in the selection box.

MATH102 Numerical and IT Literacy

Assignment 1

Name	SID	Submitted Files	Marks	Links
Chan Tai Man	012345678	A1.pdf	--	Mark
Chan Tai Ming	012345679	A1.pdf	--	Mark
Lee Tai Man	013000001	A1.pdf	--	Mark

Fig. 1. List of students in an assessment

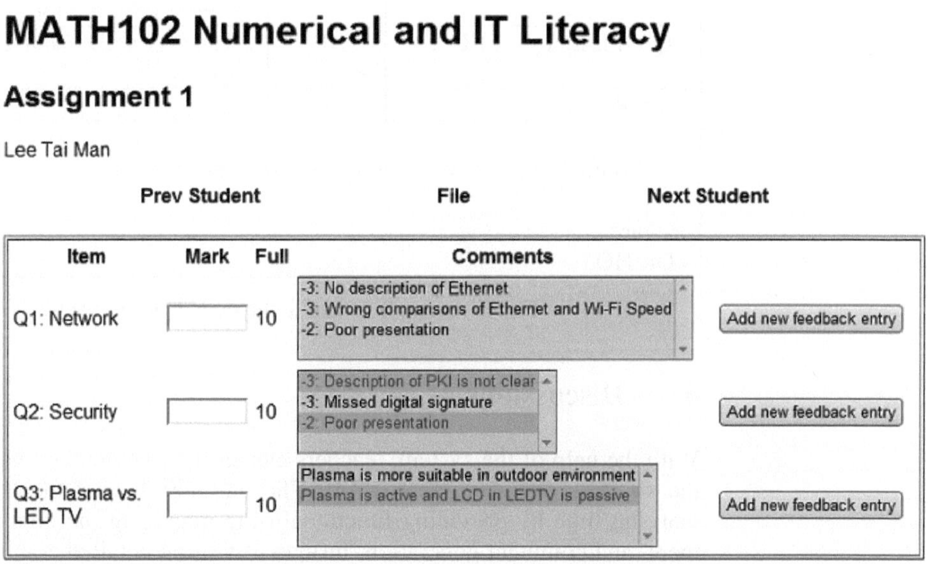

Fig. 2. Interface for marking an assessment of a student

3.3 Dissemination of Comments

After marking all the assessments, the teacher can use the system to as individual comments to every student. In the enrolment records, e-mail inf stored for every student. Fig. 3 shows a sample e-mail to a student with marks and comments. We believe that the detailed individual comments the students will improve the learning quality.

Dear Tai Man,

Here is a summary of your Assignment 1 in MATH102 Numerical anc acy.

Item	Mark	Comments
Q1: Network	10/10	Nil
Q2: Security	5/10	-3: Description of PKI is not clear -2: Poor presentation
Q3: Plasma vs. LED TV	7/10	Plasma is active and LCD in LE passive
Total	22/30	

Should you have any enquiry, please contact XXXX

Regards,
Dr. HO

Fig. 3. A sample e-mail to the student generated by the system

4 Discussions

With the help of the system, teachers can easily give detailed individual co the students on every assessment. The interface helped the teachers to marking time by providing functionality in managing the course, enrolm ment, and comment generation. Instead of writing detailed comments as te can use the interface to select common comments. With the high quality comments received by the students, we believe that the students will app efforts and learn the course materials in a better manner. Thus, the next s research is applying this system in courses and evaluate the perceptions and students on the effectiveness of the system.

References

1. Hattie, J., Timperley, H.: The power of feedback. Review of Educational Research 77(1), 81–112 (2007)
2. Paulus, T.M.: The effect of peer and teacher feedback on student writing. Journal of Second Language Writing 8(3), 265–289 (1999)
3. Weaver, M.R.: Do students value feedback? Student perceptions of tutors' written responses. Assessment & Evaluation in Higher Education 31(3), 379–394 (2006)
4. Higgins, R., Hartley, P., Skelton, A.: The concientious consumer: Reconsidering the role of assessment feedback in student learning. Studies in Higher Education 27(1), 53–64 (2002)
5. English, J., Siviter, P.: Experience with an automatically assessed course. In: Proceedings of the 5th Annual SIGCSE/SIGCUE ITiCSE Conference on Innovation and Technology in Computer Science Education, pp. 168–171. ACM, Helsinki (2000)
6. Edwards, S.H.: Using test-driven development in the classroom: Providing students with automatic, concrete feedback on performance. In: Proceedings of the International Conference on Education and Information Systems: Technologies and Applications, Florida (2003)

PMS – A Simulation Game for Interactive Lear
of Software Project Management

Richard W.C. Lui, Hareton K.N. Leung, Vincent T. Y. Ng, and Philip T

Department of Computing, Hong Kong Polytechnic University, Hung Hom, Hc
richard.lui@polyu.edu.hk
{cshleung,cstyng,cstylee}@comp.polyu.edu.hk

Abstract. Successful management of software projects requires both theor
project management knowledge as well as practical reality-like managemen
periences. Simulation Based Training provides a hands-on approach to ex
the complexity of managing projects through rapid and inexpensive experi
tation. Most of the existing project simulation game focuses only or
management of time, scope, cost, and human resource. There are relatively
products which focus on project stakeholder management, communication
agement and quality management.

In this paper, a project management simulation game, PMS, is introduc
support the interactive learning of software project management. The gam
sign, implementation and how it may support the learning of software pr
management concepts in different knowledge areas are discussed.

Keywords: Software Project Management, Project Management Simula
e-Learning, Simulation Based Teaching.

1 Introduction

IT projects are plagued by poor quality and schedule/cost overrun. To i
quality of IT projects, better education of (future) project managers is esse
lation games have been adopted by many universities throughout the worl
the teaching of project management [1]. Simulation Based Training provid
on approach to explore the complexity of managing projects through rapi
pensive experimentation. The user will take the role as a project manage
project decisions in some pre-defined project scenarios (e.g. manufacturi
building a high-tech large scale shark aquarium). Many of the existing p
agement simulation games only focus on the time, scope, cost, and hum
management in Project Management Body of Knowledge (PMBOK) [2]
fewer existing products focus on project stakeholder management, com
management and quality management of software projects.

In this paper, a project simulation game, PMS, is introduced for supporti
ing of software project management. Students will act as a project manag

management, stakeholder management, and quality management. Students are required to analyze the stakeholders' needs and expectation, properly define the project scope, and communicate with the stakeholders throughout the project. Students are also expected to conduct quality review activities early and develop prototypes for demonstration so as to improve the software quality and increase the stakeholders' satisfaction.

This paper is organized as follows. In section 2, related studies will be reviewed. The game design will be discussed in section 3. In section 4, the implementation will be discussed. In section 5, summary and future studies will be presented.

2 Related Studies

Simulation Based Training is recognized as an efficient and effective way for teaching and learning complex, dynamic systems for engineering and business curriculum [3]. Drappa and Ludewig developed a simulation game for software engineering education named SESAM [4]. The game adopts a rather low-level modeling approach. For example, bugs multiplication and additional communication effort due to more team members are simulated in the game. The game, however, interacts with students with plain texts without any graphics. The authors evaluated the educational value of the game through controlled experiment and case study, and they showed that the simulation software is a powerful tool for project manager training. Dantas et al. developed a simulation game called 'The Incredible Manager' to assist students to learn project management knowledge through experience from simulation [5]. The game has project members and project phases defined. Distinct models for each scenario with uncertain aspects were also developed.

Harvard project management simulation game[1] is designed for letting the students to explore the trade-offs among the three major project management levers: scope, resources, and schedule and the effect of team morale on project attributes. The user will take the role of a project manager who will make project decisions on some predefined project scenarios (e.g. manufacturing of printers). Project Team Builder is a project management simulation game with a scenario editor for creating custom project scenarios [6]. The game mainly focuses on time, scope, cost, human resources and risks management. SimSE is a computer-based environment that facilitates the creation and simulation of real-istic game-based software process simulation models [7]. It supports different software development processes, such as Waterfall, Extreme Programming, rapid prototyping, and Rational Unified Process. Lee proposed an Excel-based project management simulation game to facilitate the teaching of project management in a classroom setting [8].

[1] Project Management Simulation: Scope, Resources, Schedule V2. Available at `http://cb.hbsp.harvard.edu/cb/product/4700-HTM-ENG`

3 Game Design

3.1 Overview

In the game, the user plays the role as a project manager in a software d project. The user should analyze the stakeholders' expectation and prefe oritize the project requirements, and define the project scope to meet the of the stakeholders within the project constraints (e.g. scope, time, cost, qu ing project execution, the user should make appropriate decisions to m project team to achieve good morale, communicate with stakeholders to ac stakeholder satisfaction and monitor the project progress in different dime time, quality). Figure 1 shows the various entities in the simulation attributes for the different entities in the game is shown in Table 1.

Requirements: Functional and non-functional requirement which form th the project.

Stakeholders: Stakeholders are people who are involved in or affected by (e.g. project sponsors, customers, system users, suppliers, etc). Stakeholder different expectation on the functional/non-functional requirements of Each project stakeholder has their own level of *satisfaction* towards the come.

Activities: An activity is an abstraction of a unit of work to be perform members in the project. The effort required to complete activities increa non-core requirements are included in the project scope.

*Team members***:** Activities are performed by a team member. Different tea have different skill levels/expertise.

Project team: A project team is composed of one or more team members. team should communicate with stakeholders early and regularly so that understand the project's benefits and the most updated project status.

Defects: Defects are mistakes or faults that may be generated in a softwa ment project when performing project activities.

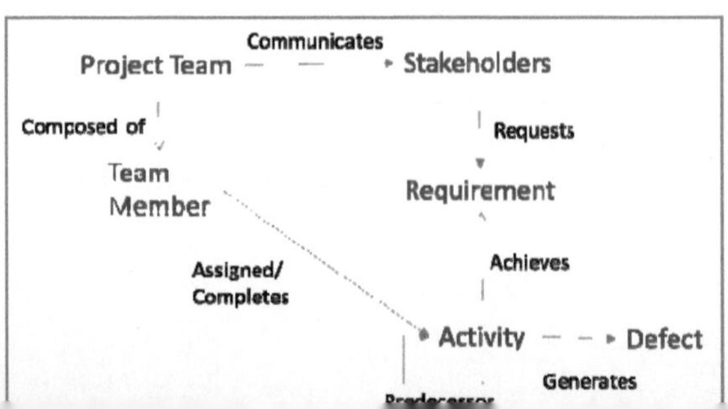

3.2 Game Decisions and Causal Model

The user should make a number of management decisions to plan for the project. Based on the analysis of the project stakeholders, the user should properly define the functional and non-functional requirements to be completed in the project. The user should also choose appropriate team members to be included in the project team and assign them to complete the project activities.

The project will start after the project planning is completed. The user should arrange management activities during the project execution to manage the project team and stakeholders. Examples of management activities are shown in Table 1.

Table 1. Game Attributes

Entity	**Attributes**	**Description**
Stakeholder	Project Understanding	The extent to which stakeholders understand about the project (expected project outcome and benefits, current project status, etc).
	Satisfaction	Stakeholders' satisfaction towards the project outcome.
	Importance	The power and level of influence of the stakeholder on project outcome or decisions.
	Project Interest	The stakeholder's level of concern for project outcomes.
	Communication Preference	Communication preference is the way the stakeholder wants to be communicated with. This includes face-to-face meeting, virtual meeting, detailed status report and prototype demonstration.
Team Member	Project knowledge	Team members' knowledge about the project objective, scope, stakeholders, most updated project status, etc.
	Morale	The level of motivation and enthusiasm of the team member towards their work.
	Fatigue	The level of tiredness of the team member. A team member may make more mistakes if he/she is tired.
	Daily Cost	Salary of the team member per day
Project team	Teamwork	How well the team members can work together as a team to achieve the project objectives
	Requirement Understanding	The extent of project team members' understanding of the stakeholder's true needs and expectation on the project or final product.

Table 2. Management activities during project execution

Category	Management activities
Team Management	Organize a Project Kickoff Meeting
	Creation of Team Slogan
	Reward and Recognition
	Half-Day Off
	Social Gathering
	Training/Coaching
Internal Communication	Internal Meeting
	Social Interaction /Management Wandering Around
External Communication	Status Review Meeting (Face to Face/Virtual Meeti
	Brief/Detailed Status Reports
Quality	Requirement Review Meeting
	Code Review Meeting
	Prototype Preparation and Demonstration
Time Management	Overtime
Others	Purchase (e.g. Project Portal)

At the end of the game, the user's performance will be evaluated base holder Satisfaction, Time, Quality, Cost, Scope and Team Morale (refer In this paper, we will focus on the stakeholder satisfaction and quality dim

Table 3. Dimensions for evaluating the game performance

Dimension	Description
Stakeholder Satisfaction	The stakeholders' perception towards the project and final product stakeholder satisfaction is affected by the project scope and the co tion with the project team. Important stakeholders (with high influ the project decisions and outcome) will have higher weight toward stakeholder satisfaction score.
Time	The time required to complete the project
Quality	The total number of defects in the final product.
Cost	The amount of financial resources spent on the project.
Scope	The requirements that are completed by the project. Users will get score if more non-core requirements are included in the project sc
Team Morale	The average morale of the team members in the project team.

Understanding project stakeholder's perception and expectation during velopment is essential for improving the chance of project success [9][10 tive project manager should analyze, evaluate, and deliver messages in dif munication channels (e.g. status meeting, status report) to ensure the effe the communications. Fig. 2 shows the causal diagram for the stakeholder

stakeholders, the student should properly define the project scope by prioritizing the needs of the different stakeholders. During project execution, management activities such as status review meetings and status report should be adopted to communicate with stakeholders early and regularly so that they fully understand the project's benefits and the most updated project status. In the game, stakeholders with higher interests to the project will require more frequent project update. If there is insufficient communication between the project team and stakeholders, the stakeholder's project understanding will decrease and this may decrease the stakeholder satisfaction.

The stakeholders may have different personality types and they may prefer different communication style [11]. In the game, different stakeholders have different communication preference (e.g. face-to-face meeting, virtual meeting, and detailed status report). Appropriate communication channel should be adopted to increase the stakeholder satisfaction.

In software projects, stakeholders often do not have a very clear understanding of what they really need or want. Due to the intangible nature of software and uncertain outcome of IT projects, it is challenging to represent the key facets of software in a way which is accessible to all stakeholders [12]. Prototype is a working replica of the system or particular functions. Through prototype preparation and demonstration, stakeholders can better understand the user interfaces and features of the final products. This helps increase the stakeholders' understanding and maintain the stakeholders' satisfaction.

Fig. 2. Causal Diagram for Stakeholder Satisfaction

Studies have shown that the majority of the defects identified in the software testing phase are introduced in the requirement or design phase [13]. Since defects generated may multiply the defects in the downstream activities, defects identified later in the software development lifecycle are more expensive to fix than defects identified at early stages. The game models three types of defects: requirement defects, user interface defects, and coding defects. In the game, the defects generated earlier in the project may increase the defect generation rate of subsequent project activities. Therefore, the defects should be discovered and fixed early by requirement review and code review. During prototype preparation and demonstration, team members can also gain

a better understanding of requirements, evaluate system feasibility and v
system design. In the game, the user interface defects can be discovered an
during prototype demonstration to the stakeholders. The development and
tion of prototypes may also increase the requirement understanding of
team. As a result, fewer defects will be generated in subsequent project acti

4 Implementation

4.1 System Components

Fig 3 shows the system components:

Project Scenario: A project scenario is an XML document which defin
ties (e.g. team member, stakeholder, activities, and their dependency, re
sudden events) and the game attributes (E.g. initial cash, target completion

Scenario Builder: Custom project scenarios can be created by scenario b

Game Rule: An XML document defining the rules for the game (e.g
management activities, number of action points per week, causal relation
different game attributes)

Game Configuration tool: Defines the game settings and causal mod
format.

Game Engine: The project scenario will be read and executed by the ga
The game rules and causal model are enforced by the game engine.

User interface: Graphical user interface for interacting with the users.

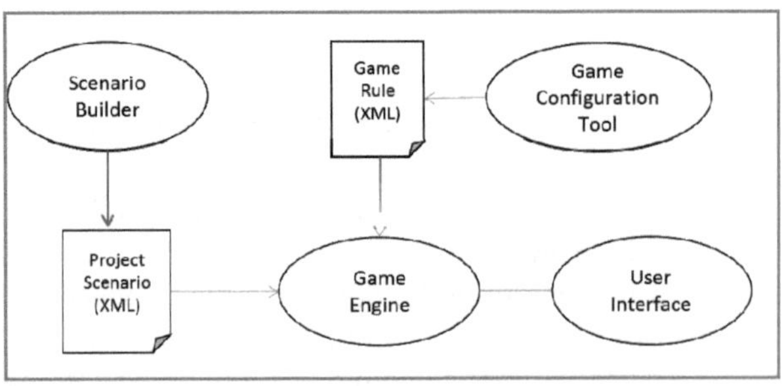

Fig. 3. System components

4.2 Game Features

A hypothetical project scenario is created to illustrate the features of the
user will act as a project manager in a company and plan for the video co
cation development project (refer to Fig. 4). In the project, there are five s
and eight potential team members.

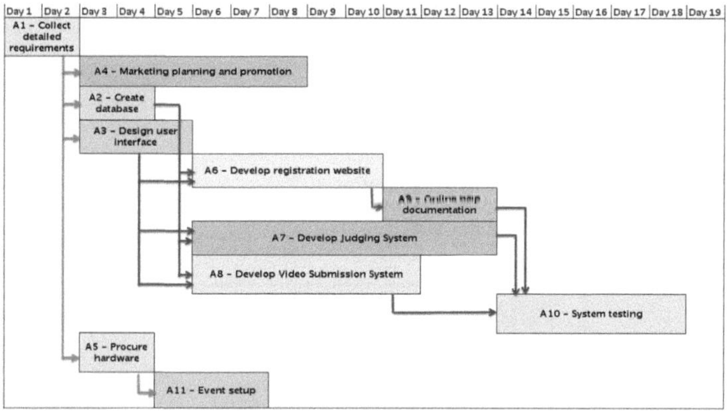

Fig. 4. Project Schedule for the hypothetical project

During the planning phase, the user may select a subset of non-core requirements to be included in the project scope (refer to Fig 5). As time and human resources are required to complete the selected optional requirements, the user should strike a balance between stakeholders' satisfaction, project duration and cost. The user should also select appropriate team members to form the project team and assign them to the project activities (refer to Fig. 6).

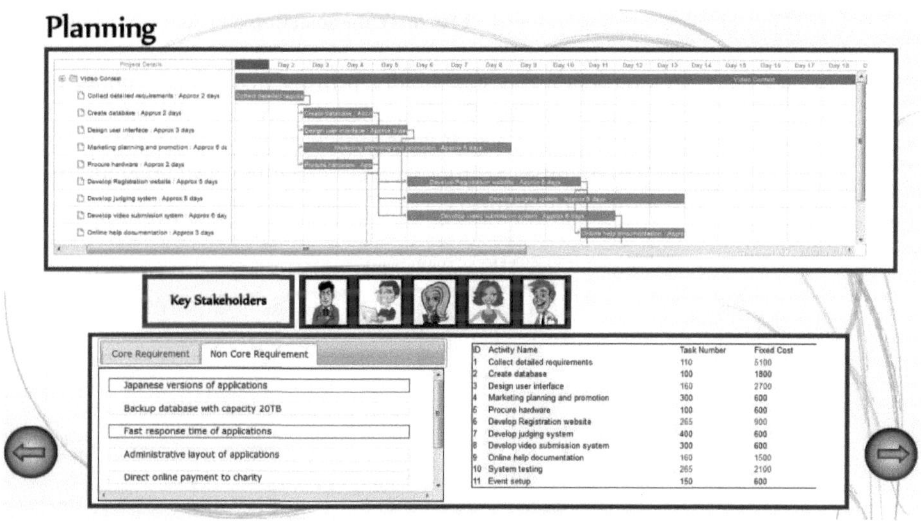

Fig. 5. Selection of non-core requirements

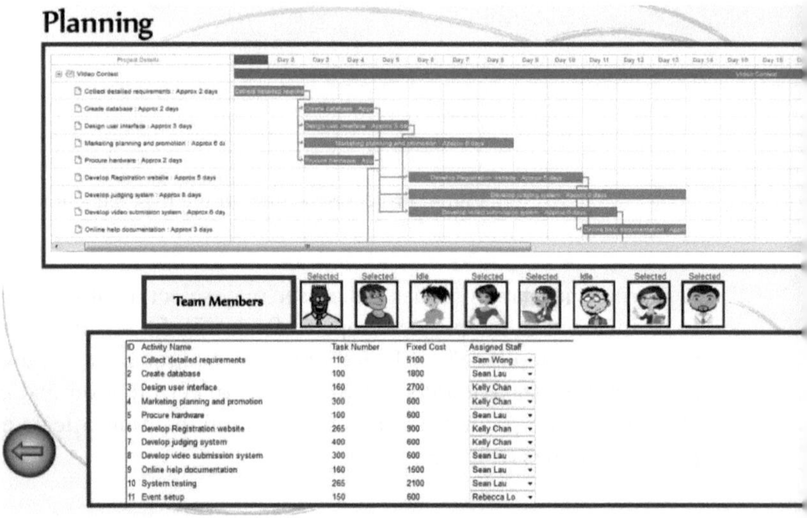

Fig. 6. Team Selection and Activity Assignment

Comprehensive stakeholder profiles and team member profiles are cre
game (refer to Fig. 7). The user may review the stakeholder profiles to
the stakeholders' needs and expectation on the project. The user may
the team member profiles to understand the skill level and the various attri
different team members.

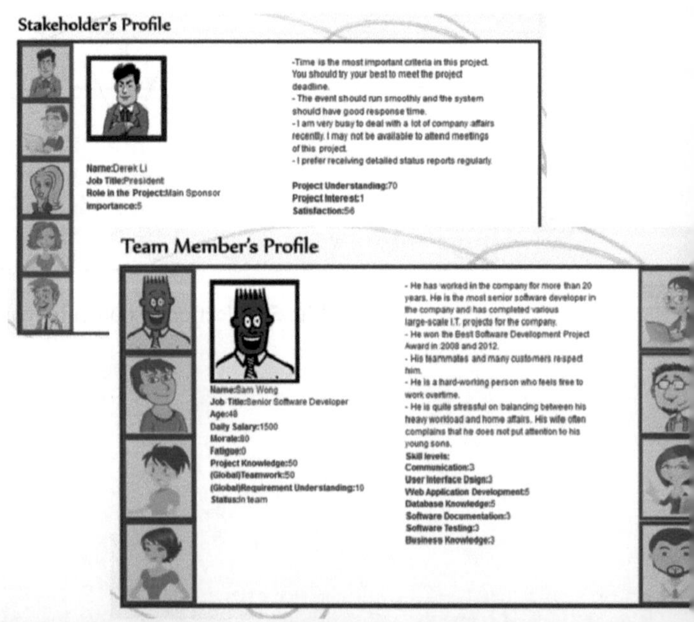

The project will start after the project planning phase (refer to Fig. 8). Different options are available for the user (e.g. adjusting team member's assignment to activity, viewing the sudden events that have occurred, reviewing charts/project information). On every Monday, the user may plan the management activities for the coming week (weekly decisions) (refer to Fig. 9). Users will be given action points for planning the management activities in the current week. For instance, suppose the user intends to prepare and demonstrate a prototype in the current week. A stakeholder should be selected for attending the presentation and a team member should be chosen as a presenter. Choosing a presenter with good communication skill has the bonus effect of increasing the project stakeholder's satisfaction.

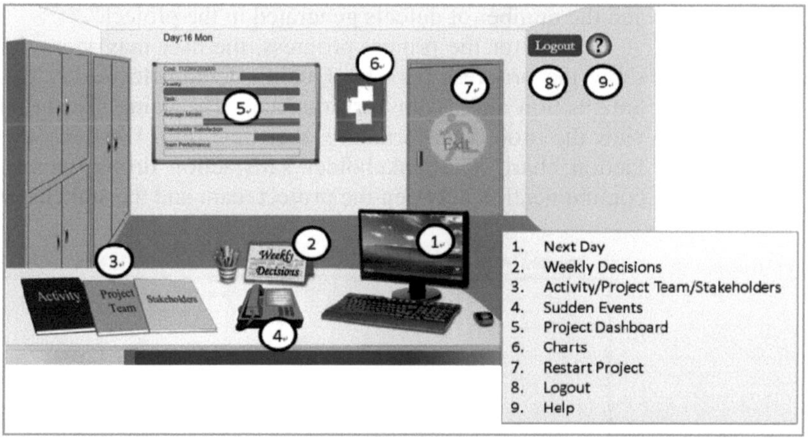

Fig. 8. Office Environment during project execution

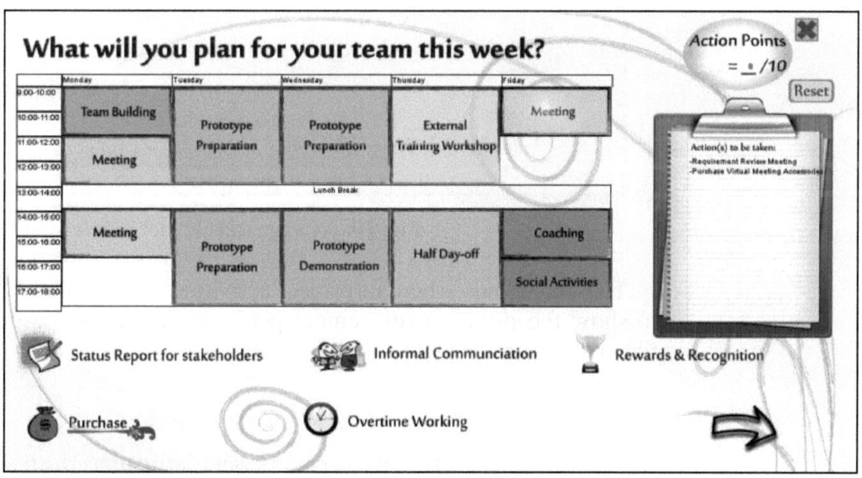

Fig. 9. Weekly Decisions Options

Users may click the next day button to proceed to the next day. A dail will be displayed to summarize the project progress. The user may review t management activities in the current week, current progress of each proje and the number of defects generated in the project.

To monitor the project progress, the user may view the project dashbc show the progress bars for Quality, Complete Tasks, Average Morale, S Satisfaction and Team performance). The game also provides charts for view the project performance over time. Fig. 10 shows the average stakeh faction chart. The stakeholder satisfaction drops over time because of communication between the project team and the stakeholders.

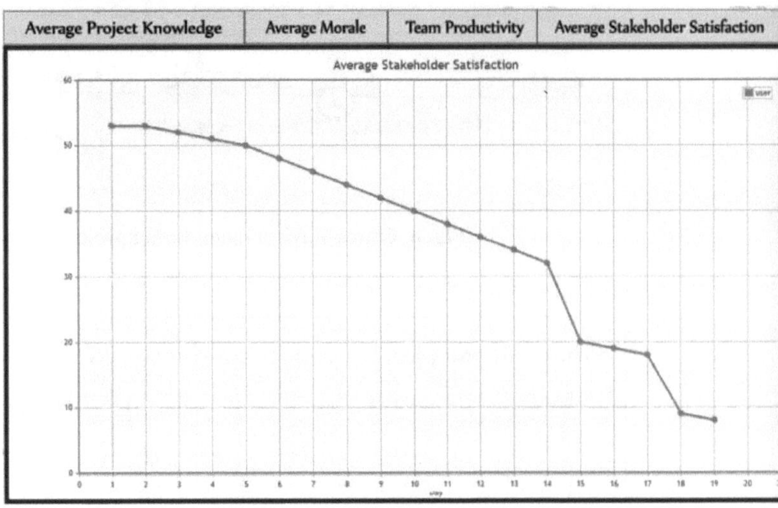

Fig. 10. Average stakeholder satisfaction Chart

The game ends when all project activities are completed. A page will b to show the project management performance under the different dimens Fig. 11).

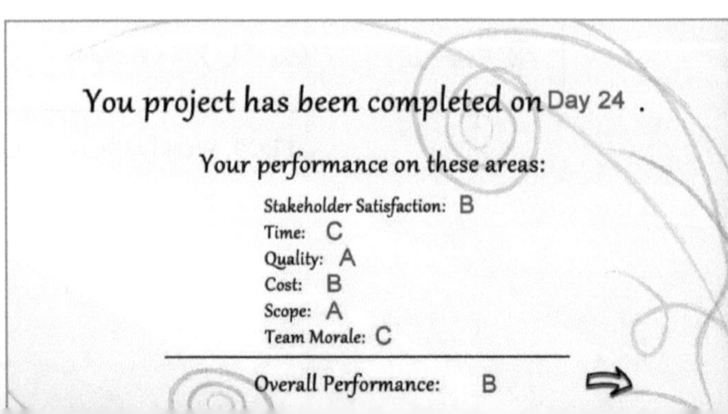

5 Summary and Future Work

In this paper, the design and implementation details of a project simulation game, PMS, is presented. In addition to scope, time, and human resources management, the game also focuses on project decisions for communication management, stakeholder management, and quality management. Our future work is to extend the game to include more project management decisions and sudden events. Also, the effectiveness of the game for the teaching and learning of software project management concepts will be evaluated.

References

1. Cohen, I., Iluz, M., Shtub, A.: A simulation-based approach in support of project management training for systems engineers. Systems Engineering 17(1), 26–36 (2014)
2. PMI.: A Guide to the Project Management Body of Knowledge: PMBOK(R) Guide. Project Management Institute (2013)
3. Salas, E., Wildman, J., Piccolo, R.: Using simulation-based training (SBT) to enhance management education. The Academy of Management Learning and Education 8(4), 559–573 (2009)
4. Drappa, A., Ludewig, J.: Simulation in software engineering training. In: Proceedings of the 22nd International Conference on Software Engineering, pp. 199–208. ACM (2000)
5. Dantas, A.R., de Oliveira Barros, M., Werner, C.M.L.: A Simulation-Based Game for Project Management Experiential Learning. SEKE 19, 24 (2004)
6. Shtub, A.: Project Management Simulation with PTB Project Team Builder. Springer (2012)
7. Navarro, E., Van Der Hoek, A.: Multi-site evaluation of SimSE. In: Proceedings of the 40th ACM Technical Symposium on Computer Science Education, pp. 326–330. ACM (2009)
8. Lee, W.L.: Spreadsheet based experiential learning environment for project. In: Proceedings of the 2011 Winter Simulation Conference (2011)
9. Pan, G.: Information systems project abandonment: a stakeholder analysis. International Journal of Information Management 25(2), 173–184 (2005)
10. Boonstra, A., De Vries, J.: Managing stakeholders around inter-organizational systems: A diagnostic approach. The Journal of Strategic Information Systems Archive, 190–201 (2008)
11. Morris, R., Sember, B.: Project Management That Works: Real-World Advice on Communicating, Problem-Solving, and Everything Else You Need to Know to Get the Job Done. In: AMACOM (2008)
12. RAENG.: The Challenges of Complex IT Projects. The Royal Academy of Engineering (2004)
13. Patton, R.: Software Testing. Sams Publishing (2005)

A Study on Students' Attitudes Towards Teach Intervention in Statistical Computing Laborat

Ken W. Li[1] and Merrilyn Goos[2]

[1] Department of Information and Commmunications Technology,
Hong Kong Institute of Vocational Education (Tsing Yi), Hong Kong SAR,
kenli@vtc.edu.hk
[2] School of Education, The University of Queensland, Queensland, Austr
m.goos@uq.edu.au

Abstract. Within an IT environment, the teacher's role has changed transmitting knowledge to managing IT resources for learning and facilit student learning. Thus, the teacher planned for improving classroom tea practice by playing these two roles, particularly in computing laboratory sions. Students within each computing laboratory session were divided small groups so as to enable teacher's intervention to offer assistance or c tives within each group more efficiently. A question which arises here is the teacher's intervention promoted learning and statistical thinking of stu when using IT in a statistics classroom. A questionnaire based survey was conducted to study the attitudes of students towards teacher's interve within IT environment. The results of the survey indicated that the te played facilitating and supporting roles in their learning to foster a learnin mosphere, restructure learning tasks and provide feedback.

Keywords: social process of learning, modelling heuristics, statistical think

1 Introduction

Within an IT environment, the teacher's role has changed from transmi ledge to managing IT resources for learning and facilitating the constructic ledge. For instance, Knutzen discussed how teachers could develop and online learning management system in which they posed the learning con cussions among students and the teachers monitored their discussion activi

The teacher planned for improving classroom teaching practice by ado tating as well as managerial roles within an IT environment. Using Taylor' refers to enabling students to have a more intuitive feel for the concepts be serving students to alleviate computational burden; and implementing con by students [2].

The teacher taught a statistics module, "Regression Modelling", follow tern of 2-hour lectures and 1-hour computing laboratory sessions in eac

own understandings, opinions, judgments or perspectives. The discussion they held was a form of interaction where they joined together to evaluate ideas their classmates brought forward in order to come up with a joint decision leading to a correct and complete answer. In computing laboratory sessions, the teacher used talk to guide the construction of students' knowledge and orchestrate learning activities. Students within each computing laboratory session were divided into 2-person or 3-person groups in order to increase students' opportunities for peer learning; and to enable teacher's intervention to offer assistance or directives within each group more efficiently and to monitor their learning progress. Each group of students was assigned laboratory exercises demanding the analysis, design or implementation of the solutions in a statistical computing laboratory. Apart from apparent uses of IT in teaching and learning, IT has an educational role in organising environment to promote interaction among students as well as students and teacher.

2 Literature Review

In Li and Ng's study, they found that students demanded peer collaboration and student-teacher interaction when learning with IT [3]. Learning with IT here refers to the way that can organise the learning environment to promote social interaction among students as well as between students and a teacher. Thus, Li proposed a model of pedagogy in an IT environment aiming at quality teaching and learning of statistics to address the significance of teacher guidance and peer collaboration [4].

Li conducted a questionnaire based survey to study how students perceived the learning activities taking place in an IT environment [5]. The survey results indicated that most students held positive perceptions of learning with IT associated with productive social interactions with their learning partners. They found their interaction with their learning partners collaborative and their communication beneficial to learning as it enabled them to verbalise their thoughts to sustain task-centred discussion.

Fisher argued that teachers played managerial and facilitating roles in classroom teaching would be beneficial to student learning [6]. Students sought assistance from their teacher to overcome learning difficulties or mediate between a student and their learning partners. That is why Hoyles and Sutherland found that learning progress is associated with teacher's interventions for maintaining control with students; offering teacher-directed tasks; and being in the form of teaching episodes [7]. They also studied the nature of the intervention and further classified the interventions as being motivational, reflectional or directional.

Mercer provided a framework to analyse talk used by teachers assisting students in knowledge construction in the following ways [8]. The teacher elicited knowledge from students; responded to what students said; and recapped to re-organise, or call attention to the significant ideas students had just presented. The recap so used can be reflectional, and may end up offering hints or directives.

Tharp and Gallimore also developed a framework for categorising ways in which teachers' talk assists their students to learn, via modelling, questioning, cognitive structuring, contingency management, feeding back and instructing [9]. Within each of these discourse categories, teachers may elicit, respond, or recap. Fo questioning can be used to elicit what students already know or how their ing develops or misunderstanding arises. Alternatively, questioning can b responding to students if the teacher wishes to extend discussions. Ques also be used to offer directions towards task improvement or accomplish recapping students' useful ideas as hints. The talk analysed by Mercer [8] and Gallimore [9] seems not focusing on student motivation.

Nevertheless, almost no research has explored how teacher's interventio tics classroom is significant, especially in the way that promoting students thinking in statistical computing laboratories. As such, an empirical stud ducted to address the research question, "How does the teacher's interventi learning and statistical thinking of students when using IT in a statistics clas

3 Empirical Study

A questionnaire based survey is a commonly used tool by education res solicit feedback from students and the findings are used for enhancing bo and learning. A questionnaire consisting of a set of organised and structure was designed and constructed as a standard format for gaining a more com understanding of student-teacher social interactions when learning with IT.

It was decided that survey data could best be gathered by means of per view. Through a personal interview, it was possible to elaborate difficult a questions; to achieve a higher response rate; and to facilitate communicatio an interviewer and interviewees in order to gather more accurate and g ponses given by interviewees [10].

3.1 Questionnaire Design

A questionnaire on learning activities in a statistical computing laborato signed and constructed to develop a deeper understanding of how social was constructed when students were learning with IT. The questionnaire clude clear instructions, optional wordings and an appropriate flow of que must be arranged in proper order and divided into parts and numbered (Fo The first four questions, Q's 1-4 were to gather students' general view teacher's intervention. Q's 5 and 6 enabled students to express the role a ance of the teacher in their learning process. Q's 7-9 wanted to know wh IT was regarded as a vehicle of education delivery that could replace huma The prime purpose of the last two questions, Q's 10 and 11 was to kno experience of interacting with their teacher.

The questionnaire was made of multiple-choice questions (Q's 1, 2, 3, 10). All multiple-choice questions were closed-ended and provided prop categories that were mutually exclusive and collectively exhaustive. Mutu

exhaustive response categories provided interviewees with all possible options to select as their answer. Most of these multiple-choice questions used a five point Likert scale for response categories so as to enable interviewees to indicate the extent of their agreement with a proposition. Some used a three point Likert scale for response categories so as to enable interviewees to indicate whether they agreed or disagreed with, or were neutral towards a proposition. All these response categories were also balanced, symmetrically about neutral alternatives.

To understand why interviewees chose their answers for closed-ended questions, open-ended questions (Q's 4, 5, 6 and 11) were also designed to collect their views and enabled them freely to express what aspects of teaching were beneficial to their learning and in what they would like the teaching to be changed to help them learn better.

3.2 Research Participants

The research participants for this questionnaire-based survey were all the 58 full-time students (whole class) enrolling in Year 2 of the Higher Diploma in Applied Statistics and Computing (HDASC) course in the Hong Kong Institute of Vocational Education. Among the students, 32 were females and 26 were males, ranging in age from 19 to 22.

3.3 Pilot Study

The format and layout of the questionnaire were initially checked with two experienced education researchers. They also scrutinised the wordings in questions to ensure the questions were clear, specific, precise and unambiguous and could be understood by most interviewees. Some questions and question wordings were rephrased for ensuring unbiasedness as well as improving clarity and conciseness.

To ensure that valid and reliable responses would be collected from the students, a pilot study was subsequently done by interviewing nine of the students enrolling in Year 3 of HDASC students. They were selected for this study because they had experience of learning with IT and learning with their learning partners as well as their teacher. They were willing to participate in this pilot study prior to the main study. This pilot study did not only provide an estimate of time taken for responding to this survey but it could also highlight what aspects in the questionnaire should be improved.

3.4 Main Study

3.4.1 Data Collection

Each of the 58 full-time HDASC Year 2 students (whole class) was interviewed by the first author. Through the personal interview, it was possible to achieve 100% response rate. As all the 58 students is the HDASC Year 2 student population, no sampling is required. Thus, the survey conducted has no error due to sampling.

3.4.2 Data Validation

To ensure data accuracy, three phases of data validation were carried ou phase of data validation took place in the process of personal intervie responses given by the interviewees were cross checked with their previou for data logic and consistency. The interviewer found no questions were unanswered and no answers were incomplete or redundant.

In the second phase of data validation, a double-check system was adop the first author of this paper and a data checker to code and input the da spreadsheets independently. A computer program was written to detect wh there was discrepancy between the two spreadsheets of the data codes There was no such discrepancy, implying that the data were properly cod rectly inputted.

The data validation tasks were basically accomplished at the first two third phase of data validation was to perform an exploratory data analysi the scrutiny of data. Its results revealed whether or not there were missing ningless data range, data inconsistency and undefined data codes.

3.4.3 Error Handling

As the response rate was 100%, there was no non-response error. If que missing or unanswered or answers were incomplete or redundant, the i were asked to answer questions or clarify their answers. However, no mis no redundant information was found. If answers were illegible, the inter asked to transcribe his writings. Some validation rules were built in a spr perform data range and consistency checks according to the content and data. If any of these checks was failed, no more data would be accepted a needed to be amended immediately. This could safeguard data to fall into range and be consistent at each time data was being inputted.

3.4.4 Data Analysis

Statistical analysis of students' responses was divided into preliminary a levels by using the statistical software SPSS. In preliminary data analy statistical insights and ideas from data was by means of descriptive statist tistical tables that provide valuable clues to what and how an in-dept analysis of students' responses ought to be carried out subsequently. C tables and Chi-square tests were used in the in-depth data analysis for ir factors that might be related to teacher's intervention.

3.4.5 Research Findings

Statistical analyses of these data were performed by examining the gener ristics and patterns of data. The analysis addressed these questions: how c perceive the educational use of IT when learning with the teacher's in How beneficial to their learning process is interacting with their teacher? H teacher's intervention prompt student learning?

Question 1 asked students "Do you need or need not teacher's intervention in your learning process?" Most students (46, 79.3%) said they needed the teacher's intervention, 12 (20.7%) students gave a neutral response but none said "No need".

Table 1 gives a summary of students' attitudes towards the teacher's intervention. A little over two-thirds (40, 68.9%) found the timing of teacher's intervention appropriate and about one-quarter (15, 25.9%), and 3 students (5.1%) gave neutral and negative responses respectively (Q2). Almost all students (54, 93.1%) thought their intervention was beneficial and none gave a negative response, while 4 students were neutral (Q3). One student found his teacher ensured he was on the right track of learning but he also felt uncomfortable when his teacher pointed out his mistake. Two students found the teacher gave constructive ideas or explained the approach to problem solving but they both found the teacher sometimes gave direction instead of answers to their questions. One student found the teacher provided well-timed feedback, as well as direction but she felt under pressure during the teacher's intervention.

Table 1. Students' attitudes towards teacher's intervention (Q's 2 and 3)

Questions	% of students responded to options (N=58)				
	1	2	3	4	5
Q2. Do you find the timing of teacher's intervention in your learning process appropriate or inappropriate?[1]	10.3	58.6	25.9	3.4	1.7
Q3. Do you find the teacher's intervention beneficial or unbeneficial to learning process?[2]	12.1	81.0	6.9	0.0	0.0

Notes.

Owing to rounding, there may be a slight discrepancy between the sum of individual responses and the total as shown in the above table.

[1]Options 1-5: "very appropriate", "appropriate", "neutral", "inappropriate" and "very inappropriate".

[2]Options 1-5: "very beneficial", "beneficial", "neutral", "unbeneficial" and "very unbeneficial".

It is of interest to investigate factors that might be related to the needing of teacher's intervention by using Contingency tables and Chi-square tests. Most of the data were found in factor 1 (i.e., Q1-needing teacher's intervention) and factor 2 (i.e., Q3-teacher's intervention beneficial to learning progress) cell of the contingency table of factor 1 by factor 2, indicating these two factors might be related. Moreover, Chi-square test (χ^2 (2, N = 58) = 7.751, p = 0.021) shows statistical evidence to support the relationship between factor 1 and factor 2 would exist. Similarly, data concentrated in the common cell of a contingency table, factor 3 (i.e., Q2-appropriate timing

of teacher's intervention) and factor 2 (i.e., Q3-teacher's intervention b
learning progress), revealing that these two factors might be related, sta
dence (χ^2 (4, N = 58) = 13.739, p = 0.008) substantiates the relationsh
factor 3 and factor 2 would also exist.

An open-ended question (Q4) was asked to explore under which cir students found the teacher's intervention beneficial or unbeneficial to th process. The students who found the teacher's intervention beneficial to th process, their responses were categorized by using Tharp and Gallimore's of offering learning assistance (see Table 2) so that their responses could than one of the categories. The teacher provided regular feedback to supp planations and clarify their misunderstanding (29 students, 50.0%). He cues and restructured learning in order to model thinking (25 students, posed questions to organise students' thoughts towards task accomplishm dents, 6.9%). He offered students cognitive structuring assistance to form for problem solving (3 students, 5.1%). When students did not respond to of learning assistance the teacher adopted, he eventually gave them ins students, 15.5%). Feeding back and modelling were the two most commo assistance the students found beneficial to their learning process, whereas c management seemed not to be adopted. Apart from these categories, sor mentioned that the teacher maintained an active dialogue with students to their participation and involvement, share their views as well as ideas and assistance they sought (8 students, 13.8%). Conversely, those few students the teacher's intervention unbeneficial to their learning process felt unc when their mistakes were pointed out.

Table 2. Circumstances under which students found the teacher's intervention ben

Circumstances	% of students (
I. Feeding back	50.0 (29
II. Modelling	43.1 (25
III. Instructing	15.5 (9)
IV. Questioning	6.9 (4)
V. Cognitive structuring	5.1 (3)

Note.
*Frequencies add to more than 58 because students' responses could be placed in more than o

The teacher's intervention is a social process within which the teacher a were engaged in various assisting means, feeding back, modelling, instru

In the context of statistics teaching and learning, the teacher found the first four means of assisting students' learning useful. It was possible to model the acts of translating the strength of data relationship and mapping the direction of data context when assisting students in interpreting a regression slope. Questioning was used to assist students in achieving specific learning objectives through free and open exchange of their ideas, and this was particularly useful as an implicit means of developing students' thinking and reasoning. Cognitive structuring was adopted to organise students' thinking associated with selecting among models and justifying model practicality as being parts of regression heuristics. Contingency management exhibited in the form of praise was used to build, maintain or bolster students' confidence before moving into more difficult learning tasks.

An open-ended question (Q5) asked students to describe how the teacher orchestrated the learning activities in the computing laboratory. Their responses to the question were summarized and could be placed in more than one category in Table 3. The teacher provided good learning materials and organised meaningful learning activities, with 52.6% (30 students). He structured learning process by reviewing key concepts, clarifying misconceptions, initiating discussions and outlining problem background and settings, and context, content and measurement of data, with 36.8% (21 students). He fostered an amusing climate for learning and told students jokes in order to reduce work stress in the computing laboratory, with 33.3% (19 students). He monitored learning activities and provided feedback to students, with 26.3% (15 students). He utilised IT resources for teaching and learning, with 14.0% (8 students). He organised students to engage with tasks, as well as peers in line with generating feelings of confidence, competence and control, with 8.8% (5 students). The responses given by the students suggest they thought that the teacher was conscientious and responsive in the ways he organised learning. They considered that he did not merely provide knowledge, but also created and maintained a positive and warm classroom atmosphere conducive to learning.

Table 3. Ways learning activities orchestrated by teacher (Q5)

Ways learning activities orchestrated by teacher	% of students (N=57)*
I. Provided good learning materials and activities	52.6% (30)
II. Structured the learning process	36.8% (21)
III. Fostered learning atmosphere	33.3% (19)
IV. Monitored learning progress regularly	26.3% (15)
V. Used IT	14.0% (8)
VI. Organized students to engage with tasks and peers	8.8% (5)

Note.

*Frequencies add to more than 57 because students' responses could be placed in more than one category.

In response to an open-ended question (Q6), which asked how well s learnt from the teacher, the following positive views were expressed. Whe ing students, the teacher monitored students' learning progress and reg learning. To respond to differing student needs, he made effective use of to check student understanding and offer directives. He did not provide di tion to his students, but encouraged them to construct their own under helping them learn how to recognise problems; and set goals and determin for solving regression problems. The teacher demonstrated the use of cor ware and provided good command of English language. He was consci enthusiastic about teaching and patient to elaborate concepts and explaine clearly. He managed class time and activities and guided effective learni effective communication skills and utilised illustrations and examples in ting laboratory, as well as the lecture theatre. He developed a rapport w and helped students build confidence. He was very statistically competen correct knowledge with ease and broadened their views of statistics le students held positive perceptions of the teacher's teaching as well as ir skills. However, a few students also had negative views about their teac they felt his presentation was sometimes boring and he did not explain con ly and answer their queries directly.

It is interesting to examine preferences for interaction with the teach partners and IT. Table 4 shows students' responses to Q's 7, 8 and 9. T (39.7%) students preferred learning with a teacher to IT, only one stude learning with IT to a teacher and 34 (58.6%) students gave a neutral resp asked to choose between learning partner and IT, about half (30, 51.7%) p former, while 24 (41.4%) students had no preference and very few preferr (4, 6.9%). Students were evenly divided in choosing to learn with a 24.1%) or the teacher (12, 20.7%), and about half (32, 55.2%) gave a sponse. The results of analysing students' responses to these three questi that students would like to interact with humans rather than IT but it is noting that significant numbers of neutral responses given by students. T of students gave favorable responses to the teacher's intervention, while a proportion of students (25.9%) neutrally responded to one item, concernin of the teacher's intervention. Apparently, students who expressed a prefer like to interact with humans, the teacher or their partners rather than IT.

Question 10 asked students "Do you have a better or a worse learni when working with your teacher in an IT environment?" Seven (12.1%) s much better learning progress when working with their teacher in an IT e 43 (74.1%) had better learning progress, and 8 (13.8%) gave a neutral re no students gave a negative response (i.e., neither much worse nor wo progress) respectively. One of the eight neutral respondents did not give reasons and another elaborated with a positive reason, "Teacher provided ing objectives so as to focus better on problem-solving task". The others variety of reasons why they sometimes did and sometimes did not experie progress. The positive reasons were similar to those in Table 2, while n

Table 4. Students' preference for learning (Q's 7, 8 and 9)

Questions	% of students selected options (N=58)		
	1	2	3
Q7. Would you like to learn with a teacher or IT?[3]	39.7	58.6	1.7
Q8. Would you like to learn with your learning partner(s) or IT?[4]	51.7	41.4	6.9
Q9. Would you like to learn with your learning partner(s) or teacher?[5]	24.1	55.2	20.7

Notes.

[3]Options 1-3: "teacher", "neutral" and "IT".

[4]Options 1-3: "learning partner", "neutral" and "IT".

[5]Options 1-3: "learning partner", "neutral" and "teacher".

To understand why the students had a better or a worse learning progress when working with your teacher in an IT environment, an open-ended question (Q11) was asked to collect their responses. Their positive responses spelt out the form of teacher's intervention as being motivational, reflectional or directional as in Hoyles and Sutherland [7]. As being motivational, the teacher was more concerned with student participation in learning activities so as to motivate students to learning. In reflectional form, the teacher checked student understanding as identifying their learning difficulty; and assisting in reasoning and enquiring about what they were doing. For the interventions being regarded as directional, their teacher posed directive questions or gave cues resulting in escalating their thoughts towards problem solving. Besides, the teacher made effective use of information and IT resources to drive student learning and demonstrated how to build regression models using IT tools. They found their teacher was communicative in learning in the way that they could interact and exchange views. One of the responses was affection, as indicated that the teacher was participative and students were accompanied by the teacher in tour of learning.

Conversely, students had worse learning progress when working with teacher because they were anxious and had less freedom and limited room for problem solving. They found wasting time for student-teacher communication that would slow down learning progress. The teacher did not provide a clear and directive approach to tackling a problem but posed questions that were demanding and created confusion.

4 Conclusion

The research findings from this study outlined the importance of the teacher's intervention in students' development of statistical understanding. Students believed that the teacher played facilitating and supporting roles in their learning to foster a learning atmosphere, restructure learning tasks and provide feedback. It was important to them that their teacher organised their interaction with tasks and peers ir facilitated their learning of regression modelling heuristics.

When the teacher adopted the role as a learning facilitator, he knew w plement his students information, knowledge and skills; when to leave solve problems on their own; and when to use questioning to stimulate t direct thoughts; or to have intellectual exchanges between the teacher an dents. He encouraged student participation, involvement and autonomy. U circumstances, IT supported and initiated learning and promoted social inte

Based on the data collected and findings from the survey, how teacher tion may facilitate student learning in an IT environment can be underst survey findings cannot lead to in-depth understanding of how different ca teacher's intervention interplays so as to develop the ownership of learn fore, it would be better to be supplemented by observation study.

References

1. Knutzen, K.B.: Driving and assessing participatory learning. Paper presen Research Symposium 2013, Hong Kong (2013)
2. Taylor, R.T.: The computer in school: tutor, tool, tutee. Teachers College Pres (1980)
   Li, K., Ng, T.: Enhancing students' understanding of regression concepts. In: Ogata, H., Arnseth, H.C., Chan, C.K.K., Hirashima, T., Klett, F., Lee, J.H.M Looi, C.K., Milrad, M., Mitrovic, A., Nakabayashi, K., Wong, S.L., Yang, Proceedings of the 17th International Conference of on Computers in pp. 792–800. Asia-Pacific Society for Computers in Education, Hong Kong (20
3. Li, K.: A pedagogy model for an IT Environment. In: Kong, S.C., Ogata, H., A Chan, C.K.K., Hirashima, T., Klett, F., Lee, J.H.M., Liu, C.C., Looi, C.K., Mi trovic, A., Nakabayashi, K., Wong, S.L., Yang, S.J.H. (eds.) Proceedings of th national Conference of on Computers in Education, pp. 890–895. Asia-Pacific Computers in Education, Hong Kong (2009)
4. Li, K.: A study on computer-supported collaborative learning in statistics cl Lam, P. (ed.) Proceedings of the 7th International Conference on e-Learning, Academic Publishing International Limited, Reading (2012)
5. Fisher, E.: The teacher's role. In: Scrimshaw, P. (ed.) Language, Classrooms a ers, pp. 51–74. Routledge, London (1993)
6. Hoyles, C., Sutherland, R.: Logo Mathematics in classroom. Routledge, Londo
7. Mercer, N.: The guided construction of knowledge. Multilingual Matters Lt (1995)
8. Tharp, R.G., Gallimore, R.: Rousing minds to life: teaching, learning and social context. Cambridge University Press, Cambridge (1988)
9. Foddy, W.H.: Constructing questions for interviews and questionnaires: practice in social research. Cambridge University Press, Cambridge (1998)

Applying "First Principles of Instruction" In a Blended Learning Course

Wing Sum Cheung[1] and Khe Foon Hew[2]

[1] National Institute of Education, Nanyang Technological University, Singapore
wingsum.cheung@nie.edu.sg
[2] The University of Hong Kong, Hong Kong SAR, China
kfhew@hku.edu.hk

Abstract. In this paper, we share our experience of using the "First Principles" of instruction [1] to design a blended learning course: (a) Learning is promoted when learner are engaged in solving real-world problems, (b) Learning is promoted when existing knowledge is activated as a foundation for new knowledge, (c) Learning is promoted when new knowledge is demonstrated to the learner, (d) Learning is promoted when new knowledge is applied by learner, and (e) Learning is promoted when new knowledge is integrated into the learner's world. We describe the five "First Principles" of instruction by Merrill and identify the specific instructional activities that support each principle in either the face-to-face mode or e-learning mode. We conducted a survey study to gather students' perspectives of the organization of the blended course as well as the ability of the blended learning course to engage student learning. Eighteen students were involved in the study. The results showed that the blended learning course was well organized to provide meaningful activities, and that the blended course provided a positive engaging learning environment for the students.

Keywords: online learning, quality assurance, student engagement, student satisfaction, first principles of instruction, blended learning.

1 Introduction

In the recent years, more and more universities are using the blended approach to deliver their courses. In the National Institute of Education, Nanyang Technological University, we have been using the blended approach to deliver our graduate courses. One of the courses in the Master of Arts in Instructional Design and Technologies (MAIDT) program has been using the blended approach supported by Merrill's First Principles of instruction for the last decade [1]. In this paper, we describe the five "First Principles" of instruction by Merrill and identify the specific instructional activities that support each principle in either the face-to-face mode or e- learning mode. We also conducted a survey study to gather students' perspectives of the organization of the blended course as well as the ability of the blended learning course to engage student learning.

K.C. Li et al. (Eds.): ICTE 2014, CCIS 494, pp. 127–135, 2015.

1.1 Background

The "Multimedia Design" course is currently offered as an elective co Master of Arts in instructional design and technologies (MAIDT) progra 39 hours face-to-face course in 13 sessions (ie 13 weeks). Each sessic includes lectures, discussion, exercises, and feedback of the students' proje classmates and instructor. The purpose of using the blended learning appr course was to cut down the face-to-face sessions. This was because ma were often late for the face-to-face sessions. As a result, they missed and other in class activities.

We took seven years to convert the face-to-face "Multimedia Design" blended learning one [2]. In 2007, we decreased the duration of the c 13 weeks to 4 days. The 4 days included 32 hours of face-to-face s 7 hours of asynchronous online discussion. In 2008, we shortened the time from 32 hours to 24 hours making it a 3-day course. In addi asynchronous online discussion activities, we also provided a com learning package for students to learn design guidelines for audio and ar 2011, we further shortened the face-to-face time from 24 hours to 20 hour a two and a half day course [3]. The other 19 hours were e-learning ac included asynchronous online discussion, computer-based learning onlir and "Skype" synchronous online consultations. In 2013, we added the u as one of our e-learning activities. An overview of the pedagogical app course is summarized in Figure 1.

The purpose of this paper is to share how we adopted the "First Pri instruction into a blended learning context. The blended learning approa using face-to-face tutorial and e-learning activities. E-learning activit asynchronous online discussions, synchronous online discussions and refl activities.

1.2 The "First Principles of Instruction"

The "First Principles of Instruction" were originally articulated by David M reviewing several instructional design theories. Essentially, the "First P Instruction" are a set of prescriptive design principles that are common to instructional design theories regardless of their theoretical or ph orientation [1].

The "First Principles of Instruction" are founded on three main premis learning will be enhanced in direct proportion to the implementation o Principles". Second, the "First Principles" can be implemented in any I delivery system. Third, the "First Principles" are design oriented instead oriented which means that they are used to create learning environments a rather than explaining how learners acquire knowledge and skill. The "Firs of Instruction" include the following [1]: (1) Learning is promoted when

promoted when new knowledge is demonstrated to the learner, (4) Learning is promoted when new knowledge is applied by learner, and (5) Learning is promoted when new knowledge is integrated into the learner's world. Table 1 describes in more detail each of the principle.

Table 1. "First Principles of Instruction" (summarized from [1], pp. 45-50)

Instructional Principles	*Corollary*
• Learning is promoted when learner are engaged in solving real-world problems.	• *Show task:* Learning is promoted when learners are shown the task that they will be able to do or the problem they will be able to solve as a result of completing a module or course. • *Task level:* Learning is promoted when learners are engaged at the problem or task level, not just the operation or action level. • *Problem progression:* Learning is promoted when learners solve a progression of problems that are explicitly compared to one another.
• Learning is promoted when existing knowledge is activated as a foundation for new knowledge.	• *Previous experience:* Learning is promoted when learners are directed to recall, relate, describe, or apply knowledge from relevant past experience that can be used as a foundation for the new knowledge. • *New experience:* Learning is promoted when learners are provided relevant experience that can be used as a foundation for the new knowledge. • *Structure:* Learning is promoted when learners are provided with a structure or encouraged to recall a structure that can be used to organize the new knowledge
• Learning is promoted when new knowledge or skill is demonstrated to the learner.	• *Demonstration consistency:* Learning is promoted when the demonstration is consistent with the learning goal: (a) examples and nonexamples for concepts, (b) demonstrations for procedures, (c) visualizations for processes, and (d) modeling for behavior. • *Learner guidance*: Learning is promoted

Table 1. (*Continued*)

	when learners are provided appropriat learner guidance including some of th following: (a) learners are directed to relevant information, (b) multiple representations are used for the demonstrations, or (c) multiple demonstrations are explicitly compare
	• *Relevant media:* Learning is promoted when media play a relevant instructio role and multiple forms of media do n compete for the attention of the learne
• Learning is promoted when new knowledge is applied by learner.	• *Practice consistency:* Learning is promoted when the application (practi and the posttest are consistent with th stated or implied objectives: (a) information-about practice—recall or recognize information, (b) parts-of practice—locate, and name or describ each part, (c) kinds-of practice—ident new examples of each kind, (d) how-t practice—do the procedure and (e) wh happens practice—predict a conseque of a process given conditions, or find faulted conditions given an unexpecte consequence.
	• *Diminishing coaching:* Learning is promoted when learners are guided in their problem solving by appropriate feedback and coaching, including erro detection and correction, and when th coaching is gradually withdrawn.
	• *Varied problems:* Learning is promote when learners are required to solve a sequence of varied problems.
• Learning is promoted when new knowledge is integrated into the learner's world.	• *Watch me:* Learning is promoted wher learners are given an opportunity to publicly demonstrate their new knowledge or skill.
	• *Reflection:* Learning is promoted whe learners can reflect on, discuss, and defend their new knowledge or skill.
	• *Creation:* Learning is promoted when learners can create, invent, and explor new and personal ways to use their ne knowledge or skill.

The effectiveness of the "First Principles of Instruction" was examinec

the "First Principles" scored the highest scores than the other two groups. All differences were statistically significant beyond the .001 level. Further, the "First Principles" group managed to complete three authentic Excel tasks in the shortest time (29 minutes), compared to the group that received the existing commercial version of the company's Excel course (49 minutes), while most of the control group (without any prior instruction in Excel) failed to finish the tasks. These differences are also statistically significant beyond the .001 level.

In Merrill's book [5], he identified a few other studies [6][7][8] which suggested that the use of 'First Principles of Instruction can improve the effectiveness, efficiency, and learner engagement when compared with other forms of instruction.

In Session 2, we will identify the instructional activities of our blended learning course that were derived from the five principles.

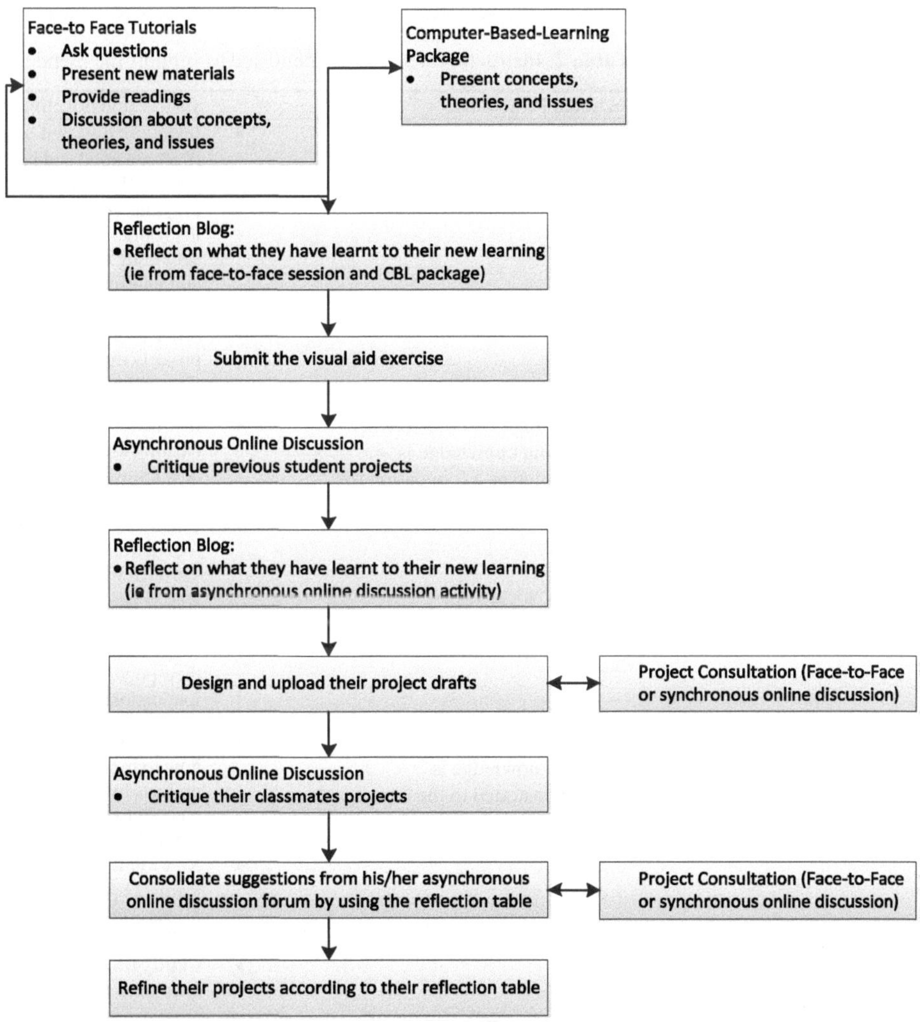

Fig. 1. An overview of the pedagogical approach of the MAIDT course

2 Instructional Activities involved the Blended Learnin Approach

In the blended learning approach, we identified the instructional ac support each instructional principles suggested by Merrill. Some of the

Table 2. Instructional activities identified to support the blended learning ap

Instructional Principles	Instructional Activities
• Learning is promoted when learner are engaged in solving real-world problems	• Instructor uses real-world examples illustrate good and bad multimedia design. (F2F, CBL) • Previous student projects are shown the learners for them to critique according to the visual design princi and multimedia design guidelines. (AOD) • Students need to get feedback about projects from the instructor and classmates (F2F,AOD,SOD)
• Learning is promoted when existing knowledge is activated as a foundation for new knowledge.	• Instructor / CBL begins with studen existing knowledge before he prese new knowledge (F2F, CBL). • In the AOD environment, students usually use their existing knowledge foundation for the discussion (AOD Through the discussion, they may be able to co-construct new visual / multimedia design principles. • In the blogs, students may show how their previous learnings serve as the foundation for their new learning (B
• Learning is promoted when new knowledge is demonstrated to the learner.	• Instructor / CBL usually demonstrat how to improve "poor" multimedia projects by applying the design guidelines (ie new knowledge) (F2F CBL SOD). • New knowledge may be demonstrat learners by their peers after having t discussion in the AOD environment (AOD). • Clarify learners' doubts when they a questions. (F2F, AOD, SOD)
• Learning is promoted when new knowledge is applied by learner.	• Make suggestions to improve others project (F2F, AOD) • Apply new knowledge in designing projects (P)
• Learning is promoted when new knowledge is integrated into the learner's	• Apply new knowledge in designing projects (F2F, AOD) • In the blogs, students may show hov

F2F	Face-to-Face Environmen
CBL	Computer-Based Learning package (ie interactive multimedia learning software)
AOD	Asynchronous Online Discussion Activity (ie It is not a real time activity. Individuals can login an online discussion forum anytime and anywhere) [9]
Blog	Reflection Blogs
SOD	Synchronous Online Discussion Activity (ie It is a real time activity. Individuals can be anywhere but they have to login the online discussion system at the same time.)
P	Project Activity (ie Each student has to design a multimedia educational package.)

the face-to-face mode while others were in the e-learning activities. The latter included activities such as blog, asynchronous online discussion (AOD), computer-based learning tutorial (CBL), synchronous online discussion (SOD) such as Skype, project activity. Table 2 summarizes the instructional modes and activities used to support each instructional principle.

2.1 Evaluation of the Blended Learning Approach

The data was collected from an evaluation survey at the end of student course evaluation. We identified two relevant closed ended items and one open ended item from the survey. The two closed items were students' perspectives of the organization of the blended course, and the ability of the blended learning course to engage student learning. The open ended item was to get general feedback from students. There were 18 students involved in the study.

Students seemed to have a positive perspective upon the organization of the blended course (M = 3.8, SD = 0.8). The following students made comments regarding the blended learning approach (ie face-to-face activities, and e-learning activities).

> Student A, "It's blended learning which has provides opportunity for learner to be self-directed. .... Also the CBL (Computer-Based Learning) package was very well done for this module".

> Student F, "The instructor always provides his real life past experiences for us to think. He has created a multimedia package for this course for the students to go through during the student's free time. I find that the multimedia package enhances my learning and guides me with my assignment".

Some students made some positive comments about the face-to-face sessions. For example, here are some comments of the face-to-face sessions:

> Student D, "The instructor is passionate and knowledge in the field of his expertise. I have learnt a lot from him. I like the way he teaches and he is very approachable in terms of learning. Overall, I have a good experience learning from him."

Student E, "He always relates the session with his experience whic Sometimes he tends to repeat. Probably I see this is an important me him".

Some students also made comments about the e-learning activities. He of the comments.

Student B, "He (the instructor) has a multimedia package for this students to go through during the student's free time. I find that the package enhances my learning and guide me with my assignment".

Student C, "The exercise of going through peers' works allows me to to many various perspectives and the (asynchronous online) provided important information that are transferable to my own learnin

Students have a positive perspective about the ability of the blend course to engage student learning (M = 3.7, SD = 0.7). Student D poin "The teachings help the learners to think and learn the subject in depth".

In addition, students also provided some positive comments to sho valued the use of the real life examples in the sessions such as "linking course to real life", and "sharing of practical life experience". From comments, we believe students really value the principle, "Learning i when learners are engaged in solving real-world problems [1].

Student A also pointed out that "the visual aid exercise is a good learners to understand the basic multimedia". This indicates that Stu support the principle, "Learning is promoted when new knowledge is ap learner" [1].

3 Conclusion

We converted a face-to-face course to a blended learning course. The process takes many cycles for us to reach the current blended learning m blended learning model for solving design problems.

In this paper, we share the organization of the blended learning cours we use the "First Principle" of Instruction to design instructional activi course. According to our survey study, it seems students liked the organiz blended learning course. They also tended to agree that the instruction could engage them in their learning. This implies that the "First Pr instruction may be a good guideline for instructors to design blended learnin

However, we also learned two key points regarding applying "First P Instruction" in a blended learning course. First, the "First Principles of can be applied in most of the disciplines and / or various learning outcom the "First Principles of Instruction" does not provide any actual gu instructional designers to decide if the instructional activities should be sessions or e-learning activities. Hew and Cheung's evidence-based blend

Foo's blended learning framework may help instructional designers to make a wise decision [11].

There are several limitations in the current study. First, only a small sample size of 18 students was used. This limits the transferability of the findings reported in this study. Future research should use larger samples of students from various discipline areas to examine the validity of the findings. Second, this study relies mainly on students' perceptual data. It would be useful to examine if students' learning multimedia concepts improved after the blended learning course is completed. Future research could perhaps conduct a randomized experiment using a treatment group (Merrill's First Principles) and a control group to test the effectiveness of the First Principles of Instruction.

References

1. Merrill, D.M.: First Principles of Instruction. Educational Technology Research & Development 50(3), 44–59 (2002)
2. Cheung, W.S., Hew, K.F.: Our journey from face-to-face to blended learning approach: Important lessons learned. In: Lam, P. (ed.) Proceedings of the 7th International Conference on e-learning, pp. 27–31. Hong Kong Academic Publishing International Limited, Hong Kong (2012)
3. Cheung, W.S., Hew, K.F.: Design and evaluation of two blended learning approaches: Lessons learned. Australasian Journal of Educational Technology 27(special issue, 8), 1319–1337 (2011)
4. Merrill, D.M.: A Pebble-in-the-Pond model for instructional design. Performance Improvement 41(7), 39–44 (2002)
5. Merrill, D.M.: First Principles of Instruction: identifying and designing effective, efficient and engaging instruction. Pfeiffer, San Francisco (2013)
6. Frick, T., Chadha, R., Watson, C., Wang, Y., Green, P.: College student perceptions of teaching and learning quality. Educational Technology Research and Development 57, 705–720 (2009)
7. Frick, T., Chadha, R., Watson, C., Wang, Y.: Theory-based evaluation of instruction: Implications for improving student learning achievement in postsecondary education. In: Orey, M., Jones, S.A., Branch, R.M. (eds.) Educational Media and Technology Yearbook, vol. 35, pp. 57–58. Springer, New York (2010)
8. Frick, T., Chadha, R., Watson, C., Zlatkovska, E.: Improving course evaluations to improve instruction and complex learning in higher education. Educational Technology Research & Development 58, 115–136 (2010)
9. Chan, C.C., Hew, K.F., Cheung, W.S.: Asynchronous Online Discussion Thread Development: Examining Growth Patterns and Peer-Facilitation Techniques. Journal of Computer Assisted Learning 25(5), 438–452 (2009)
10. Hew, K.F., Cheung, W.S.: Using blended learning: Evidence-based practices. Springer
11. Foo, K.L.: Exploratory study on blended learning. Unpublished master's thesis, National Institute of Education, Nanyang Technological University, Singapore (2014)

The Greater the Online Participation, the Bet the Learning Achievement? A Study of Integra Moodle into Learning

Gary Cheng and Hin Leung Chui

Department of Mathematics and Information Technology
The Hong Kong Institute of Education
10 Lo Ping Road, Tai Po, N.T., Hong Kong SAR, China
{chengks,mikechui}@ied.edu.hk

Abstract. This study aimed to explore the relationship between students' o participation in Moodle and their learning achievement. Participants i study were 78 undergraduate full-time students who were enrolled in a ge education course entitled "Digital Citizenship" at a higher education institu Hong Kong. They were required to choose from and participate in diff types of Moodle activities including information access (e.g., reading o supplementary resources), interactive learning (e.g., running online sir tions), networked learning (e.g., discussing in online forums), and mat development (e.g., writing reflective journals). The online participation student was measured by the number of completed activities, while the lea achievement of a student was determined by his/her essay grade. This stud plied the Partial Least Squares (PLS) method to the collected data in ord identify whether there was a link between online participation and lea achievement. The results indicate that online participation in networked l ing or in materials development, but not in information access nor in intera learning, was positively and significantly related to learning achievement. finding highlights the importance of social interaction and individual cons tivism for effective online learning.

Keywords: online participation, learning achievement, learning manage system.

1 Introduction

Moodle is one of the open source Learning Management Systems (LMS vides a wide range of resource and activity modules to support online a learning [1]. The resource modules are designed to support the online delive ing materials, while the activity modules are used to evaluate studen achievement (e.g., through the use of assignment and quiz modules) and f building of online learning communities (e.g., through the use of forum an

there have been over 77 million Moodle users worldwide and over 8 million courses on Moodle. Given the huge user base of Moodle and its continued development as a free, customisable LMS, Moodle has become popular and competitive in education over recent years. It is no surprise that a growing body of blended learning studies has chosen Moodle as a platform for research [3][4]. This study is one example.

LMSs offer tools to support the interactivity between student and content, between student and teacher, and among students [5]. Such interactivity can promote learning in two ways. First, through independent online activities, the interactivity between student and content engenders a shift from teacher-centred to student-centred learning and also fosters constructivist learning [6]. Second, through online learning communities, the interactivity between student and teacher as well as among students encourages students to assume greater learner responsibility and peer collaboration [7][8].

However, despite recognition of their benefits for student learning, LMSs face concerns that may impinge upon their implementation. A major concern relates to the effectiveness of online participation in improving learning achievement. Prior research was carried out to explore this issue, but mixed results were produced. For example, some studies found that there was no significant difference in course grades between students in the face-to-face group and those in the online group, suggesting that no apparent link exists between online participation and learning achievement [9][10]. In contrast, some others showed that online participation (e.g., peer-to-peer discussion in online forums) was significantly correlated with learning achievement [11][12].

Given the mixed results, it remains unclear whether there is a positive impact of online participation on learning achievement. Therefore, this study was designed to explore their relationship. To address the limitations of some previous studies, this study involved a statistically acceptable number of participants, categorised online participation into a range of the commonly used online activities, and provided students with a number of online activities to choose from.

2 Related Work

In his theory of online learning as online participation, Hrastinski emphasised that online learning and online participation are intricately interrelated [13]. He also added that online participation can take different forms, for example, from resources access to knowledge co-construction. Oliver and Herrington identified four common forms of online participation [14]. The first is called information access, which is characterised by the way that students use technology to gain access to online resources such as online video clips. The second is called interactive learning, which means that students are engaged with interactive learning elements such as online self-test tool with automatic feedback. The third one, called networked learning, refers to using technology to support communication and collaboration among students and teachers such as online discussion forums. The last is known as materials development, which means that students use technology as a tool to build and present their own artefacts such as online multimedia presentation.

Prior studies were conducted to investigate the relationship between onl pation and learning achievement. Some reported that no significant relati found between them. Zacharis found in his study that there was no signifi ence in course grades between students in the face-to-face group and t online group [10]. This finding was consistent with the results of some o [9][15]. However, a few recent studies have indicated that online partici significantly correlated with learning achievement. Huang et al. develope to evaluate students' online participation by a set of indicators (e.g., the posts created in forums, the number of files viewed, the time spent on bro interactive pages and the number of pages read) [11]. Their results reveal line participation was positively related to learning achievement in te scores. In a study carried out by Shaw [12], a total of 144 undergraduates e computer programming course were involved. He measured learning achi terms of examination scores. Moreover, he evaluated online participation b number of forum posts created, the number of forum posts viewed and the questions asked. The results validated that online participation was signific ciated with learning achievement.

Owing to the inconclusive results obtained in the literature and the mult ture of online participation, more studies are needed to further investigate tion between online participation and learning achievement.

3 Research Model and Hypotheses

3.1 Research Model

Fig. 1 illustrates the research model of this study. It comprises four type participation and learning achievement. As discussed in the previous secti types of online participation include information access, interactive lea worked learning and materials development [14]. Due to the potential th would get more access to learning resources and receive more learning su peers in Moodle, it was assumed that online participation would have a po on learning achievement.

3.2 Hypotheses

Previous studies reported mixed results on the relationship between onlin tion and learning achievement. Morris, Finnegan, and Sz-Shyan argued t quency of online participation was important for successful online learning found that the number of forum posts and content pages viewed by stu significant predictors for their course grades. By contrast, Palmer, Hol found that the number of forum posts viewed by students contributed v their course grades, suggesting that the link between passive participatic achievement [18]. To further explore the relationship between online participation and learning achievement, four hypotheses were developed as follows:

Hypothesis 1. Participation in information access is significantly related to learning achievement.

Hypothesis 2. Participation in interactive learning is significantly related to learning achievement.

Hypothesis 3. Participation in networked learning is significantly related to learning achievement.

Hypothesis 4. Participation in materials development is significantly related to learning achievement.

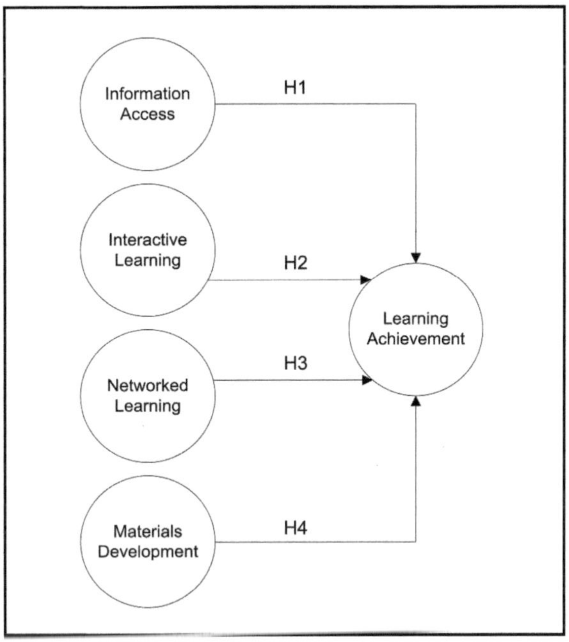

Fig. 1. Research model

4 Research Method

4.1 Context

Participants in the study were 78 undergraduate full-time students who were enrolled in a general education course entitled "Digital Citizenship" at a higher education institute in Hong Kong. The participants were all sophomores in the Bachelor of Education (Chinese Language) programme. Most of them were female and in the age group of 21 to 23 years. The course was delivered via a mix of face-to-face (f2f) sessions and online instructional activities over a period of eleven weeks in the academic year of 2012/13, with each f2f session lasting approximately 2.5 hours. Four major parts were covered in the course: (i) introduction to digital culture and citizensh essential elements of digital citizenship, (iii) appropriate use of technolo spect to elements of digital citizenship, and (iv) impact of digital citizen society.

Since the time for each f2f class was limited, online activities was strengthen and extend students' understanding of several important concep not discussed in detail during class. Students could choose and particip preferred online activities after class. Specifically, four types of online act developed in Moodle every week: (i) information access - students we access online materials and write a summary about the materials, (ii) intera ing - students were asked to participate in an interactive quiz or webpag worked learning - students were asked to create a post and give someone discussion forum or to update a group wiki page twice, and (iv) materia ment - students were asked to write a reflective journal or prepare a multi entation using MS PowerPoint.

In the course, there were three assessment items: online participation, entation and individual essay. The items constituted 10%, 30% and 60% of course grade, respectively. In order to obtain a full score of online partici dents were required to complete a minimum of four activities, each from topic. Figure 2 illustrates different types of online activities designed for a "Digital Commerce". Eight other topics featured the same number and ty activities.

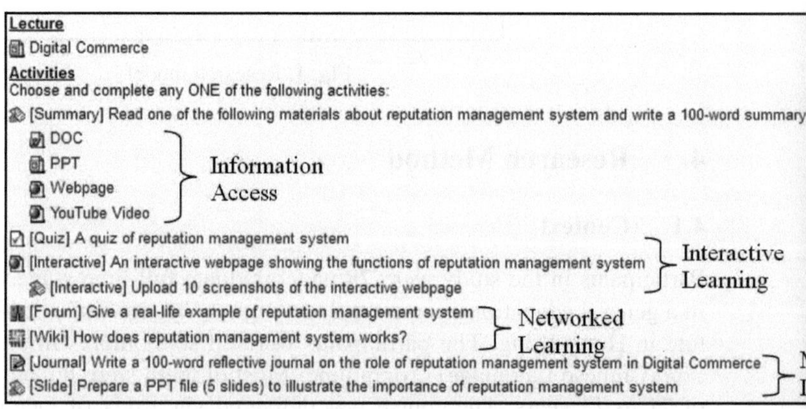

Fig. 2. Different types of online activities

4.2 Measures for Online Participation and Learning Achievement

Table 1 summarises a list of indicators used for online participation a achievement in this study. Online participation was measured by the fr student participation in online activities. Specifically, the number of sumr online quizzes taken and the number of interactive webpages accessed were used as the indicators. To measure participation in networked learning, the count of forum postings (i.e., one post and one response were expected in the same forum for each count) and the count of wikis updated (i.e., a wiki should be updated twice for each count) were used as the indicators. Lastly, to measure participation in materials development, the number of reflective journals created and the number of presentation files completed were used as the indicators.

At the end of the course, students were required to submit an individual essay of 2,000 words on discussing the characteristics of digital citizenship and its impact on our society. A marking scheme was developed to cover a number of assessment areas including introduction, evidence and analysis, concluding remark, style and use of references. Based on the marking scheme, all essays were marked by the course instructor. To ensure consistency of marking, a sample of the marked essays with high, medium and low grades were reviewed by another teacher with experience in teaching the same course. The essay grade was used as an indicator of learning achievement.

Table 1. Indicators for online participation and learning achievement

Construct	Indicator
Information Access (IA)	IA1. Number of summaries written about documents
	IA2. Number of summaries written about slides
	IA3. Number of summaries written about static web page
	IA4. Number of summaries written about videos
Interactive Learning (IL)	IL1. Number of quizzes taken
	IL2. Number of interactive web pages accessed
Networked Learning (NL)	NL1. Number of forum posts and replies created
	NL2. Number of wikis updated
Materials Development (MD)	MD1. Number of reflective journals created
	MD2. Number of presentation files completed
Learning Achievement (LA)	LA1. Essay grade

5 Results and Discussion

A variance-based structural equation modeling (SEM) technique called Partial Least Squares (PLS) was used to explore the research model illustrated in Fig. 1 [19]. PLS estimates the path relationships in a model with the objective of minimising the residual variance of all dependent variables rather than explaining the covariation, so it was widely used for theory development and prediction of key constructs [20][21]. In this section, the results of PLS are discussed in terms of the relationship between online participation and learning achievement (i.e., the path coefficient) and the impact of online participation on learning achievement (i.e., the effect size). The results are shown in Table 2.

Table 2. Results of PLS

Hypothesis	Path	Path coefficient	f^2 effect size	t-value	H S
H1	IA → LA	.078	.009	0.848	N
H2	IL → LA	.012	.000	0.106	N
H3	NL → LA	.408	.194	3.253 ***	Y
H4	MD → LA	.355	.159	2.907 ***	Y

*$p < .10$, **$p < .05$, ***$p < .01$

Hypotheses 1 to 4 suggested that students' participation in online ac significantly associated with their learning achievement. As shown in Tab theses 3 and 4 were supported by the data while hypotheses 1 and 2 were n words, online participation in networked learning was significantly related achievement (H3, $p < .01$), and online participation in materials develo significantly related to learning achievement (H4, $p < .01$). An analysis o sizes of networked learning ($f^2 = .194$) and materials development (f^2 = cates that their impact on learning achievement was medium [22]. The res that students' learning achievement was influenced by their frequency of ticipation in networked learning or in materials development.

In this study, networked learning (e.g., online discussion and wiki de required students to interact with peers through comments about and re ideas of each other. This kind of social interaction was recognised as a contributing to the cognitive and intellectual growth of individuals [23] a deep learning and understanding [24]. Our results are consistent with the [16], highlighting the importance of social interaction to learning achi LMSs.

Unlike networked learning, materials development focused on individu such as creating one's own digital artefacts in forms of reflective j multimedia presentation. It involved students in a learning process to col organise, and present their understanding. Such a process was underpin constructivist learning theory, in which learning is perceived as a proc structing meaning and students learn best when they construct their know active way [23]. In this regard, our results add evidence to support the pos of individual constructivism on learning achievement in LMSs.

6 Concluding Remarks

To recapitulate, this study was designed to explore the relationship betw participation in Moodle and learning performance in a blended learning c the Partial Least Squares (PLS) method. Participants in the study were 7 duate full-time students who were enrolled in a general education cou

(e.g., running online simulations), networked learning (e.g., discussing in online forums), and materials development (e.g., writing reflective journals). The online participation of a student was measured by the number of online activities completed, while the learning achievement of a student was determined by his/her essay grade.

The results of the PLS analysis indicate that online participation in networked learning or in materials development, but not in information access nor in interactive learning, was positively and significantly related to learning achievement. In the study, networked learning required social interaction among students while materials development required individual construction of artefacts. With theoretical and empirical support, both social interaction and individual constructivism have an impact on fostering deep learning. Our findings further illuminate the importance of social interaction and individual constructivism for effective online learning.

Several limitations of this study can be identified. First, the sample was taken from a general education course only. In order to generalise the findings, more research should be conducted in various courses. Second, the results of this study were derived from the frequency of online participation and the essay grade, but the quality of online participation was not taken into account. In future research, both the quantity and quality of online activities should be evaluated to gain a fuller understanding of online participation.

Acknowledgement. This research was financially supported by the departmental small research grant from the Hong Kong Institute of Education (Ref: MIT/SRG02/12-13).

References

1. Moodle: What is Moodle? (2014), `https://moodle.org/about/` (retrieved April 25, 2014)
2. Moodle: Moodle Statistics (2014), `https://moodle.org/stats` (retrieved April 25, 2014)
3. Escobar-Rodriguez, T., Monge-Lozano, P.: The acceptance of Moodle technology by business administration students. Computers & Education 58(4), 1085–1093 (2012)
4. Lambropoulos, N., Faulkner, X., Culwin, F.: Supporting Social Awareness in Collaborative E-learning. British Journal of Educational Technology 43(2), 295–306 (2012)
5. Lonn, S., Teasley, S.D., Krumm, A.E.: Who needs to do what where?: Using learning management systems on residential vs. commuter campuses. Computers & Education 56(3), 642–649 (2011)
6. Lonn, S., Teasley, S.D.: Saving time or innovating practice: Investigating perceptions and uses of Learning Management Systems. Computers & Education 53(3), 686–694 (2009)
7. Garrison, D.R., Kanuka, H.: Blended learning: Uncovering its transformative potential in higher education. The Internet and Higher Education 7(2), 95–105 (2004)
8. Naveh, G., Tubin, D., Pliskin, N.: Student satisfaction with learning management systems: a lens of critical success factors. Technology, Pedagogy and Education 21(3), 337–350 (2012)

9. Brittan-Powell, C., Legum, H., Taylor, E.: The relationship between student le selection of course delivery format, and academic performance. Internation Instructional Technology and Distance Learning 5(5), 41–46 (2008)
10. Zacharis, N.Z.: The effect of learning style on preference for web-based cours ing outcomes. British Journal of Educational Technology 42(5), 790–800 (201
11. Huang, E.Y., Lin, S.W., Huang, T.K.: What type of learning style leads to onli tion in the mixed-mode e-learning environment? A study of software usage Computers & Education 58(1), 338–348 (2012)
12. Shaw, R.-S.: A study of the relationships among learning styles, participatic performance in programming language learning supported by online forums. C Education 58(1), 111–120 (2012)
13. Hrastinski, S.: A theory of online learning as online participation. Compute tion 52(1), 78–82 (2009)
14. Oliver, R., Herrington, J.: Teaching and learning online: A beginner's guide and e-teaching in higher education. Edith Cowan University, Western Australi
15. Buerck, J.P., Malmstrom, T., Peppers, E.: Learning environments and learning traditional student enrollment and success in an Internet-based versus a lecture puter science course. Learning Environments Research 6(2), 137–155 (2003)
16. Morris, K.V., Finnegan, C., Sz-Shyan, W.: Tracking student behavior, per achievement in online courses. Internet and Higher Education 8(3), 221–231 (
17. Palmer, S., Holt, D., Bray, S.: Does the discussion help? The impact of a form online discussion on final student results. British Journal of Educational Techn 847–858 (2008)
18. Davies, J., Graff, M.: Performance in e-learning: online participation and stu British Journal of Educational Technology 36(4), 657–663 (2005)
19. Wold, H.: Systems analysis by partial least squares. In: Nijkamp, P., Leitner, N. (eds.) Measuring the Unmeasurable, pp. 221–252. Martinus Nijhoff, Dordre
20. Chin, W.W.: The partial least squares approach to structural equation modeli coulides, G.A. (ed.) Modern Methods for Business Research, pp. 295–33 Mahwah (1998)
21. Hair, J.F., Hult, G.T.M., Ringle, C.M., Sarstedt, M.: A Primer on Partial L Structural Equation Modeling (PLS-SEM). Sage, Thousand Oaks (2013)
22. Cohen, J.: Statistical power analysis for the behavioral sciences. Lawren Mahwah (1988)
23. Vygotsky, L.: Mind in Society. Harvard University Press, Cambridge (1978)
24. Donnelly, R.: Online learning in teacher education: Enhanced with a problem ing approach. AACE Journal 12(2), 236–247 (2004)

Reconceptualizing a Creative and Specific Learning Environment by Using Web-Based Automated E-Quizzes as a Guiding Tools for Accountable Study Behaviour

Alice M.L Li

Programme Director, College of Life Sciences and Technology, The HKU SPACE
alice.mla.li@hkuspace.hku.hk

Abstract. Web-based automated e-quizzes provides the better ways to transform a creative learning environment to ensure students can manage learning by reinforcing their practices through e-learning and guiding their study behaviour towards the demand for improving quality education. This paper proposed a specific focus on using Web-based automated e-quizzes exercises system (WE system) as an enabling automated learning environment to monitor and guide students' self-study and revision, with an approach of 'Assessment For Learning' as a learning process, and the design of using this WE system will be in line with the four required aspects under the paradigm of our HK Government's Qualifications Framework in Education. This pragmatic approach is used to cultivate and reinforce students' accountable study behaviour. Whether this approach of using WE system as compulsory or supplementary in the practical sense of operation or as a catalyst for cultivating student's study behaviour in the process of learning are further discussed, together with different integrated conceptual frameworks of learning and study behaviours are being empirically reviewed.

Keywords: study behavior, web-based e-quizzes, accountable learning.

1 Introduction

As the advancement of technology becomes more mature, the utilization of educational technology to optimize teaching and learning activities is now a worldwide phenomena for using such creative and specific learning environments. Many studies have been conducted with research efforts to determine the impacts of web-based automated learning tools for supporting various functions in education.

There is a need for ongoing guidance and support to monitor students' learning activities in a more effective means for tracking outcome of their study behaviour. Moreover, the utilization of this proposed Web-based automated e-quizzes exercise system ("this WE system") can also facilitate our role and function in programme monitoring into a more effective means in enhancing and shaping students' way of learning and the subsequent trends of their resultant learning outcomes are also being easily identified. This proposed WE system can also serve as the measures for guiding

K.C. Li et al. (Eds.): ICTE 2014, CCIS 494, pp. 145–155, 2015.

students' study behaviour in the process of doing revision in an ongoing basis, as in accordance with the expected quality criteria of estimated a self-studying time, which was generated in compliance with the HK Go Qualifications Framework System in Hong Kong Education Bureau.

Nowadays, the students are becoming increasingly exposed to Web- ronments for automated learning, and how willing did students in Web-based environments in their automated learning practices, and what terminants of students' study behaviour in web-based practices for learn discussed from the perspectives of different theoretical models of empiri and literature studies.

Smith pointed out that most behaviorists also reckon the students' learn can be viewed as a change in behavior and the learning environment sh ranged to elicit the desired responses through such educational devices behavioural objectives for competency-based learning, and training for sk ment [1]. Kim and Axelrod agreed that the educational approaches such behaviour analysis and curriculum-based measurement should be embra direct instruction of learning criteria served as the accountable task that stu be engaged in during their studying, including the use of this proposed WE automated learning, as an integral part of students' commitment to be in this guided episodes of learning [2].

A good quality education should be and is one that enables all learner the capabilities they require, and therefore the infrastructure of the inter-r ronment must be sophisticated enough to blend our educational practices from both perspectives of pedagogical effects and technologically capab ment, in order to enable an accountable interventions for the student process. And therefore, this paper proposed a WE system and employed re-engage students for such an accountable learning, under this WE s homework approach of 'Assessment For Learning' with built-in conceptua as expected and required from the 4 aspects: (i) Knowledge and Intellectua Processes; (iii) Application, Autonomy and Accountability and (iv) Comm IT and Numeracy, under the paradigm of the HK Government's Qu Framework in Education (HKGQF). The enabling factors will be discussed cultivate an accountable learning by shaping students' study behaviour proposed WE system.

In another word, this outcome-focused learning can also be seen as int tivities between parties-involved within our educational system, which responsible for blending education as accountable learning in practice by of the technological tools, with the intended purposes of integrating the fc aspects under the paradigm in our HK Qualifications Framework in Educa of my newly constructed concept of "Knowledge about knowledge" as a tional strategies of the automated learning with the approach of 'Asse Learning' via this proposed WE system.

This of my concept of "Knowledge about knowledge" is derived from t

tional system, which also in line with the paradigm of HKQF, through the embracement of technological educational tools as the platform to equip the pedagogy needs and quality expectations of the Intended Learning Outcomes (ILO) for blending accountable learning in practice, as in this concept of interventional strategies. One of these efforts in this paper is to discuss different theoretical frameworks that permit a more systematic accumulation and evident-based research studies to support and guide the design of effective educational practices by using this proposed WE system, to produce efficient efficacious and effective quality learning for the ultimate educational goal at large.

In support of this ultimate educational goal, the basic and balanced flows from different levels and aspects of knowledge learning is an important determinants in mounting my constructed concept of "Knowledge about knowledge" as an interventional strategies. Through this transformative automated learning activities that specifically designed to encourage an accountable study behaviours in learning, as in line with the ILO that generated in the fulfillment of the four required aspects under the paradigm of the HK Qualifications Framework in Education, which in turn, should be incorporating with different levels and aspects of knowledge learning, namely with the following components and focuses on:

- Declarative knowledge(knowledge-zero)
- Cognitive knowledge (know what)
- Procedure knowledge or Applied skill (know-how)
- Reason knowledge or Systematic understanding (know-why)
- Condition-knowledge (know-when)
- Relation-knowledge (know-with)
- Affective-knowledge (ways to learn knowledge)

As a result of such advances in information technology in education, this proposed WE system, should become an integral part of our educational system, which allows and optimizes the desirable functions to serve the vital role in the areas of reconceptualizing a creative and specific learning environment by using this proposed Web-based automated E-quizzes exercise system to, yet again, encourage an accountable study behaviours in learning.

2 The Effective Use of this WE System – Creating Accountable Automated Learning Environments

This paper proposed the use of this **WE system** to guide study behaviours and translate such usage into educational practice for encouraging students' study behaviours in doing e-quizzes exercise as their revision or homework and which is part of the integral informal 'Assessment for Learning' strategies on a continual and regular-basis to promote students' accountable learning habits.

The principal characteristic of utilizing this WE system is embedded with 'Assessment For Learning' Strategy as an accountable educational practice for their

educative automated learning that blended with pedagogical criteria w
concepts of an innovative technological tools for:

a. reinforcing students' practices of utilizing the existing e-lear
tools;
b. doing and performing revision as their homework on regular-b
Web-based automated e-quizzes exercise system, the WE system
c. facilitating e-based monitoring students' pattern of learning acti
d. providing effective means for tracking students' learning ou
their progress; in which it can provide the monitoring capabilit
ing who has read, and also automated e-quizzes to determine
learners have grasped the contents of learning materials;
e. integrating the four required aspects as in the paradigm of HKG
cation into this WE system.

A parameter to identify the situation by simply observing the records in which each data log gives an indication related to: (i) overall interaction f log activities; (ii) overall pattern of e-quizzes attempts; (iii) knowledge a overall results of attempted e-quizzes, as the basis for indicating students' viours. As Cocea and Weibelzhal pointed out that log activity has been co a source of information for assessing students' motivation [3]. Furtherr educational theorists and researchers consider learning styles as an importa the learning process, as learning styles can be seen as "a description of t and behaviours which determine an individual's preferred way of learning that incorporating them in education has potential to facilitate learning [4].

In order to support students' e-Learning process, Sfenrianto, Hasibuan tanto proposed the Triple-Characteristic Model (TCM) in e-learning sys which the e-Learning process should accommodate students' in their style, (ii) motivation and (iii) knowledge ability embraced as their persona ing activities.

In this sense, it further sustains the usage of this WE system in an or regular-basis for facilitating such blending into educational practice and g dents' study behaviour by providing the stimulation of innovation that emb the overall benefits of flexible accessibilities that makes catching up and fo possible at an individual student's own pace of learning for supporting th of learning activities, as well as allowing the effective use of time with au instant feedback that makes students' self-review or self-evaluation possibl

3 Determinants of Study Behaviour as an Accountable Automated Learning in Educational Practices

In fact, there are many influential factors affecting students' attitudes towar

factors such as 'attitudes towards e-learning'; 'intention to adopt e-learning'; 'availability of resources'; 'pressure to use e-learning'; 'ease of e-learning use' and 'usefulness' would affect the students' intention to adopt e-learning practices [6].

Lu, Stokes and Zhu generated a MUST Model to analyze a Web-based Learning Process, in which they propose four key elements that impacted students' web-based learning practices, which composed of Motivation; Usage; Satisfaction and Task performance in their MUST model [7]. Smith et al describe the learning style theory as the individuals learn in different ways that can be categorized into four distinct learning styles, namely – feeling, watching, thinking and doing, in which they found that knowledge of a learner's preferred learning style, will lead to faster and more satisfactory improvement in facilitating their e-learning practices [1].

As according to Ndubisi, the factors that affect students' intention to adopt e-learning practices by using the Decomposed version of Theory of Planned Behaviour (DTPB), in which he illustrates specific salient beliefs that may influence technology usage in his research framework as shown in Figure 1 [8].

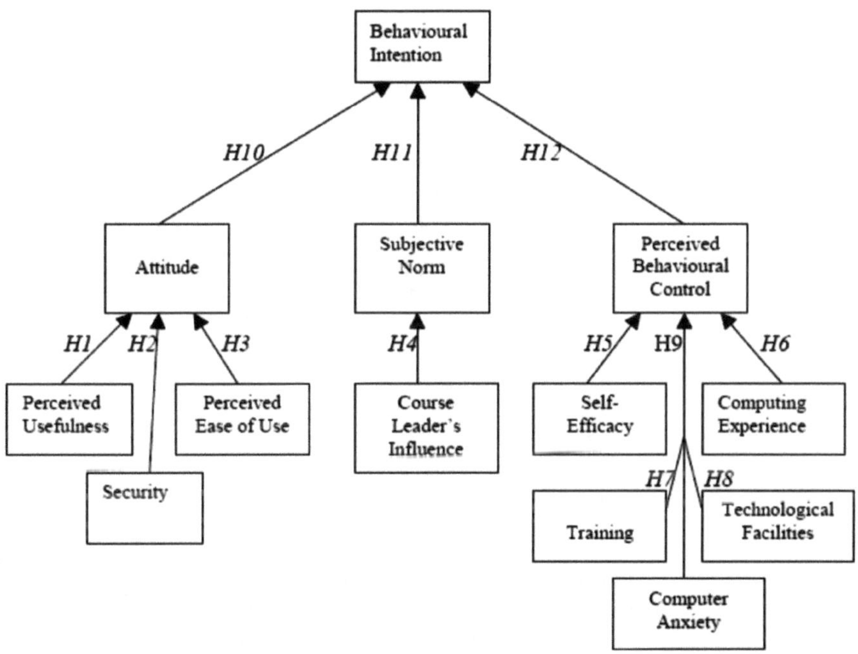

Fig. 1.

Kraft, Rise, Sutton and Roysamb tried to identify whether behaviour was regressed on intention by using the theory of planned behaviour (TPB), in which it indicated that no interactions between attitude and perceived behavioural control (PBC) components in terms of predicting intentions were being identified, and no interaction between intentions and PBC components in predicting behaviour were identified neither [9]. Whereas, Siragusa and Dixon highlighted merits of this applic TPB and subsequently anticipated the need to continue trialing of thi planned behaviour as it pertained to the practice of ICT-based intera learning [10]. Siragusa [11] has adopted Hrubes, Ajzen and Daigle, 2001's framework of TPB is shown in Figure 2.

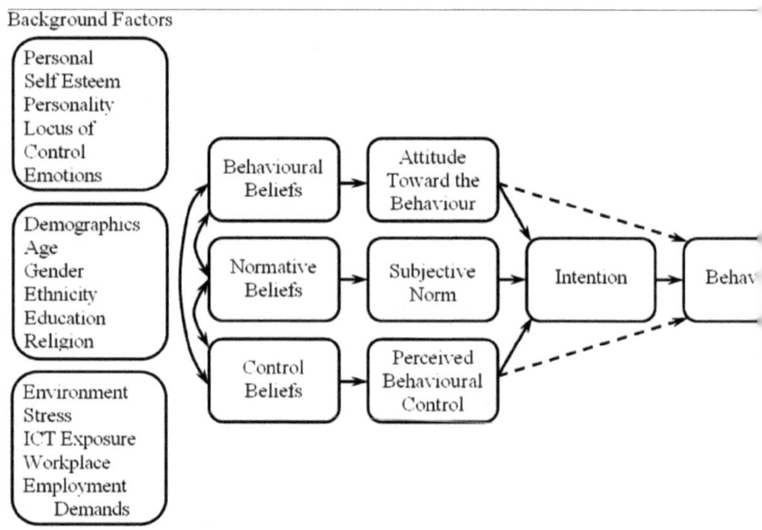

Fig. 2.

Jan, Lu and Chou have explored several models in their research study generate the understanding of e-learning's acceptance as environmental promoting the beliefs in the adoption of e-learning practices [12]. They strated there are two systemic beliefs in Technology Acceptance Model included (i) perceived usefulness and (ii) perceived ease of use are the dete students' attitude for the adoption of using e-learning practices. However proposed determinants of attitude are only on technical and individual leve

In this study, they [12] in fact, has also postulated a significant facto tional forces is the most important determinants of attitude on the a e-learning practices. This Institutional Theory accentuates the significanc stitutional environment as to the students' attitudes and their subsequent viours and practices in using e-learning. They have further agreed and cit two types of coercive pressures that exerted on the students' attitudes, beh practices, which are regulations and competition.

According to Ndubisi [8], understanding the factors that influence i adopt e-learning in general will help to create a more favourable envir

adoption of e-learning practices and subsequently suggested certain criteria for making the successful implementation of e-learning practices in an educational system. He further proposed the focus of those criteria including (i) the acquisition of adequate technological infrastructure (ii) an adequate educational content of learning, and (iii) a developed culture for such learning activities, including sharing of knowledge and skills.

In the study by Phillips, McNaught and Kennedy [14], they reckoned that learning processes are the ways in which students engage with the learning environment and the learning activities embedded in it may also include interaction between students and technology, in which they have produced the LEPO framework to describe the characteristics of the learning process, as shown in Figure 3:

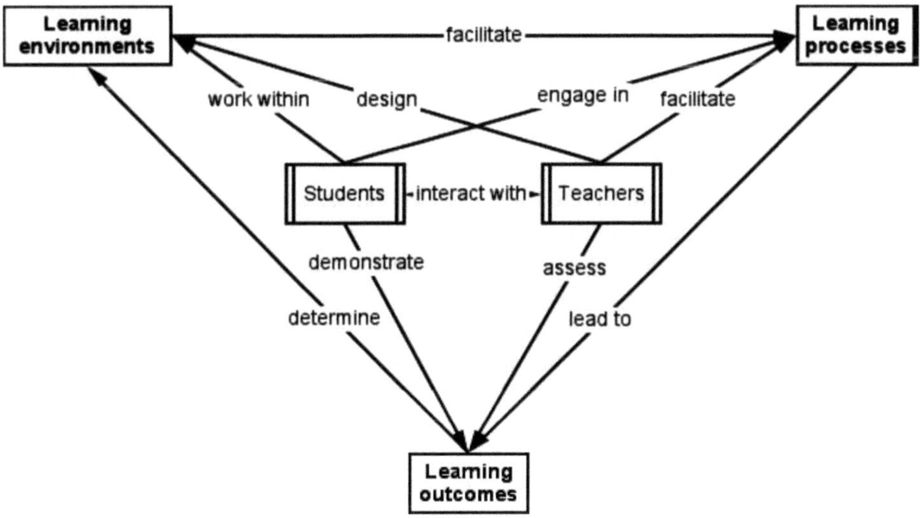

Fig. 3.

In this Figure 3, the LEPO framework is showing the interrelationships between learning environments, learning processes and learning outcomes. It "conceptualizes learning as having three components: the environment which facilitates learning (Learning Environment), the activities which are part of learning (Learning Processes) and the knowledge, behaviours, skills or understanding which can be demonstrated (Learning Outcomes) [14].

4 Accountable Demand and Obligated Study Behaviour – 'Assessment for Learning' Approach

Assessment is a process of gathering a variety of evidence to identify a student's performance of attainment of the intended learning outcomes, and the purpose of assessment is mainly to promote learning based on a philosophy of using 'assessment for learning' as a strategy to further transform and optimize the functionalities for reconceptualizing a creative and specific learning environment for a goo education arises from the correct mix of enabling inputs and processes t proper, relevant and educative interactions to produce desired learning Watson and Angus described that "Assessment is the most powerful le have to influence the way students respond to courses and behave as learn 1999 p.41)", and also found the regular usage of online learning tools s and positively contribute to students' performance of learning and also ac ble identifier for 'at-risk' students as well [15].

As insofar the confirmatory factor analysis revealed that there are s riables could be empirically distinguished on the effects of perceived control and self-efficacy on behavioural intentions and actual behaviour the e-learning practices. However, the quality of learning with the sup technological educational tools in e-learning will not just depend on stud tion to adoption e-learning practices, but most importantly is the learnin behaviours through this practices of e-learning can, in turn, produce or o best results for educative and accountable learning for knowledge and skills development.

As learning aims for its quality, Biggs identified that students hav processed the text for meaning and focus on themes and main ideas becam types for the "deep" approach to learning; rather than just focused on wo tences as the "surface" approach to learning [16]. In fact, there are many f for using the appropriate technological educational tools in a way to fa educational practice and guide students' study behaviour of such quality learning. He has also postulated that "the highest form of understanding, tivation driving it, creates a personal commitment to learn, with consequ of 'ownership'. Such a commitment involves processes of a higher cog than rote learning" [16].

This WE system is in a position to reconceptualize this kind of com processes, to become more foremost 'Assessment Literate' through the er of an integrative conceptual frameworks for supporting the development o ble educational practices, which blended with pedagogical criteria and to an innovative technological educational tools, in creating this WE syste students' study behaviours towards the quality education of accountab Nacheva-Skopalik and Green supported that such a system responds to providing inclusive learning for a learners and is an important agenda iten education institutions [17].

5 Recommendations for the Need to Transform Educat Practices in More Accountable Learning -Mandatory Optional

The main strategic considerations and implications for establishing an eng

factors of monitoring changes in Information and Communication Technology (ICT) strategy and its use in higher education, which in turn requires a significant change in pedagogy and a related shift in use technology platform of this proposed WE system for positively enhancing students' learning outcomes by enabling a Web-based environment to monitor and guide students' self-study and revision as an accountable study behaviours in learning.

In fact, accountability for learning can be seen as a personal virtue and this property of virtue will function as a positive quality in learning and intrinsic factor or determinant for self-motivated and accountable study behaviour. The existence of such personal virtue also serves as a synonym for a student or learner to self-initiated for taking 'responsibility', 'involvement' and 'participation' in their accountable learning, which is construed as the broader sense in the concept of 'accountability' with the presence of such genuine virtue. And therefore, one of the ways of unpacking the overall problems in recommending whether this WE system should be used mandatory or as supplementary for helping students to focus on an outcome-based learning for blending this strategic concept of using technological tools in educational practices as accountable study behaviour will be very much responding to the situation of the students' entry behaviour in this regard. Whereas a mandatory approach for students to make use of this proposed WE system on a compulsory basis could be the solution towards those students with a much narrower concept in exercising their sense of 'accountability'. And therefore, a mandatory approach can only be viewed as a forcible mechanism, another alternative to induce and shape the students for cultivating accountable study behaviour in learning as preconditions to this educational intervention.

Without compromising the expected learning quality, and for the avoidance of misnomer of the intended purposes of the four required aspects under our HK Government's Qualifications Framework in Education, this proposed WE system should be used mandatory as the integral part of homework under the philosophy of 'Assessment For Learning' strategy, in an attempt to optimize the beneficial effects of an accountable educational learning practices for the students' study behaviours.

6 Conclusion

Viewed separately or perhaps more importantly, is to rethink the fundamental processes of learning is not just a simple matter of using a technological educational tools, but more significantly is to support and facilitate students by cultivating their personal learning habits and accountable styles in practicing and managing their learning in accountable manner. What exactly these web-based technologies mean for blending learning and educational practices, in fact, have to be broadened by reconceptualizing a creative and specific learning environments' driving vehicle – that is students' accountable study behaviour in utilizing this inclusive e-learning tools integrating into the processes of learning as a blending educational practices.

The empirical review of those combinations of determinants of study behaviour that contributed to our overall understandings on the implications in formulating the subsequent remediate educational and beneficial approaches for streng areas of weakness for students to adopt this proposed WE system as part o ble study behaviour for their automated learning. Interventional strategies f and facilitating this outcome-based or outcome-focused learning can be co interactions between students' study behaviours and the professional ob support of this quality delivery from the role of academics and/or the affirn ations from the higher educational institutions as part of the quality assur ism through web-based learning technologies.

Despite the proliferation of web-based technologies in the educational produced and projected wide-spread changes in our blended learning and practices for more than a decade, however the vast impact of these educa nologies on education need to be further strengthening up by references to reviewed studies and/or models that generated the pursuits of consideratio in-depth understandings into the determinants of students' study behav different perspectives of the reviewed conceptual frameworks, together wi cal basis for determining how to have a proliferation of rule-based an based system that embedded with factors arising from the studies and liter as TCM; DTPB; TPB; TAM; MUST model; Institutional Theory and LI works that provided theoretical preconditions and justifications in enhancir ways of learning by optimizing and shaping a creative and specific learni ment to cultivate and reconceptualize accountable study behaviour as blen tional practices in learning.

References

1. Smith, M.K.: Learning Theory, the encyclopedia of informal education. The of informal education (2011)
2. Kim, T., Axelrod, S.: Direct Instruction: An Educators' Guide and a Plea for Behavior Analyst Today 6(2), 111 (2005)
3. Cocea, M., Weibelzhal, S.: Can log files analysis estimate learners' level of In: Proceeding of the 14th Workshop on Adaptivity and User Modeling i Systems, University of Hildesheim, Germany, pp. 32–35 (2006)
4. Graf, S., Kinshuk, Liu, T.C.: Supporting Teachers in Identifying Students' Le in Learning Management Systems: An Automatic Student Modelling Appr tional Technology and Society 12(4), 3–14 (2009)
5. Sfenrianto, H.Z.A., Suhartanto, H.: An Automatic Approach for Identifying in e-Learning Process. International Journal of Computer Theory and Engi 371–376 (2013)
6. Eke, H.N.: Modeling LIS Students' Intention to Adopt E-learning: A case fro of Nigeria, Nsukka. Library Philosophy and Practice (2011)
7. Lu, A., Stokes, M., Zhu, J.J.H.: Motivation, Usage Behaviour, Satisfactio Performance: A MUST Model of a Web-based Learning Process. A proje supported by UGC teaching development grant and quality enhancement fund
8. Ndubisi, N.O.: Factors influencing e-learning adoption intention: Examining

9. Kraft, P., Rise, J., Sutton, S., Roysamb, E.: Perceived difficulty in the theory of planned behaviour: Perceived behavioural control or affective attitude? British Journal of Social Psychology 44, 479–496 (2005)
10. Siragusa, L., Dixon, K.C.: Theory of planned behaviour: Higher Education students' attitudes towards ICT-based learning interactions. In: Proceedings Ascilite Auckland, pp. 969–980 (2009)
11. Siragusa, L.: Theory of Planned behaviour: Higher Education students' attitudes towards ICT-based learning interactions. Presentation at Ascilite (2011)
12. Jan, P.T., Lu, H.P., Chou, T.C.: The Adoption of E-Learning: An Institutional Theory Perspective. The Turkish Online Journal of Edcational Technology 11(3), 326–343 (2012)
13. Psycharis, S.: Presumptions and actions affecting an e-learning adoption by the educational system complementation using virtual private networks (2005), http://www.erodl.org/materials/contrib/2005/sarantos_psycharis.htm
14. Phillips, R.A., McNaught, C., Kennedy, G.: Towards a generalized conceptual framework for learning: the Learning Environment, Learning Processes and Learning Outcomes (LEPO) framework. In: Herrington, J., Hunter, W. (eds.) ED-MEDIA 2010, pp. 2495–2504 (2010)
15. Watson, J., Angus, S.D.: Does regular online testing enhance student learning? Evidence from a large first-year quantitative methods course. University of New South Wales (2014)
16. Biggs, J.: The psychology of educational assessment and the Hong Kong scene. Bulletin of the Hong Kong Psychological Society 28/29, 5–26 (1992)
17. Nacheva-Skopalik, L., Green, S.: Adaptable Personal E-Assessment. International Journal of Web-Based Learning and Teaching Technologies 7(4), 29–39 (2012)

Reflective Practice with Digital Portfolio for Te[a]
Readiness and Maturation of Prospective Tea[c]
within the TPACK Framework

Hin Leung Chui, Ho Kong Christopher Au-Yeung, and Gary Che

The Hong Kong Institute of Education
{mikechui,cauyeung,chengks}@ied.edu.hk

Abstract. This study explores the influence of digital portfolio on refle practice of prospective teachers (PTs) with the Technological Pedago Content Knowledge framework (TPACK). A total of 36 PTs studying teacher education course (one-year full-time) at a tertiary education institu Hong Kong took part in the study. Blended learning approach was adopt facilitate the completion of digital portfolio with various applications of services as a pedagogical tool. At the end of the course, the PTs complete same questionnaire again as a post-test. Results showed that engaging P digital portfolio integrated with different levels of Web services can inc their degree of readiness and maturation in different dimensions unde TPACK framework. The findings shed light on the development of te readiness for their entering of teaching profession in terms of technical, gogical and content knowledge individually and holistically, and further vated a higher degree of sustainability in reflective practice for the prospe teachers.

Keywords: reflective practice, digital portfolio, teacher readiness, TPACK

1 Introduction

This study focuses on knowledge construction of prospective teachers (PT year teacher education programme leading to become qualified teacher enrolled in the programme were to equip themselves as professional subj ists. In particular, they would be taking a course and to prepare themselv ers, who would be able to integrate technologies into content or subject and pedagogies, based on their learning and teaching experiences. Reflect is one of key processes on skill development for prospective teachers in t cation programme [1] and it has been suggested in recent years that PTs use digital portfolios to capture learning experiences [2][3]. However, no have developed competent technical skills to store teaching artefacts sys that may lead to the loss of invaluable materials during their trainings and discrepancies while receiving teacher education [4]

found, the term "teacher readiness" was not precisely defined. Thus, the idea of enhancing "teacher readiness" became the objective of the present study, i.e. to explore ways for the professional development of prospective teachers, through the cyclic process of reflective practice with technologies related to digital portfolio with Web services. Such skill would be essential for them to become confident and be ready to become professional teacher in the future.

2 Literature Review

2.1 TPACK and Teacher Readiness through Reflective Practice

In consideration of an integration of subject knowledge, pedagogies, and technologies, the TPACK framework was adopted to conceptualise our proposition of using Web services and blog. TPACK was built upon Shulman's notion of pedagogical content knowledge (PCK) [5], [6][7] suggesting prospective teachers (in our context) to plan learning and teaching activities by 1) blending technologies (TK), 2) learning content (CK), and 3) teaching strategies for the appropriate audience in the suitable learning contexts (PK).

Reflective practice is another crucial factor in the personal aspect of a teaching professional. PTs are academically trained to be effective reflective practitioners by evaluating their own teaching performance through different opportunities such as field experience [8]. Among the digital tools on the Web, blogs provide an easy platform for effective reflection on their own or with each other [9]. Whenever there is Internet access, blog content can be created conveniently with the help of varies online resources and widgets such as speaking avatar and games for learning, and be allocated clearly in an anti-chronological order for the readers [10].

The idea of teacher readiness and teacher maturation are about the ability of a trained teacher to master the content knowledge (CK), pedagogical knowledge (PK), and technological knowledge (TK) in terms of the TPACK framework. This study aimed at articulating how the integration of various Web services into one's blog could contribute to increase teacher readiness and to help the PTs facilitate their reflective practices.

3 Methodology

3.1 Participants and Setting

This is a questionnaire-based study design aiming at investigating teacher readiness and maturation by using blog and other Web services. The participants are one group of Postgraduate Diploma in Education (PGDE) PTs (19 male and 17 female) specialised in various subjects of secondary education (i.e. Business Studies, Chinese Language, Information Technologies, Mathematics, Music, Physical Education, Science, and Visual Art) at the Hong Kong Institute of Education.

3.2 Validity of the Questionnaire

Before disseminating the questionnaire to the prospective teachers, face v measured by inviting four volunteers (Table 1) to evaluate and give indiv back to reduce bandwagon effect and halo effect for the clarity of wordi logical sequence of the questions. This was followed by the undertaking validity by two independent scholars who are familiar with research in (English) and quantitative research in physical education respectively. T further ascertain the content of the questionnaire was appropriate and rel study.

Table 1. Profile of four volunteers testing the validity of the questionnai

Volunteer	Level	Major	Mother
1	Postgraduate Diploma (Primary Education)	Information Technology	Chinese
2	Postgraduate Diploma (Primary Education)	Chinese Language	Chinese
3	Postgraduate Diploma (Primary Education)	English Language	English
4	Postgraduate Diploma (Primary Education)	Mathematics	English

The selected volunteers were full-time students of the institute compa target students (e.g. similar educational background by institutional entra ments). They were admitted into a different full-time one-year programm independent to our target students' course. This reduced the interference ment error such as the disclosure and discussion of the questionnaire con the study.

3.3 Blended Learning Course Design

The one-year teacher preparation programme for teaching in secondary s Sec. Ed) admitted 48 PTs in the 2011-12 academic year. One PT withdre programme while another 11 PTs in English major were excluded in this s conflict of interest with another study [11]. Thus, a total of 36 full-tim included in this study. They completed a questionnaire early in the cours firmed that they had little experience using blogs for teaching or learning. adopted a blended-learning approach for training the PTs in ten topics rela mediated teaching and learning (Table 2). Topics one and five were cond to-face while the other eight topics were delivered through the instructor's Moodle and blog content with TPACK framework for PTs' self-directed le

Table 2. Blended learning scheme of work

Semester	Topic	Content covered
1	1	• register and create a basic blog for teaching and learning
1	2	• add a single image and a YouTube video in one's blog for a meaningful lesson
1	3	• register an account from an online slide host • upload and share slides by embedding codes into one's blog or a learning Web site
1	4	• upload and share a photo album by embedding codes into one's blog or a learning Web site
1	5	• identify and embed royalty free music in the blog • understand the pros and cons of using Flash games in the classroom • create and embed Flash games that could be constructive in your classroom
2	6	• upload MS Word document in Google Drive • embed Google Drive document in one's blog
2	7	• create and embed one's voice as a speaking avatar in blog • develop one's listening comprehension learning materials with the speaking avatar • search and embed Google Calendar for collaborative learning schedules • create and download brainstorming diagrams with an online application
2	8	• create and embed a quick poll widget in blog for feedback collection • create an online questionnaire with theme effectively with Google Drive • co-edit an online questionnaire (by using Google Drive) with group members
2	9	• enable synchronous communication with instant messaging tool in your blog
2	10	• record one's voice for audio reflection • edit sound with proper effects and background music • create a photo story with sound files and images • upload the finalised photo story to YouTube

3.4 Data Collection

Quantitative data collected included pre-test (at the beginning of semester one), post-test (at the end of semester two). On the other hand, selected blog posts (at the end of semester two) served as another set of quantitative data to triangulate the first set of quantitative data (i.e. pre-/post-test). A total of 180 blog posts (five representative posts from each PT about reflective practice of teaching and learning) were extracted and evaluated for the teacher readiness throughout the one-year teacher t gramme. For research ethics, all PTs were informed either with verbal or claimer to reach consensus that all their responses and profiles would not b (or by using pseudonyms in particular data presentations).

3.5 Data Analysis

The response rate for the pre-test and post-test was 100%. For quantitative sis, a table of rubric by integrating the seven dimensions of TPACK fran literatures related to teacher readiness was created (Table 3). Content a carried out by counting the number of blog posts that matched each dimen TPACK framework (Figure 1). Two coders with common understanding c integrated with seven dimensions of TPACK and teacher readiness (Table blog posts independently followed by discussions to further reach consens ond part of quantitative data collected from pre-test (at the beginning of ser post-test (at the end of semester two) were also analysed by paired t-test (Ta

Table 3. The rubric integrated with seven dimensions of TPACK and teacher rea

Dimension	Indicators
Content Knowledge teacher readiness (CK-tr)	Develop awareness with actions as a teacher masters subject matter through teaching and theories and practices.
Pedagogical Knowledge teacher readiness (PK-tr)	Develop awareness with actions as a teacher masters various methods/ strategies in teachi
Technology Knowledge teacher readiness (TK-tr)	Develop awareness with actions as a teacher adapts changes of technologies and masters v technologies for one's learning and teaching tivity.
Pedagogical Content Knowledge teacher readiness (PCK-tr)	Develop awareness with actions as a teacher internalises methods/ strategies of teaching a present subject matter in multiple ways.
Technological Content Knowledge teacher readiness (TCK-tr)	Develop awareness with actions as a teacher applies right technologies for specific subjec learning.
Technological Pedagogical Knowledge teacher readiness (TPK-tr)	Develop awareness with actions as a teacher applies right technologies for specific subjec teaching and presentation.
Technological Pedagogical Content Knowledge teacher readiness (TPACK-tr)	Develop awareness with actions as a teacher learns and teaches/ presents subject matter w technologies in consideration of pedagogical dances so to strengthen and transcend the exi knowledge.

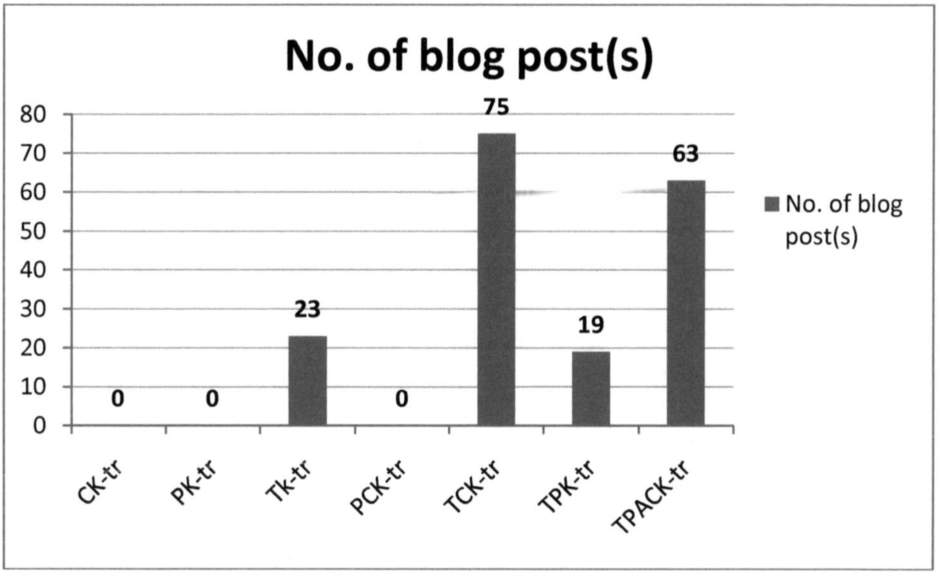

Fig. 1. Results from blog posts related to teacher readiness under TPACK

We further looked at the TPACK-tr dimension and found that 60 out of 63 blog posts were generated in semester two in the one-year programme. In other words, the PTs developed better understanding the TPACK framework through educational theories and practices while the instructor did not emphasise on the mandatory use of the TPACK framework throughout the blended learning course.

Table 4. The Results of ST readiness before and after using blog (N=36)

	Pre-test mean(SD)	Post-test mean(SD)	t
Q1: Your perception of effectiveness by using blog as a platform for knowledge construction.	2.89(0.78)	5.22(1.24)	-12.21**
Q2: Your perception of effectiveness by using blog as a platform for teaching and learning.	3.11(0.62)	5.94(1.29)	-11.61**
Q3: The recognition of yourself as a professional teacher by using blog.	3.50(0.56)	6.11(1.14)	-13.58**
Q4: The extent you developed your own teaching and learning framework blended with content knowledge, pedagogical knowledge, and technology knowledge after using blog.	2.86(0.54)	5.08(0.81)	-14.85**
Q5: The extent you are confident to enter the teaching profession after using blog.	3.69(0.62)	6.17(1.25)	-11.63**

**p <.01 Paired t-tests were used for analysing the survey data. The results indicated that readiness of the PTs had significantly improved through the blended learning course design ($p < .01$).

4 Discussion and Conclusion

The first set of quantitative data analysis showed that engaging PTs in blc grated with Web services increased their degree of teacher readiness to b fessional teachers. The second set of data also attained a positive result the PTs had developed gradually from single element of TPACK (e.g. T integrative intrinsic understanding of TPACK (i.e. TPACK-tr). We perceiv of the PTs had become more mature in terms of teaching and learning p The PTs actually developed awareness including attitude of being a teach tainable learning from reflective teaching practice in consideration of te However, our study was limited to a technology-mediated teaching and lea ronment, therefore three of TPACK dimensions (i.e. CK-tr, PK-tr, PCK-t observed. This warrens further studies on the semantic analysis and in-de of blog content in the seven areas of TPACK.

References

1. Schön, D.A.: The reflective practitioner: How professionals think in action. New York (1983)
2. Killeavy, M., Moloney, A.: Reflection in a social space: Can blogging supp practice for beginning teachers? Teaching and Teacher Education 26(4), (2010)
3. Wopereis, I.G., Sloep, P.B., Poortman, S.H.: Weblogs as instruments for action in teacher education. Interactive Learning Environments 18(3), 245–26
4. Chui, H.L.: Educational blogfolio - exploring student teacher's concepts and of integrating Web applications and blog features for knowledge construct lished paper presented at CITE Research Symposium 2010, Hong Kong (2010
5. Shulman, L.S.: Those who understand: Knowledge growth in teaching. Edu searcher 15(2), 4–31 (1986)
6. Koehler, M.J.: What is TPACK (2011), `http://tpack.org/` (retriev 2014)
7. Mishra, P., Koehler, M.J.: Technological pedagogical content knowledge: A for teacher knowledge. Teachers College Record 108(6), 1017–1054 (2006)
8. Cochran-Smith, M., Lytle, S.L.: Relationships of Knowledge and Practice: Te ing in Communities. Review of Research in Education 24, 249–305 (1999)
9. Huffaker, D.: The educated blogger: Using weblogs to promote literacy in th AACE Journal 13(2), 91–98 (2005)
10. Absalom, M., Leger, D.D.S.: Reflecting on reflection: Learner perceptions o blogs in tertiary language study. Arts and Humanities in Higher Education 10 (2011)
11. Chui, H.L., Mak, B.C.N., Li, C.X.: Reflective inquiry practice of Engli teacher: Blogging as e-portfolios within the TPACK framework. In: Procee 13th Global Chinese Conference on Computers in Education (GCCCE) (2013)

If You Comes* to Guangzhou: Pedagogical Implications of Typical Errors Committed by Students with Mainland Chinese Background as Revealed on an e-learning Platform

Sui Chi Kwan, Hoi Man Dorothy Chow, and Sin Ying Sharon Wong

Caritas Institute of Higher Education
Hong Kong SAR, China
{sckwan,dchow,sywong}@cihe.edu.hk

Abstract. This article aims at revealing the inadequacy of an e-learning platform by examining a number of language errors found among a batch of freshmen (the participants) studying in a self-financing higher education institute in Hong Kong. The participants were selected since they share a common Mainland Chinese background. Meta-linguistic analysis of the errors compiled indicates that the students have both inter-language and intra-language errors, i.e. having difficulties in shaking off the interference from L1 as well as being unable to acquire a number of grammatical rules pertaining to forming syntactically legitimate sentences in L2. Given the dramatic increase of students with such background over the last few years within the tertiary realm, this article may help shed light on how future pedagogical preparations for more effective teaching can be enhanced with regards to such a platform. This article advocates that, it should better be equipped with the capability to issue automatic responses for students to engage themselves in self-studying.

Keywords: E-learning platform, students with Mainland Chinese background, L1 interference, automatic electronic responses.

1 Introduction

Tertiary education in many respects is a paradigmatic shift from secondary and primary education for students. One of its salient features is that students are no longer pampered throughout their learning process with teachers escorting them each step of the way. It is natural therefore that students have to be capable of studying on their own. And as a matter of fact, this is the manner in which education is conducted across the entire spectrum at this level. Language, among others, holds the key to such mode of independent learning. As the majority of learning resources accessible to students both in the forms of traditional printed materials and electronically across the Internet is written in English, it follows that being able to master this language is a necessary condition for students to be successful in their studies. As English is not the mother tongue of most students here in Hong Kong, anyone who commands a high

K.C. Li et al. (Eds.): ICTE 2014, CCIS 494, pp. 163–174, 2015.

proficiency of it would definitely have a comparative advantage over th not. For the less competent, they would probably become the unprivileged their way with double efforts.

For one to be an effective leaner of English, grammar plays a role so vi other factors can compare with. Yet, it is precisely in this area that many s yielded a pessimistic picture. Many students in Hong Kong, even at the tiary education, are at the relentless mercy of grammar and syntax, bac framework out of which a legitimate English sentence is constructed. T ment becomes even more serious when what is at center of the issue co dents having a Mainland background (henceforward, SMBs) where En even a second tongue and their exposure to it has been kept to a minimum dents brought up in the Mainland have little chance to learn the 26 alpha they reach Primary Four, as they claimed, and even after they have starte English education, their pace in learning the language is still painstakingly result, with the exception of a few, most of these students are badly in nee form for learning on which they can endeavor to rectify and redress the d This article reports the implementation of such platform for SMBs as e Caritas Institute of Higher Education, a self-financing higher education Hong Kong which offers both degree and sub-degree programmes.

Background

This article focuses on a group of SMBs with respect to their English com such, it is perhaps in place to give an account of why there is this group of the first place.

Currently there are more than 60 students with such background enrolle programmes and it is expected to be numbered at 100 next years. CIHE not alone in admitting SMBs. In an article, dated 11 Nov, 2013, on the S Morning Post, it was reported that 'places on graduate programmes at un Hong Kong are increasingly being filled by mainlanders, who are flood courses with applications.'[1] With local enrollment being on a decline more SMBs are taking courses that to some extent they can safely claim th instance, 99% of students taking the Master of Science in Finance progra Chinese University of Hong Kong are SMBs.

Like graduate programmes, those at the undergraduate levels are also fi SMBs. A similar report on a local Chinese newspaper had a cover story f secutive years which claimed that the trend of SMB intake has sped [2][3]. The following figures are taken from these coverage:

Table 1. Number of intake of students with Mainland background at UGC-funded
* undergraduates and postgraduates inclusive

Academic years	Numbers of SMBs
2008 - 2009	4,348
2009-2010	4,562
2010-2011	4,638
2011-2012	4,583

From the table, it is clear that there has been an upward trend of SMBs coming to study at local tertiary institutes and the speed seems to be accelerating with 6,315 in the 2012-13 academic year, a rise by 38% over the previous year. This trend continues to rocket by a great leap forward to a total of 11,374, undergraduates and postgraduates inclusive.

While this has raised some eyebrows among the legislators and commentators, it represents a very clear wake-up call for tertiary educators. What concerns them primarily is certainly administrative. But equally pressing is how to provide adequate support for this group of students who have specific needs in their studies, especially that which is concerned with their English competency.

Methodology

The Electronic Writing Platform

Funded by Quality Education Grant Scheme (QEGS), Education Bureau of the SAR Government, the e-platform under review (fig 1) operates under a system known as OASISS 2.0, itself also funded by QEGS, with a purpose to cater for the specific needs of all SMBs as regards their English competency.

Participants

15 undergraduates from Mainland China at CIHE participated in this study. All of them had their secondary education in Mainland, in which Chinese was the medium of instruction. English was taught as an additional subject in the curriculum.

Context and Data Collection

All participants in this study took a non-credit bearing course in the first semester in the academic year 13-14 for 3 hours each week. During meetings with the instructor, they were given a 90 minute lecture on a great variety of topics, including among others:

- cities they have traveled,
- movies they liked,
- personal hobbies,
- formal letter & email writing,
- describing architectural sites,
- describing your life,
- holiday pastimes,
- student life,
- studying habit,
- life aspiration.

Immediately following the lecture was writing practice in a computer laboratory, taking another 90 minutes, in which they were required to produce write-ups on a corresponding topic related to the lecture that day and post their writings on the e-platform. The data gathered for analysis in this study was collected from this platform written by the participants.

Fig. 1. the electronic writing platform for students with Mainland Chinese backgro

Research Question

This article is guided by three questions:

1. What are the typical errors recurrent in the writings of the SMBs?
2. How far is the set of errors a product of L1 transfers?
3. What areas are there in the platform that needs enhancement?

Literature Review

The Value of Error Analysis

The pedagogical value for the study of error analysis (EA) has been w mented in the literature. Errors made by students in their compositions ments can be useful indicators of the effectiveness of teaching [4], whi teachers with valuable evidence to determine which level of language pro language learner has reached [5], which areas of focus should be reinforce that follow (Richards 1971), whether the scope and difficulty levels of t materials need to be further modified and what kind of remedial learni should be provided to individual students [6]. In other words, student er died systematically, can be used for dual purposes, both diagnostic and pro It is diagnostic because EA is a valuable device to help identify learning pr difficulties encountered by students; and it is prognostic in in the sense t provide teachers with not only guided insights on how to modify their te learning materials, but also how to design a remedial teaching plan for st specific learning problems [4][5][6][7].

Sources of Errors

As regards the source of ESL errors, three types of writing errors were i the extant literature, namely, Inter-language errors, Intra-language errors lopmental errors.

Errors that are caused by the interference from L1 are called "inter-la rors", a term introduced by Selinker [8] deriving from the interlanguage she proposed referring to a linguistic system that has structurally interme between the learner's L1 and Target language. It is also interchangeable w cept of *Approximate System* proposed by Nemser [9] and the terms such *cratic Dialect* and *Transitional Competence* employed by Corder [4].

effects can be either positive or negative, depending on the level of similarity between the two language systems in terms of phonological, lexical and structural patterns.

Intra-language errors specifically refer to those errors produced by learners mainly due to their misunderstanding of the grammatical rules of the target language. According to Richards (1971), these errors are caused by "faulty generalization, incomplete application of rules and failure to learn conditions for rule application, the learner attempting to build up hypothesis about English from his limited experience of it in the classroom or textbook". Past researches reported that L2 learners were more likely to make inter-lingual errors at the early stages of second language acquisition but they would have a larger tendency to produce more intra-lingual errors once they have got more familiar with the new language system. Unlike inter-language and intra-language errors, developmental errors occur as a result of a learner's less than satisfactory language competence at a particular stage compared with the learning pace of their peers (Richards 1971). It has nothing to do with any transfer effect from another language system.

Related Hong Kong Literature on Error Analysis involving Chinese ESL Writers

There have been a number of empirical studies on common ESL errors made by Chinese writers in the past decades. In these studies, different syntactic, lexical and structural patterns were under investigation, ranging from the use of transitive verb and the passive construction, through spelling and choice of words, to the acquisition of subject-predicate structures and topicalization. Below are some examples:

In a study conducted by Bunton [10] on a comparison of English errors made by Hong Kong Cantonese-speaking students and those made by non-native learners of English internationally, it was found that a group of Hong Kong errors were not in the international sample that can probably be attributed to LI transfer. These include pluralisation of uncountable nouns *(e.g. 'a camping' and 'transports')*, use of double connectives (*e.g. although/but and because/so are used together*), incorrect choice of lexical items *(e.g busy time from 繁忙時間 (faan mong si gann) for rush hour), use of wrong word class (e.g. *China is a communism country) and inappropriate use of voice (e.g. *A strange person was appeared and That company situates in Hong Hom).*

Webster and Lam (1991) in another study of similar nature found that a considerable proportion of English errors Hong Kong Chinese students made in their essays were due to their first language interference. Several types of recurring writing errors were identified. For example, some Hong Kong students were used to putting an unnecessary *'to'* after a number of verbs which are followed by infinitive without 'to' *(e.g. 'suggest', 'see', 'hear', 'feel', 'watch' and 'notice').* It is also evident that they demonstrated difficulty in the use of causative 'have" as such expression does not appear in Cantonese. This seems to lead to few common errors such as '**I cut my hair at the barber's shop*' and '**I made my clothes at the tailor's*' in which simple verbs were incorrectly selected by students. In addition, the problem of redundancy in English expression seemed to be influenced by transfer from L1 Cantonese: *'according to my opinion', 'the reason is because…'*. The use of intrusive preposition *'*I went <u>to</u> shopping' and '*we need to discuss <u>about</u> our future plan'* also can be seen as first-language induced errors produced by local Chinese students in English writing.

Chan was interested in examining the effect of mother tongue Chinese writing of Hong Kong students, particularly those erroneous sentences inv sitive verbs and passive construction [11]. Form six students from five schools in Hong Kong were invited to take part in her study and 156 cc were collected. In terms of the transitive verbs, it was shown that studer use them with an appropriate object or even forgot to put any object after s tive verbs in a complete sentence. One of the examples Chan cited wa *are many facilities, but people don't use'*, where in English 'them' is re use, but in spoken Cantonese, the pronoun for facilities is omitted. Apa monstrating confusion in verb transitivity, students in Chan's study also e difficulty in the use of the English passive sentences. Negative transf Chinese was ascribed to some of the errors made. Two types of common ing from language transfer impact with regard to the concept of passivity v fied. They included 'inappropriate use of the passive' *(e.g. *some proble happened),* and 'failure to use the passive where appropriate' *(e.g *The pr not solve).* The latter error type was called as "pseudo passives" or "putativ in the previous literature (Li 1976; Schacher and Rutherford 1979, cit (1991), pp. 49).

In a study based on data collected from 710 Hong Kong Chinese ESL different proficiency levels, Chan reported that the surface structure of ma sentences produced by participating students, whether collected through task or grammaticality judgment test, were largely similar to the normati structures of Cantonese (that is, their first language) [12]. The influence transfer is remarkably apparent among learners of lower proficie particularly when they dealt with complex target structures. Evidence of relating to syntactic transfer generated from this study include: (1). O English copula in sentences with modal verbs *(e.g.*If I fail the exam mother will very angry)*; (2). Placement of the intensifying adverb before ** he very like dancing)*; (3). Use of *'there have'* instead of *'there be'* in constructions *(e.g. * There have many Japanese tourists on the ship)*; (4). in the transitivity patterns of high-frequency verbs *listen* and *care (e.g. care the old people)*; (5). Inability to use relative clause *(e.g. she is the pe came to see me yesterday).*

Data Analysis and Discussion

The study started with collecting written works by a group of SMBs from platform for text analysis. Bunton pointed out that "there are many diff errors can be categorized and some errors could come under two or more [10]. Error types customized by Bunton were adapted in this study and should still be open to any interpretation and not restricted by the categoriz

Example of errors from students' works under seven categories are pres following table:

Table 2. Samples of Common Language Errors

Error Categorization	**Identification of Errors**	**Correct Sentences**
1. Noun Countability (Singular / Plural)	1. The soup inside **make** it tasted good. 2. The winter **are** cold and the summer **are** hot.	1. The soup inside **makes** it taste good. 2. The winter **is** cold and the summer **is** hot.
2. Verb- Tense Simple present instead of simple past	1. I **do** the economic assignment at the weekend.	1. I **did** the economic assignment at the weekend.
Missing of verb after model	1. Today I **would to** introduce my classmate, Hei.	1. Today I **would like to** introduce my classmate, Hei.
Simple present instead of infinitive/ misuse of infinitive	1. Today I would **like introduce** my classmate Stephanie. 2. She likes **to goes** the library to study alone. 3. She likes **to makes** some notes. 4. Who can teach me how **to sent** photos?	1. Today I would **like to introduce** my classmate Stephanie. 2. She likes to **go** the library to study alone. 3. She likes to **make** some notes. 4. Who can teach me how **to send** photos?
3. Verb- Active/passive	1. The dish 'fishskin' **can make** after we dry the fishskin under the sun.	1. The dish of 'fshskin' **can be made** after we dry them under the sun.
4. Verb- Subject-verb Agreement (wrong combination of subject and verb)	1. If you **comes** to Guangzhou,… 2. Sometimes she **study** in the school library. 3. She **come** from Zhong Shan. 4. She **study** hard, I should learn from her.	1. If you **come** to Guangzhou…. 2. Sometimes she **studies** in the school library. 3. She **comes** from Zhong Shan. 4. She **studies** hard, I should learn from her.
5. Lexical Choice	1. I **am very like to eat** this porridge. 2. At the beginning of **every** week she makes a study plan.	1. I **like to eat** this porridge **very much**. 2. At the beginning of **each** week she makes a study plan.

Table 2. (*Continued*)

6. **Word Class**	1. The assignment is very **difficulty** for me. 2. In my city, football is **the more important** culture than others.	1. The assignm very **difficu** 2. In my city, **the most in** culture.
7. **Preposition** (a preposition is misused, omitted or added)	1. She likes to study **in** home by herself. 2. We shared our experience how to solve our problems **from** our life. 3. He is the member **in** International Practical Shooting Confederation.	1. She likes to home by he 2. We shared rience how our problem life. 3. He is the m Internationa al Shooting ration.

Noun Countability (Singular / Plural)

One of the most common errors found in participants' writings is 'Noun co Students failed to recognize that there are plural and singular forms for En or they were not sure when they should apply the plural form. When the in the singular form they applied the plural form to the noun as shown in th below. A possible reason for the failure to use plural noun forms can accounted for by the absence of plural markers for a noun in Chinese.

Example 1: **The soup** inside **make** it tasted good.

Example 2: **The winter** **are** cold and the summer **are** hot.

***Verbs** -Tense*

Errors in verb tense is another type of common errors found in students' w instance, in example 3 below, the simple present tense was used instead of past when the student was talking about something in the past. This result prising and it is very likely affected by L1. English notion of tense is c participants, a group of L2 learner, since Chinese verb itself does not in while tenses, as expressions of time, is predominant in English.

Example 3: I **do** the economic assignment at the weekend.

In addition, some students did not seem to fully understand or master verb. For example, errors were found in students' writings on the use of modals and the use of the infinitive. These types of errors are illustrated b 4-8 below:

Example 4: Today I **would to** introduce my classmate, Hei.

Example 5: Today I would **like introduce** my classmate Stephani

Example 6: She likes **to goes** the library to study alone.

Example 7: She likes **to makes** some notes.

Example 8: Who can teach me how **to sent** photos?

***Verbs** – Active/Passive*

Another common error found in participants' writing is that of verbs in use of 'active /passive' form. For instance, example 9 below shows that the student put the active form of verb 'can make' for the subject 'the dish', in which a passive form of verb 'can be made' should be used in the sentence.

Example 9: The dish 'fishskin' **can make** after we dry the fishskin under the sun.

***Verb-** Subject-verb Agreement (wrong combination of subject and verb)*

Errors in Subject-verb Agreement can be seen in students' writings in the study. Participants failed to apply appropriate verb form to the noun in a sentence. This can be a result from the absence of agreement between subjects and verbs in L1 as there is no change on verb according to the subjects in Chinese. Examples in this category are shown below:-

Example 10: If **you comes** to Guangzhou,…
Example 11: Sometimes **she study** in the school library.
Example 12: **She come** from Zhong Shan.
Example 13: **She study** hard, I should learn from her.

Lexical Choice

Students had problem with correct choice of word in their writings. Some samples of errors seem to be a direct translation of Chinese expression. For instance, in example 14, the student wrote 'I am very like' to express the idea of 'I like ....very much'. L1 transfer can be seen from this example as the sentence pattern in example 14 is indeed a common sentence pattern used in Chinese '我是很愛吃…'.

Example 14: I **am very like to eat** this porridge.
Example 15: At the beginning of **every** week she makes a study plan.

Word Class

Errors on 'Word class' are also commonly found in data gathered in this study. Example 16 below shows the wrong word class of the word 'difficulty' was used instead of putting an adjective form of word 'difficult' in the sentence. Example 17 is another sample error on word class, in which 'each' should be used instead of 'every' in the sentence.

Example 16: The assignment is very **difficulty** for me.
Example 17: At the beginning of **every** week she makes a study plan.

Bunton explained the presence of this type of error because 'Chinese characters do not change' [10]. Particles may be used before or after the Chinese characters, but if a Chinese word is to be used as a noun instead of a verb, it will not change its form.

Preposition

Most of the prepositional errors found in the study included omissions, additions and wrong selection. The cause of prepositional errors is interference from students' L1, i.e. Chinese. Darus pointed out that 'some of the Chinese prepositions are similar in meanings and functions with the English prepositions' [13]. Darus also mentioned that sometimes, a single Chinese preposition can be translated into various English prepositions. For instance, Chinese preposition '在' and '的' can refer prepositions 'in', 'at' and 'on' for '在', and 'of' and 'in' for '的'. Therefo were incapable of choosing the appropriate prepositions when more than preposition corresponds to a single Chinese preposition and created errors lowing in examples 18-20-

Example 18: She likes to study **in** home by herself.

Example 19: We shared our experience how to solve our problem life.

Example 20: He is the member **in** International Practical Shooting Co

Conclusion: Limitations and Recommendations

Students' writings on the platform are continuously being recorded and e for evaluative purposes. However, given the fact that the platform has onl ning for two semesters and that admittedly the total student population their works for the present research may not be considered large enough premature at this stage for the present research to be taken to have reache litatively and quantitatively, a high level of significance. Apparently more at an empirical level have to be conducted in future so that the tentative that this paper has reached can be verified, revised or, if necessary, fal said, at this stage, we have already observed that some lights have been routine operation of the platform that can presumably guide us in modifyin signing it in such a way as to provide more substantial support for stude learning. In what follows, we would like to sketch out some lines of th which the platform can be further developed.

As mentioned, whenever the students commit any mistakes, it is the du structor to point them out and discuss them with the students concerned. T be very tedious if we take into account the following facts:

1. It is very difficult sometimes to explain to students the mistakes th in terms that they can understand and to such an extent that they know avoid committing it again on the one hand and to form grammatically sentences on the other. This is partly due to the complexity of the involved and partly to the limited grammatical knowledge database dents have. And do not forget that most mistakes they commit are of t language type, i.e. those that clearly are the results of the interferenc negative transfers, in which cases it is doubly difficult to make them inviting them to migrate to a linguistic paradigm with different sets of

2. Workload would become increasingly heavy if the number of i mainland students keeps growing in future. And 'fortunate' enou seems to be the trend. In view of the ongoing demand on the part o structor, something must be done to alleviate her burden.

But on top of it, there is a third consideration as well. Many language te the experience (frustrating at times) that despite repeated explanations c

is right on our own. In other words, we learn by mistakes; but this has to be done with sufficient awareness of such needs. Being lectured seems to accomplish little in this. Thus, if the students are exposed to a setting in which they are encouraged to study their mistakes on their own, the pedagogical outcome should presumably be more fruitful.

It is with this in mind that we are proposing here that an I.T. assisted automatic error-checker be installed onto the platform, which is precisely what is lacking currently. This checker will be automatic in two senses. First, once an error is committed by any student writing on the platform, it will be detected instantly. To facilitate this, the system will have to be constantly on guard against any grammatical and/or syntactical errors, which in turn demands that installed in it is a vast reservoir of grammatical rules that forms a huge database (let us call this D1) against which every sentence students make is checked. Second, not only will a student making mistakes be alerted, but he or she will also be directed to another database (let us call this D2) that has pooled up all the teaching resources and materials that all faculty responsible for language courses have compiled during their lectures. And if D2 proves to be insufficient in anticipating the great variety of the mistakes to be made, materials capable of being found on the Internet can be provided as well in the form of hyperlinks.

Such features can serve dual purposes. One, the burden the instructor is currently shouldering up will be much reduced, which in turn keeps her less inclined to make mistakes herself when supervising students. Two, and more significantly, students would be given immediate responses as to what mistakes they are supposed to be making, thus keeping them in a state of constant alert of the important consideration of grammaticality. And by prompting them to D1 and D2, they will be directed to a big repertoire of resources from which they can tap as much as needed for self-study purposes. As we have observed through interacting with students on the platform, we believe that they will find these enhanced features effective and efficient in their studies.

References

1. South China Morning Post: Chinese students flood Hong Kong universities' graduate programmes (2013), http://www.scmp.com/news/hong-kong/article/1352943/chinese-students-flood-hong-kong-universities-graduate-programmes?page=all (retrieved)
2. Apple Daily: 八大本學年6,315內地生 急增38% (2013),
3. http://hk.apple.nextmedia.com/news/art/20130428/18242744 (retrieved)
4. Apple Daily:港研究院 68%內地生 ((2014)), http://hk.apple.nextmedia.com/news/art/20140404/18679004 (retrieved)
5. Corder, S.P.: The significance of learners' errors. International Review of Applied Linguistics 5(4), 161–169 (1967)
6. Sercombe, P.G.: Learner language and the consideration of idiosyncrasies by students of English as a second or foreign language in the context of Brunei Darulsalam. In: Proceedings of the International Conference on Teaching and Learning (2000)
7. Weireesch, S.: How to analyze interlanguage. Journal of Psychology & Education 9, 113–122 (1991)

8. Vahdatinejad, S.: Students' error analysis and attitude towards teacher feedb selected software: a case study, Unpublished Masters thesis,Univeristy Malaysia, Bangi (2008)
9. Selinker, L.: Interlanguage. International Review of Applied Linguistics (1972)
10. Nermser, W.: Approximate systems of foreign language learners. In: Richa Error Analysis: Perspectives on Second Language Acquisition, pp. 55–63 Essex (1974)
11. Bunton, D.: A comparison of English errors made by Hong Kong students and by non-native speakers internationally,Institute of Language in Education Jou issue no. 2), 9–22 (1991)
12. Chan, B.: A study of errors made by F6 students in their written English with ence to structures involving the transitive verb and the passive construction Language Education Journal 2, 43–51 (1991)
13. Chan, Y.W.: Syntactic Transfer: Evidence from the Interlanguge of Hong K ESL Learner. The Modern Language Journal 88, 56–74 (2004)
14. Darus, S., Ching, K.: Common Errors in Written English Essays of Form Students: A Case Study. European Journal of Social Science 10(2), 242–253 (2

A Framework for Effectiveness of Institutional Policies on Technology-Enhanced Learning

Beryl Yuen-Yee Wong, Billy Tak-Ming Wong, and Sam Pang

The Open University of Hong Kong
30 Good Shepherd Street, Homantin, Kowloon, Hong Kong SAR, China
{byywong,tamiwong,scpang}@ouhk.edu.hk

Abstract. For institutional policies associated with technology-enhanced learning (TEL) instruments, such as blended learning, mobile learning, massive open online courses, and open educational resources, their policy effectiveness is to a large extent affected by how 'effectiveness' is conceptualized. Studies on effectiveness of institutional policies reveal that a diverse conceptualization has been employed.

This paper proposes a framework based on the instrumental perspective summarizing different approaches of assessing institutional policy effectiveness and the variables involved in each approach. A systematic literature survey of institutional policies on TEL is conducted, showing that the framework is highly comprehensive in terms of capturing different dimensions of policy effectiveness. This study will provide a point of reference not only on assessing the effectiveness of relevant polices but also for formulating relevant policies by educational administrators.

Keywords: technology-enhanced learning, effectiveness of institutional policies, instrumental perspective.

1 Introduction

The use of technology in education, i.e., technology-enhanced learning (TEL), has been commonplace in the education world as shown in relevant institutional policies. Examples include blended learning [1], mobile learning [2], massive open online courses (MOOCs) [3], open educational resources (OER) [4], social media [5] and other e-learning modes [6][7]. Such wide application of technologies, in a sense, can be attributed to the purpose of enhancing efficiency and cost-effectiveness of delivery of education [8]. For institutions which have spent tremendous amount of resources in providing TEL, it is critical for them to evaluate the effectiveness of their relevant institutional policies [9].

Contemporary studies on effectiveness of institutional policies employ a diverse conceptualization of effectiveness, resulting in a wide variety of foci of analysis for understanding the concept. To illustrate a few, a focus of analysis lies in the effect of TEL on learning outcomes in terms of student performance. Comparative methods are commonly used in this kind of analysis, e.g. effectiveness of online versus traditional

K.C. Li et al. (Eds.): ICTE 2014, CCIS 494, pp. 175–186, 2015.

classroom training [6]. Another focus is on the design of a TEL device a design suits a particular teaching and learning context. Zhang et al, for e: serve that integrating interactive instructional videos into an e-learning enhance learning effectiveness [7]. Analysis can also be focused on perc attitudes of TEL stakeholders in general and learners and teachers in part an assumption that institutional policies would not be effective without considerations stakeholders' needs and wishes. For the case of OER, Gı emphasizes that "it is important to spend time exploring student perceptic tudes on OER", in order to "explore ways in which personalization can when lecturers use OER created outside their institutions" [10] (p. 2). T foci of analysis reveal the dynamic nature of policy effectiveness, which need of systematic summarization of its diverse conceptualization to facili tion of TEL-related institutional policies.

This paper presents a preliminary conceptual framework, based on the of instrumentalism, for analyzing effectiveness of institutional policies on depicts the core of instrumentalism, and then reports the findings of a litera illustrating the comprehensiveness of instrumental perspective in terms c the diverse conceptualization of policy effectiveness. Accordingly the and variables of the framework are outlined and the values of the framew research and formulation of relevant institutional policies are discussed.

2 Effectiveness of Institutional Policies on TEL: An Instrumental Perspective

Institutional policies refer to methods or means used by institutions to achi effects in line with their own visions and/or missions. This section intr different approaches to assessing effectiveness of institutional policies wi to instrumentalism [11][12][13].

2.1 Classical Approach: Character of Instruments

This approach stems from the 'classical' theory of instruments, focusing of character of instruments. It assumes that an instrument has its own natur ristics and logics of operations and functions, and hence own line of effect limitations. Each instrument brings distinctive effects on different institu cies, such as the choice of instrument and implementation design. In lin school of thought, the key questions of evaluating policy effectiveness re instrument, i.e., a TEL device, may include:

- What is the nature of the TEL device?
- How does the nature of the TEL device determine the implementation
- What is the impact of the TEL device on teaching and learning?
- What are the expected effects of the TEL device on learning outcome

2.2 Contextual Approach: Implementation Process

This approach is rooted in the 'contextual' theory of instruments that places its emphasis on the influence of the implementation process of a policy. It holds that there may be differences between instruments and no policy is universally applicable. Factors to address are contextual ones such as decision-making arena and policy network, with particular attention to the implementation process. The point of departure in examining policy effectiveness, according to this approach, is not so much about the TEL device *per se*, but how the implementation of the TEL device shapes the intended effects of the device. In this line of thinking, the key questions of evaluating policy effectiveness may include:

- What is the nature of the TEL implementation setting?
- What barriers and/or enablers are there in the TEL implementation process?
- How do the barriers and/or enablers shape the TEL device in the implementation process?
- How does the implementation process affect the expected effects of the TEL device?

2.3 Instrument-Context Approach: Requirements of a Problem Setting

This approach is rooted in the 'instrument-context' theory of instruments. Its focus of analysis is on the matching or 'good fit' between instrument and context. The choice of instruments depends on the requirements of a problem setting in the context. Once the requirements are identified, instruments that are considered most appropriate in satisfying the requirements can be chosen. Hence there are two tasks in this approach, i.e., to figure out the requirements of a particular problem setting, and to choose the instruments in accordance with the requirements. In line with this approach, questions of evaluating policy effectiveness may include:

- What is/are the problem(s) of teaching and learning in a particular setting?
- What are the requirements of the problem setting? That is, how can the problem(s) be solved?
- What are the options (solutions) available for solving the problem(s)?
- Is TEL the way out? If so, which kind of TEL device?

2.4 Constitutive Approach: Subjective Meaning of Instruments

This approach is vested upon the 'constitutive' theory of instruments which holds that effectiveness of policy instruments may be hampered or supported by subjective factors. It is interpretive and constructive in nature, with a starting point lying in the 'meaning' of instrument which can only be understood subjectively and therefore differently. The subjective meaning of instruments can be socially constructed and reconstructed over time and changes with value systems. Therefore, to study TEL policy effectiveness in this line of thinking, the following key questions can be raised:

- What do institutional leaders think about TEL?
- What do teachers think about TEL?
- What do learners think about TEL?
- To what extent is TEL accepted by institutional leaders, teachers and le

In sum, the four approaches of policy instruments, as elaborated above the core of instrumentalism, which offers the basis of developing a concep work for evaluating policy effectiveness.

3 Comprehensiveness of the Instrumental Perspective

To examine the power of the instrumental perspective in offering a con framework for analyzing TEL policy effectiveness, a survey of relevant conducted to investigate the extent to which the instrumental perspective capture various conceptualizations of effectiveness in evaluating institutio on TEL.

3.1 Data Collection and Analysis

This study adopts Price and Kirkwood's approach to collecting data for an Google Scholar was used to dig out relevant papers published in 2000- keywords used were: 'institutional policy', 'technology enhanced learnin learning', 'blended learning', 'massive open online courses', 'open edu sources', and 'social media'. Abstracts of the retrieved papers were exam sure that they satisfy the following inclusion criteria:

1. The paper involves an institutional policy in one or more of the follo associated with applications of technology in higher education instituti
   - Mobile learning
   - Blended learning
   - Massive open online courses
   - Open educational resources
   - Social media
2. The paper presents a study that was implemented and evaluated to inf tional policy on applications of technology in education.
3. The paper involves some forms of evaluation of institutional policy.
4. The paper provides a literature review of existing studies that fulfill th this list.

In addition, the following exclusion criteria were applied:

1. Technology applications in schools;
2. An institutional policy on TEL in schools;
3. An institutional policy on TEL that was proposed but had not been imp

Given the above criteria, a total of 101 papers were collected and rev following aspects were considered in the process of reviewing the papers u plified thematic analysis:

3.2 Findings

Table 1 shows the frequency of the dimensions of policy effectiveness applied in the papers. The results show that all the dimensions can be captured by one or more of the four instrumental approaches. A few papers adopt more than one dimension within the purview of the instrumental perspective, thus the accumulated total number of dimension (i.e., 114) is larger than the total number of papers reviewed (i.e., 101).

Table 1. Frequency of the dimensions of policy effectiveness applied in the collected papers

TEL device	Instrumental perspective			
	Classical	Contextual	Instrument-context	Constitutive
Blended learning	3	6	0	11
Mobile learning	4	2	0	2
MOOCs	4	6	0	4
OER	6	20	1	6
Social media	14	4	0	2
General*	13	0	0	6
Total	44	38	1	31
Accumulated total	114			

* This TEL device refers to studies on e-learning or online learning.

As shown in the data, the instrumental perspective is able to penetrate all of the TEL devices collected in this study, suggesting that the instrumental perspective is by and large not hindered by any type of TEL device.

There is only one paper falling in the instrument-context dimension. It does not, however, imply that this dimension is not useful given the small sample of papers reviewed. A possible reason for the lack of attention to this dimension which focuses on requirements of the teaching and learning setting is that TEL has largely been commonplace in the educational world [8]. This seems to have discouraged further exploration into whether there is a need for TEL in an institutional setting. On the other hand, it is observable that most papers fall into the other dimensions of effectiveness, i.e., what TEL device can produce effective learning outcomes, what barriers and enablers are in the implementation process, and what people think about TEL.

4 Towards a Framework for Analyzing the Effectiveness of Institutional Policy on TEL

Table 2 outlines a framework for evaluating TEL policy effectiveness based on the four dimensions in institutional perspective. The following discusses the variables related to each dimension of effectiveness.

4.1 Character of TEL Devices

The purpose of institutional policies on TEL should not be about the technology involved, but teaching and learning. However, as the classical approach would suggest,

Table 2. A framework for evaluating TEL policy effectiveness

Dimension of effectiveness	Variables of TEL policy effectiveness
Character of TEL devices	*Effects on institutions, learners and teachers* · Efficiency and cost-effectiveness · Learning outcomes (e.g. students' performance) · Impacts on teachers (e.g. teachers' freedom, ident dibility) *Technological, pedagogical and content designs* · Technological and pedagogical 'good fit' · Interoperability and compatibility of TEL devices · Culture issues and 'localization' · Language barriers
Implementation process	*Institutional and structural settings* · Internal institutional policy and structure; knowl nior management · Government regulatory framework · Availability of resources (financial, time, staff wi expertise) · Technology infrastructure; quality and stability of service provider · Intellectual property right and licensing *Quality assurance* · Content and pedagogical quality assessment/assur *Role of learners and teachers* · Students' understanding and knowledge, techniqu rience of TEL described, students' age · Students' self-confidence in mastery of technolog ing · Level of teacher and student engagement in the d of TEL described *Assessment and evaluation* · Student assessment and teacher evaluation
Requirements of a teaching and learning problem setting	*Relevant requirements of a teaching and learning problem s* · Demand for supply of teachers or educational serv
Acceptability of TEL	*Institutions* · Institutional norms and values *Stakeholders* · Institutional leaders, teachers and students' perce tudes and preferences · Teachers' field of teaching or students' field of lea

the TEL device definitely matters in shaping the effectiveness of TEL in p
fects of TEL devices on institutions such as cost-effectiveness and efficien

although they did not always do positively [17]. Effects of TEL on teachers have also been an important aspect of concern. In applications of social media such as Facebook in education, for example, the requirement of teacher participation in the use of this social media to enhance communication and interaction between students and teachers has raised concerns about teachers' freedom, identity and credibility [18][19].

There have been tremendous efforts in technological, pedagogical and content design in order to procure positive effects of TEL devices on learning outcomes. Technically, interoperability and compatibility have been identified as critical variables that affect the effectiveness of communication in virtual TEL environments [20]. Another key aspect is how TEL can be designed to suit pedagogical needs and to ensure a technological and pedagogical 'good fit' [21]. For example, the nature of Facebook makes it a popular platform for social networking but it is also this nature that often makes it not always suitable pedagogically to be used for academic purpose [22].

Culture issues and 'localization' embedded in TEL device (the extent in which the understanding of educational materials is not hampered by cultural difference) and language barriers have appeared to be an important variable swaying whether or not there could be proper communication between learners and TEL materials (e.g. [23][24]). A possible way to overcome cultural effects, as Kanuka and Gauthier have suggested in the case of OER, is to employ strategic use of surveys, interviews and evaluation frameworks to ensure that OER are culturally relevant to local learners [25].

4.2 Implementation Process

Studies in TEL have also looked at variables under the purview of the contextual dimension of effectiveness. Variables may be on institutional and structural settings, i.e., whether or not internal institutional policies and structures are in conflict with a policy on TEL and the friendliness of government regulatory framework [21][26] as well as knowledge of senior management [27]. Following closely, the availability of resources and technology infrastructure is an aspect of concern in the implementation process [3]. Al-Fahad has found that while students perceived mobile learning as a useful means to enhance learning experiences, the process of implementing this mode of learning was hindered by various contextual factors such as poor networking in the city [28]. Closely associated with resources and infrastructure is the quality and stability of technologies by service providers. Phillips has observed, for instance, that "there is the monitoring of hyperlinks, as after a period of time some of them become 'broken' for various reasons, such as the movement of web servers. Hence, it is the task of the subject-matter expert to promptly replace these 'dead' links with equivalent alternative links" [29] (p. 184), and therefore, informal and just-in-time support for users [30] was considered imperative and necessary in the process. Another resources related variable is about intellectual property right and licensing issues, which is an immensely imperative issue especially for OER (e.g. [31]). van Wyk has pinpointed that "OER alone cannot increase access and quality in higher education", and that governments should play a role in supporting "the principle that products of publicly funded work should carry such licenses" [32] (p. 13).

Content and pedagogical quality assessment and assurance issues hav
be a critical concern in the TEL implementation process [33][34]. A prim
is about who are involved in the development of online contents and wh
sure that those contents are relevant and pedagogically sound. Misra has
many TEL enthusiasts who worked with some support from institutions to
develop OER-based courseware were in many cases without any related tr
proper quality control is needed to prompt the production of TEL materia
sonable quality [33].

The role of learners and teachers are key variables in the implementati
Students' understanding, knowledge, techniques and experience of TEL [3
confidence in mastery of technology in learning [36] are important aspects
in the learning process. White and Manton have observed that students a
sure about their ability to choose appropriately the abundance of materia
online and "recognise how easy it is to become 'lost' in the web and to r
significant amounts of time engaging with resources that prove later to b
or unreliable" [35] (p. 26). On the other hand, level of teacher and stud
ment and empowerment in the development of TEL described has also
important part in the process of teaching and learning [37][38], while stu
ment [34][39] and teacher evaluation [40] have also imposed great challe
effectiveness of TEL.

4.3 Requirements of a Teaching and Learning Problem Setting

For the connection between this theory of instrument and TEL, it is helpf
that TEL is a means to an end, not an end in or by itself. For an educa
there can be various means to achieve it, and TEL may be only one of
should ask, therefore, before adopting TEL as a means: Why should T
means in the first place, and, if TEL is deemed necessary, which TEL m
suitable? Wolfenden's study on OER in Sub-Saharan Africa, as one of th
vant studies, focuses on the teaching and learning problem setting that th
mendous demand for new teachers to provide school services, and OER w
means to solve the problem [26]. It is found that the creation and use o
vided ample opportunities for teacher education and helped alleviate the
the huge demand for school teachers.

4.4 Acceptability of TEL

The extent to which TEL in general is accepted as a mode of learning i
variable swaying the degree in which a TEL policy is effective. Ezer
guished two thoughts about technology – "what [technology] can do, wh
interaction it invites, what properties it has" and "the idea of technology, v
think of it, how they see it helping their situation, how they shape its mea

mobile devices can be considered as 'boundary objects', the meaning of which is influenced by discourse and practices.

A variable of this dimension of effectiveness stems not from people but institutions *per se*. Wallace and Young have observed that taken-for-granted institutional values and norms hinder the implementation of blended courses, and in some case blended delivery was bounded to serve existing values and norms and long accepted protocols are often ill-fitted to make the most potential use of blended delivery within the new learning context [44].

Institutional leaders', teachers' and students' perceptions, attitudes and preferences towards TEL have often been observed as critical variables shaping or determining the extent to which TEL devices are accepted [45][46], which is often reflected in terms of degree of participation in the learning process and course dropout rates. Al-Fahad studies students' attitudes towards mobile learning and found that the primary advantage of this technology is that "it can be used anywhere, anytime and adopt their mobile learning systems with the aim of improving communication and enriching students' learning experiences in their open and distance learning" [28] (p. 111). In the context of OER, however, White and Manton have observed that one of the challenges of implementing OER is that "there is still a sense among students that non-textual online sources have less academic legitimacy than books or journals" [35] (p. 26).

5 Conclusion

Existing studies of institutional policies associated with TEL have provided a broad range of variables for analyzing TEL policy effectiveness. Through a literature survey, this study has examined the extent to which the instrumental approach to policy effectiveness is able to capture those variables for developing an encompassing conceptual framework for analyzing the effectiveness of TEL policy. Findings of the survey have demonstrated that the dimensions in instrumental perspective are comprehensive enough for this purpose, that all literature reviewed can be categorized into one of the four dimensions.

The conceptual framework presented in this paper thus potentially serves as a useful lens for analyzing the effectiveness of institutional policies on TEL and a point of reference for formulating relevant institutional policies. Nevertheless, we do not deny the possibility that a good number of relevant studies which have looked at TEL policy effectiveness beyond the four dimensions have not been covered in this survey. The proposed framework remains extensible to encompass more dimensions and variables for further improving its usefulness.

References

1. Singh, H.: Building effective blended learning programs. Educational Technology 43(6), 51–54 (2003)
2. Kneill-Boxley, S.: Towards a mobile learning strategy to support Higher Education. Innovative Practice in Higher Education 1(2), 1–19 (2012)

3. Yuan, L., Powell, S.: MOOCs and open education: Implications for higher edu White Paper (2013)
4. Glennie, J., Harley, K., Butcher, N., van Wyk, T. (eds.): Open Educational R Change in Higher Education: Reflections from Practice. Commonwealth Vancouver (2012)
5. Fagerstrom, A., Ghinea, G.: Co-creation of value in higher education: Usin work marketing in the recruitment of students. Journal of Higher Educatio Management 35(1), 45–53 (2013)
6. Jeannette, K.J., Meyer, M.H.: Online learning equals traditional classroom master gardeners. HortTechnology 12(1), 148–156 (2002)
7. Zhang, D.S., Zhou, L., Briggs, R.O., Nunamaker Jr, J.F.: Instructional video i assessing the impact of interactive video on learning effectiveness. Informa agement 43(1), 15–27 (2006)
8. Mars, M.M., Ginter, M.B.: Connecting organizational environments with the technology practices of community college faculty. Community College R 324–343 (2007)
9. Wiley, D.: On the Sustainability of Open Educational Resource Initiatives in cation (2007), http://www1.oecd.org/edu/ceri/38645447.pdf
10. Gruszczynska, A.: HEA/JISC Open Educational Resources Case Study: Development from OER Practice. Higher Education Academy, York (2012)
11. Bennear, L.S., Stavins, R.N.: Second-best theory and the use of multiple p ments. Environmental and Resource Economics 37, 111–129 (2007)
12. Lascoumes, P., LeGales, P.: Introduction: Understanding public policy th struments—from the nature of instruments to the sociology of public policy tion. Governance 20(1), 1–21 (2007)
13. Peters, B.G., van Nispen, F.K.M. (eds.): Public Policy Instruments: Evaluati of Public Administration. Edward Elgar Publishing, Northampton (1998)
14. Price, L., Kirkwood, A.: Technology enhanced learning—where's the eviden culum, Technology & Transformation for an Unknown Future. In: Proceeding Sydney 2010, Sydney, Australia (2010)
15. Dean, P., Stahl, M., Sylwester, D., Peat, J.: Effectiveness of combined delive for distance learning and resident learning. Quarterly Review of Distance Ed 247–254 (2001)
16. Omollo, K.L., Rahman, A., Yebuah, C.A.: Producing OER from Scratch: health sciences at the University of Ghana and the Kwame Nkrumah Universi and Technology. In: Glennie, J., Harley, K., Butcher, N., van Wyk, T. (eds.) tional Resources and Change in Higher Education: Reflections from Practic wealth of Learning, Vancouver (2012)
17. Vamosi, A.R., Pierce, B.G., Slotkin, M.H.: Distance learning in an accounti course – student satisfaction and perceptions of efficacy. Journal of Education 79(6), 360–366 (2010)
18. Li, L., Pitts, J.P.: Does it really matter? Using virtual office hours to enha faculty interaction. Journal of Information Systems Education 20(1), 175–185
19. Mazer, J.P., Murphy, R.E., Simonds, C.J.: The effects of teacher self-disclosu book on teacher credibility. Learning, Media and Technology 34(2), 175–183
20. Feliz, T., Ricoy, C., Feliz, S.: Analysis of the use of Twitter as a learning master's studies. Open Learning: The Journal of Open, Distance and e-Le

21. Harishankar, B.V.: Tracing the trajectory of OER in India: Reflections on three initiatives. In: Glennie, J., Harley, K., Butcher, N., van Wyk, T. (eds.) Open Educational Resources and Change in Higher Education: Reflections from Practice, Commonwealth of Learning, Vancouver (2012)
22. Mendez, J.P., Le, K., De La Cruz, J.: Integrating Facebook in the classroom: Pedagogical dilemmas. Journal of Instructional Pedagogies 13, 1–10 (2014)
23. Badarch, D., Knyazeva, S., Lane, A.: Introducing the opportunities and challenges of OER: The case of the Commonwealth of Independent States and the Baltic States. In: Glen-nie, J., Harley, K., Butcher, N., van Wyk, T. (eds.) Open Educational Resources and Change in Higher Education: Reflections from Practice. Commonwealth of Learning, Vancouver (2012)
24. Yuan, L., MacNeill, S., Kraan, W.: Open Educational Resources – Opportunities and Challenges for Higher Education (2008), `http://muele.mak.ac.ug/file.php/1/Student_Reading_Resource/oer_briefing_paper.pdf` (retrieved)
25. Kanuka, H., Gauthier, G.: Pedagogical content knowledge in higher education and open educational resources: A case study on course design. In: Glennie, J., Harley, K., Butcher, N., van Wyk, T. (eds.) Open Educational Resources and Change in Higher Education: Reflections from Practice. Commonwealth of Learning, Vancouver (2012)
26. Wolfenden, F.: OER production and adaptation through networking across Sub-Saharan Africa: Learning from TESSA. In: Glennie, J., Harley, K., Butcher, N., van Wyk, T. (eds.) Open Educational Resources and Change in Higher Education: Reflections from Practice. Commonwealth of Learning, Vancouver (2012)
27. Armstrong, J., Franklin, T.: A Review of Current and Developing International Practice in the Use of Social Networking (Web 2.0) in Higher Education (2008), `http://www.franklin-consulting.co.uk/LinkedDocuments/the%20use% 20of%20social%20networking%20in%20HE.pdf` (retrieved)
28. Al-Fahad, F.N.: Students' attitudes and perceptions towards the effectiveness of mobile learning in King Saud University, Saudi Arabia. The Turkish Online Journal of Educational Technology 8(2), 111–119 (2009)
29. Phillips, J.A.: Experiences in finding and using OER in teacher education programmes: Pedagogical approach and challenges. In: Glennie, J., Harley, K., Butcher, N., van Wyk, T. (eds.) Open Educational Resources and Change in Higher Education: Reflections from Practice. Commonwealth of Learning, Vancouver (2012)
30. Olney, I., Lefoe, G.: Introducing mobile technologies: Preparatory staff development issues. In: ICT: Providing choices for learners and learning, Proceedings Ascilite Singapore 2007 (2007)
31. Mawoyo, M., Butcher, N.: Sharing existing teaching materials as OER: Key considerations from practice. In: Glennie, J., Harley, K., Butcher, N., van Wyk, T. (eds.) Open Educational Resources and Change in Higher Education: Reflections from Practice. Commonwealth of Learning, Vancouver (2012)
32. van Wyk, T.: Taking OER beyond the OER community: Policy issues and priorities. In: Glennie, J., Harley, K., Butcher, N., van Wyk, T. (eds.) Open Educational Resources and Change in Higher Education: Reflections from Practice. Commonwealth of Learning, Vancouver (2012)
33. Misra, P.K.: Pedagogical quality enrichment in OER based courseware: Guiding principles. Open Praxis 5(2), 123–134 (2013)
34. Voss, B.D.: Massive open online courses (MOOCs): A primer for university and college board members. In: An AGB White Paper. Association of Governing Boards, Washington, D.C (2013)

35. White, D., Manton, M.: Open Educational Resources: The Value of Reuse in cation. JISC funded OER Impact Study, University of Oxford (2011), http://www.jisc.ac.uk/media/documents/programmes/elea er/OERTheValueOfReuseInHigherEducation.pdf (retrieved)
36. Miligan, C., Littlejohn, A., Margaryan, A.: Patterns of engagement in MOOCs. Journal of Online Learning & Teaching 9(2), 149–159 (2013)
37. Afnan-Manns, S., Medrano, R., Mickelsen, K.F.: OneClick Digital and t Project: OER as Content, OER as Pedagogy (2013), http://www.educa ero/article/oneclick-digital-and-medrano-project-oer- content-oer-pedagogy
38. Petrides, L., Jimes, C., Middleton-Detzner, C., Howell, H.: OER as a model teaching and learning. In: Open ED 2010 Proceedings. UOC, OU, BYU, Barce
39. Chen, Y.: Investigating MOOCs through blog mining. The International Research in Open and Distance Learning 15(2), 85–106 (2014)
40. McClure, M.W.: MOOCs: Hope and hype in viral technologies and policies. F Higher Education 4, 7–24 (2013)
41. Ezer, J.F.: The Interplay of Institutional Forces behind Higher ICT Educat Doctoral dissertation, London School of Economics and Political Science (20C
42. Corbeil, J.R., Valdés-Corbeil, M.E.: Are you ready for mobile learning? Quarterly 30(2), 51–58 (2007)
43. Beddall-Hill, N.L., Raper, J.: Mobile devices as 'Boundary Objects' on field of the Research Center for Educational Technology 6(1), 28–46 (2010)
44. Wallace, L., Young, J.: Implementing blended learning: Policy implications ties. Online Journal of Distance Learning Administration 13(8) (2010), http://www.westga.edu/~distance/ojdla/winter134/walla g134.html (retrieved)
45. Cross, S.: Evaluation of the OLDS MOOC Curriculum Design Course: Part pectives, Expectations and Experiences. OLDS MOOC Project, Milton Keyne
46. Lane, A.: Design and development of OER: A student perspective. In: Glenni K., Butcher, N., van Wyk, T. (eds.) Open Educational Resources and Chan Education: Reflections from Practice. Common-wealth of Learning, Vancouve

Effectiveness of Technology Enhancement in Blended Learning: An Instrumental Perspective

Kam Cheong Li, Helen Lam, and Terry Lee

The Open University of Hong Kong
30 Good Shepherd Street, Homantin, Kowloon, Hong Kong SAR, China
kcli@ouhk.edu.hk

Abstract. Studies on institutional policies on the use of technology in blended learning reveal that technology choices and policy implementation are largely governed by three common perceptions: (1) technology *per se* has its own logic of effectiveness and operation, (2) the choice of technology is based on its utilities across contexts, and (3) the application of technology is pre-determined. However, this commonality overlooks the existence of various factors that shape the effectiveness of technology at different stages of application.

This paper examines, via the perspective of policy instrument, various factors that may hinder or facilitate the effectiveness of technology in blended learning. The use of technology is conceptualized as a policy instrument in the process of formulating and implementing institutional policies on blended learning. Its effectiveness is analyzed using four theories of policy instrument, namely the 'classical', 'contextual', 'instrument-context' and 'constitutive' approaches to instrument. Results of the analysis show the dynamic nature of effectiveness which should be considered when formulating institutional policies on technology-enhanced learning.

Keywords: Institutional policies, technology as policy instrument, effectiveness of policy instruments, blended learning.

1 Introduction

In virtually all aspects of education, application of technology has become commonplace in educational institutions. Mars and Ginter summarize a variety of reasons for the increasing use of technology in education [1]. First, technology-based models of learning are adopted by educational institutions to make operations more efficient and cost-effective. Second, these models are used as alternative methods of course-delivery to expand student markets and reach those students who would otherwise not be able to attend conventional face-to-face on-campus classes due to geographical or other difficulties. Third, their use enables programmes and courses to be regularly updated to enhance student enrolment capacities and in many cases to bring course content more in line with the increasingly high-tech economy.

The notion that 'technology can do' stems in part from the vast number of studies that have reported relatively positive effects of the use of technology on learning outcomes,

K.C. Li et al. (Eds.): ICTE 2014, CCIS 494, pp. 187–198, 2015.

e.g. [2][3][4][5]. In particular, Ali and Elfessi investigated the performance o
of student by offering virtual and conventional settings respectively, where n
difference was observed in performance between the two groups, implying th
setting could serve as an alternative to the conventional one [6].

However, an increasing number of studies have also reported that tech
not necessarily bring about positive effects on teaching and learning [7][8
times there are even negative experiences and outcomes [10][11][12][13]
there is a need to understand the factors that influence the effectiveness
gy-enhanced learning in order to properly utilize technology in education.

This paper examines various factors that may hinder or facilitate the e
of technology in the context of blended learning as a 'critical case'. Arg
pared to full e-learning models such as 'massive open online courses', the
of technology used in blended learning is smaller as it normally consists o
tional face-to-face classroom setting and some form of e-learning. The s
portance of a 'critical case' is that "if this is valid for this case, then it a
cases" [14]. Thus, if the factors examined in this study impact on the effe
blended learning, (to deduct logically) it is then likely that the same fa
also influence the effectiveness of other learning models that embrace ful
settings. An analysis of the case of blended learning is, therefore, strategic
tive for understanding the effectiveness of learning models based ent
learning environments.

To understand different factors that influence the effectiveness of blend
this study as a preliminary endeavour borrows the concept of 'policy instru
the field of social sciences and conceptualizes this mode of learning as
accomplish the policy objectives of an educational institution. This conce
allows an analysis of the effectiveness of technology use in blended le
policy instrument by using theories in the social sciences field which,
shown, produce distinctive factors that shape its effectiveness.

2 Blended Learning as an Institutional Policy Instrume Technology-Enhanced Learning

The concept of 'policy instrument' is commonly used in studies of gove
public policy [15][16], referring to a method or means used by gove
achieve a desired effect. For example, 'assessment' has been used by
authorities to accomplish educational success in terms of reportable risi
attainment[17].

However, the use of 'policy' and 'policy instrument' is not limited to go
institutions. Educational institutions have their own visions and/or missio
formulate various institutional policies to achieve them. In Utah Valley
(UVU), for instance, 'policy' is defined as "a set of principles intende
actions" which "can represent the strategic direction or operating philos

- It is a governing principle that mandates or constrains actions.
- It has institution-wide application.
- It will change infrequently and sets a course for the foreseeable future.
- It helps ensure compliance, enhances the University's mission or reduces institutional risk.
- It is approved at senior levels of the institution [18].

Technology is in many ways a policy instrument used by institutions to achieve a variety of institutional policy goals. For example, information technology was introduced as a policy instrument by the UK Department of Health and Social Security in 1959 for modernizing the nation's social security system. The goal was to improve operational efficiency and flexibility, reduce administrative costs, replace repetitive and routine tasks, allow a greater degree of information disclosure, and enhance the quality of public services [19]. Cohen has observed that information technology such as the Internet might decrease the cost of information dissemination and enable information to reach a large population of targeted beneficiaries [20].

Technology-enhanced learning tools or materials, such as open educational resources (OER), have been seen as policy instruments which help to achieve various educational purposes at an institutional level. Ferran et al regard OER as a policy instrument of higher education institutions to facilitate flexible learning experiences, enhance transparency in learning paths, and enable greater accessibility to the learning materials in order to reinforce the concept of lifelong learning [21].

Blended learning as a technology-enhanced learning model can, therefore, be viewed as a policy instrument to achieve institutional policy goals. Colis and Moonen refer blended learning to the instruction taking place both in the classroom and online environment [22]. Harding, Jaczynski and Wood have observed that blended learning is "a mixture of online and face-to-face learning using a variety of learning resources and communications options available to students and lecturers" [23] (p. 56). This mode of learning as an institutional policy instrument thus offers institutions an alternative to pursue their intended policy objectives.

3 Effectiveness of Blended Learning: Four Instrumental Factors

By conceptualizing blended learning as a policy instrument, its effectiveness could be analyzed through various theories of policy instrument in policy studies. Peters and Van Nispen classify these theories into four types: 'classical', 'contextual', 'instrument-context' and 'constitutive' [15]. Table 1 summarizes their foci of analysis.

Table 1. Overview of focus of analysis by type of instrumental factor

Instrumental factor	Focus of analysis
Classical	Nature and character of educational technology
Contextual	Implementation process
Instrument-context	Requirements of a teaching and learning problem setting
Constitutive	'Subjective meaning' of educational technology

The 'classical' theory of instruments [24][25] values the importance o
and character of policy instruments in determining the course of the policy
the context of technology enhancing learning, this theory explores the na
learning mode—how its characteristics or features determine the teaching
ing setting, its impact and expected effects on teaching and learning expe
outcomes. The underlying assumption of this theory is that instruments p
tinctive characteristics and nature attached to their logics of operations and
Each instrument by its very nature determines the design of the impleme
tivities with distinctive effects on teaching and learning as well as outc
nature and character of instruments can be applied across contexts. Instituti
makers can be informed about the application and choice of instrument
their utility across contexts which in reality are predetermined in most case

The analysis of the 'contextual' theory focuses on factors relevant to th
in which the policy is applied, especially those within the complex process
instruments operate [25][26]. Substantial emphasis is placed on examining
the implementation process, identifying various contextual factors such as
of technology infrastructure and level of support for technology users.
argues that while instrumental differences may exist, it is questionable
struments of any kind can be applied universally as contextual factors are
swaying the way they operate and their intended level of effectiveness.

The focus of analysis of the 'instrument-context' theory locates som
tween the above two. This school of thought places a lot more attention
over contextual problem settings and instruments as solutions, i.e., to unde
vant teaching and learning problems and identify suitable solutions to ther
ogies may provide options from which institutional policy makers may ch
is not, as this theory may argue, the only option. In line with this theory, t
foremost task is to identify relevant requirements of a teaching and learn
and to make instrumental choices based on the extent to which the instrum
to fulfill the requirements.

For the 'constitutive' theory, it is argued that understanding instrumenta
ness should go beyond all objective evidence and consider subjective m
instruments. "What do people think" is the central question of this theory.
cultural and normative, and is therefore subject to social construction and
tion. The focus of this theory is in many ways about the extent to which pe
the use of technology in education.

4 Institutional Policies on Blended Learning

The four types of instrumental theory, in essence, shape or determine the
ness of blended learning as a policy instrument of technology-enhanced lea
section reviews relevant studies on institutional policies on blended learni
to examine how the various instrumental forces sway differently the effec

4.1 Character of Blended Learning

In line with the classical theory of instruments, the character of blended learning renders a critical factor that determines its effectiveness. An integration of traditional face-to-face classroom setting and some form of e-learning has been considered as the primary characteristics of blended learning [27][28]. Mitchell and Honore define blended instruction as "learning involving multiple methods and approaches, commonly a mixture of classroom and e-learning" [29] (p. 149). Delialioglu and Yildirim suggest that blended instruction refers to the mix of classroom instruction and online instruction with which benefits of both instructional modes could be achieved [30].

Relevant studies have attempted to explore explicit and observable benefits of blended learning. For example, Garrison and Kanuka claim that blended learning provides large numbers of learners with interactive learning experience in an accessible and cost-effective way through the Internet [31]. Dowling, Godfred and Gyles consider blended learning a teaching model allowing flexibility by delivering learning contents electronically while keeping regular face-to-face classes [32]. To maintain their economic competitiveness, many countries have developed policies to increase the participation of adults in higher education. Broek and Hake have observed that distance and blended learning has been one of the policy instruments that governments employ to increase the participation of adults in higher education by reducing the costs of learning and making higher education more accessible [33].

Studies have also examined the cost-effectiveness and direct impact of blended learning on learning outcomes. Dean et al. show that blended learning programmes "can be completed in approximately one-half of the time, at less than half the cost, using a rich mix of live e-learning, self-paced instruction, and physical classroom delivery", and that this programme design was also able to contribute to "an overall 10% better learning outcome than the traditional classroom learning format" [34] (p. 247).

The character of blended learning, therefore, justifies its utility as an alternative learning mode in the teaching and learning process and its existence as a key component of educational administrators' 'toolkit'.

4.2 Implementation Process

The implementation of blended learning involves a set of contextual factors determining the effectiveness of this policy instrument. A contextual factor of this kind is availability of resources. Wallace and Young's case study shows that blended courses at the early stage were delivered with existing resources or given 'special project' status, and they in general lacked an implementation plan to cover institutional resources, reward structures, and priorities [35].

The ability of students to learn independently has been identified as a crucial factor that shapes the effects of blended learning on learning outcomes. Snodin assessed the effectiveness of blended learning by involving learners to autonomously organized resources in a course management system, and found that such effectiveness depends on how well learners' autonomy is inspired [36]. Kemmer finds that learners need to take responsibility for their learning in order to fully benefit from blended learning [37].

A suggestion is thus made to enhance students' understanding of the deman
learning and its contribution to their learning. Napier, Dekhane and Smi
qualitative feedback from students after trying a computing course in the bl
[38]. Participating students responded that being responsible for their o
and managing time properly are key factors to the success of blended learn

Learners' understanding of the use of technology and ability to maste
technology component of blended learning play an important role in dete
success of blended learning in the implementation process. Kemmer ob
learners' understanding of the use of technology to facilitate their indepe
ing is one major factor towards the success of blended learning [37]. Carte
ers highlight the significance of technological readiness in the blended mc
they reviewed, learners who are self-confident in mastery of technology t
form better in and be more satisfied with blended and online learning e
than those with lesser skill with technology" (p. 444). Ratz observes the
between readiness in technology and learners' interest in blended learnin
cording to her findings, higher confidence level is shown in younger and n
pants, who are also more interested in adoption of blended learning. Kim
Oh find that, among the various obstacles to adopting blended learning, fa
technology is rated as the most significant one [41]. They suggest that b
and practitioners have to keep themselves updated about the latest techr
teaching and learning.

Another critical concern lies in the extent to which pedagogical design
fits a learning setting that consists of both traditional classroom and onlin
well as teachers' ability to master both platforms. Precel, Eshet-Alkalai a
highlighted that the importance of completing the pedagogical design of o
ing component of blended learning in advance was acknowledged by stu
Werth, Werth and Kellerer's study on the impact of blended learning on s
teachers has shown that the ability of teacher to be innovative was positi
lated with (1) his or her ability to provide one-to-one instruction
efficacy/confidence; (3) ability to monitor student learning; and (4) en
teaching [43]. Their study also pinpointed the importance of identifying a
rating pedagogical strategies particularly pertinent to blended and online te
teacher preparation for new modes of education.

Planning and monitoring of staff workload has also been a key to effect
learning. McIntyre, Watson and Larsen pointed out that the balance of w
gether with time management was, among others, a problematic issue rele
large-scale implementation of blended learning [44]. Tynan et al. observed
load planning for staff is an essential part of the process of designing ble
ing, and that most universities did not have at the early stage centralized pr
guidelines for allocating academic workload on blended learning [45]. Ru
that the move from traditional campus university teaching to blended lear
hampered by lack of planning and monitoring of staff workload [46].

The interplay of barriers and enablers in the implementation process

4.3 Requirements of a Teaching and Learning Problem Setting

According to the instrument-context theory, central questions may involve whether relevant requirements of a teaching and learning problem setting allow technology-enhanced learning to play a role in that setting, and if so, whether it necessarily means blended learning. Blended learning, as mentioned earlier, is primarily characterized by a combination of some degree of traditional face-to-face classroom-based and some form of off-campus online-based settings. Programmes or courses that are considered better delivered by either one of the two settings may not provide the necessary institutional incentive for a policy on blended learning.

Rolfe et al. documented that science staff conceived their academic subjects as suitable for the use of e-learning and were more aware of the potential benefits of e-learning, whereas staff in the arts subjects tended to hold that their academic subjects were based on more in-depth analysis and discussion that could hardly be supported by e-learning activities [47]. Given such difference in staff's perception, Rolfe et al conclude that application of e-learning in arts subjects does not bring as much benefit as that in science subjects in terms of learning the subject matter [47].

The increasing transformation of course-delivery from conventional in-class to e-learning setting through the use of technology-enhanced learning device may mean that using blended learning for a full delivery of relevant courses would be hindered by this instrument's nature to request for some elements of conventional in-class environment. To take an example, international partnerships such as 'OpenupEd' [48] were established to deliver educational services for lifelong learning by providing programmes or courses that are fully delivered online (and can be completed for free for an informal credit). Lifelong learners may well opt for this kind of online and conditionally free learning mode rather than blended learning for which they often have to settle a payment at least for the usage of classroom equipment and facilities.

Thus, while blended learning may be found in education administrators' 'toolkit', it may be just a tool 'ready for use only' and may not be used at all. Its application, in accordance with the instrument-context argument, depends on what a teaching and learning problem setting would call for in the first place.

4.4 Acceptability of Blended Learning

The extent to which blended learning is accepted by educational stakeholders (especially learners) has been a critical factor for the effectiveness of blended learning in terms of participation and course dropout. Learners' and teachers' perceptions, attitudes and preferences have therefore been crucial variables in examining the acceptability of blended learning, which provides the necessary legitimacy for an institutional policy on blended learning.

For instance, in a comparative study that Chen and Jones reported on business students' assessments of course effectiveness and their overall satisfaction with an accounting class, one group of students were offered a traditional face-to-face classroom setting and another group a blended-learning setting in which online method was supplemented by a few occasions of in-class meeting [49]. They summarized the following relatively encouraging results:

> "Overall perceptions of the course, instructor and learning outcomes positive for both groups. …However, some interesting differences noted. Specifically, students in the traditional setting were more sati with the clarity of instruction. On the other hand, students in the blen learning section felt more strongly that they gained an appreciation c concepts in the field. Blended-learning students also indicated strongly that their analytical skills improved as a result of the course. results suggest that the two delivery methods were similar in terms nal learning outcomes, but that both may be improved by incorpor aspects of the other." (p. 1)

However, as the constitutive theory of instruments would argue, the meaning of blended learning can be constructed and reconstructed from t and across contexts, resulting in various levels of effectiveness of this accordingly. Learning style preferences have been an important variable bility of blended learning. Akkoyunlu and Soylu find that students' per blended learning are affected by their learning styles [50]. Following Kolb Style Inventory [51], Akkoyunlu and Soylu categorized students into fo styles, namely divergers, assimilators, covergers and accommodators [50]. ings reveal that, for example, divergers who prefer concrete experience tend to be in favor of more interactions with peers and teachers. In contras tors who prefer abstract conceptualization in learning prefer a lecture setti laar, Rienties and Giesbers also observed the difference of students' learni relation to learning effectiveness [52]. According to their findings, less ac inclined students, such as those taking a "surface" approach to learning, b from learning statistics in a blended environment. Banerjee surveyed stu ception on blended learning [53]. It is found that students who are vis prefer seeing things done as an example rather than figuring them out on Banerjee also finds that only certain disciplines are preferred in blended Computer science, for example, is a discipline involving complicated cc students prefer learning it with face-to-face interactions with a teacher.

Teachers' orientations and preferences are equally, if not more, impera erations in making technological choices and putting it into practice. Benso and Ooms documented that academic staff's perceptions, attitudes and blended learning can be varied [54]. In the case of business and managen tion, they developed a typology of three distinct approaches to blended le the staff's perspective, namely "technology is all", "Bolt-ons" and "purely each of which represents a different degree of participation in blended learni

Cultural variances as a result of geographical differences may render tion for various views of teachers about the integration of online collabor ing in blended learning [55], but the existence of pluralistic perspectives cept of blended learning is also not surprising even in monistic cultural cc highlights the importance of introducing proper mechanisms to sustain th

Thus, even though blended learning as a tool is preferred by education administrators, its applicability is still affected by other educational stakeholders' acceptability.

5 Conclusion

This paper has attempted to argue that some common assumptions underlying institutional policies on technology-enhanced learning (i.e., technology *per se* has its own logic of effectiveness and operation; the choice of technology is based on its utilities across contexts; and the application of technology is predetermined) overlook the existence of various factors that shape the effectiveness of technology at different stages of its application from technological choice to implementation.

Through the instrumental perspective, this study has examined various instrumental factors that may hinder or facilitate the effectiveness of the use of technology in blended learning as an institutional policy instrument of technology-enhanced learning. A review of relevant studies has revealed that such effectiveness is influenced not only by the character of blended learning, but also the implementation process, requirements of a teaching and learning problem setting and teachers' and learners' acceptability of this particular form of technology-enhanced learning.

The integration of technology-enhanced learning in education has been an ongoing trend and formulation of relevant policies remains a top item in the agenda of institutional policy making. Deliberation of educational administrators in making technological choices should focus on, in addition to the character of educational technologies, whether there is a need for such a technology in education, and if so, which form and type of the technology, what possible barriers and enablers are likely to happen in the implementation process and the extent to which applications of technology in educational services are accepted by learners and staff members as well as other relevant stakeholders.

References

1. Mars, M.M., Ginter, M.B.: Connecting organizational environments with the instructional technology practices of community college faculty. Community College Review 34(4), 324–343 (2007)
2. Omollo, K.L., Rahman, A., Yebuah, C.A.: Producing OER from scratch: The case of health sciences at the University of Ghana and the Kwame Nkrumah University of Science and Technology. In: Glennie, J., Harley, K., Butcher, N., van Wyk, T. (eds.) Open Educational Resources and Change in Higher Education: Reflections from Practice. Commonwealth of Learning, Vancouver (2012)
3. Garrison, D.R.: Elearning in the 21st Century, 2nd edn. Routledge Falmer, New York (2011)
4. McLoughlin, C., Loch, B.: Scaffolding conceptual learning in mathematics with technology enhanced pedagogy—a preliminary evaluation of student engagement with screencasts. In: Proceedings of World Conference on Educational Multimedia, Hypermedia and Telecommunications 2013, pp. 259–265 (2013)

5. Glance, D.G., Forsey, M., Riley, M.: The pedagogical foundations of massive courses. First Monday 18(5) (2013)
6. Ali, A., Elfessi, A.: Examining students performance and attitudes towards t formation technology in a virtual and conventional setting. Journal of Intera Learning 2(3), 1–9 (2004)
7. Merino, D.N., Abel, K.D.: Evaluating the effectiveness of computer tutorials vers lecturing in accounting topics. Journal of Engineering Education 92(2), 189–194 (
8. Minocha, S.: Role of social software tools in education: A literature review and Training 51(5/6), 353–369 (2009)
9. Vamosi, A.R., Pierce, B.G., Slotkin, M.H.: Distance learning in an accounti course – student satisfaction and perceptions of efficacy. Journal of Education 79(6), 360–366 (2004)
10. Connell, R.S.: Academic libraries, Facebook and MySpace, and student out vey of student opinion. Libraries and the Academy 9(1), 25–36 (2009)
11. Hewitt, A., Forte, A.: Crossing boundaries: Identity management and student tionships on the Facebook. Poster presented at the Annual Meeting of Comput Cooperative Work. Banff, Alberta, Canada (2006)
12. Li, L., Pitts, J.P.: Does it really matter? Using virtual office hours to enha faculty interaction. Journal of Information Systems Education 20(1), 175–185
13. Mazer, J.P., Murphy, R.E., Simonds, C.J.: The effects of teacher self-disclosu book on teacher credibility. Learning, Media and Technology 34(2), 175–183
14. Flyvbjerg, B.: Five misunderstandings about case-study research. Qualita 12(2), 209–245 (2006)
15. Peters, B.G., van Nispen, F.K.M. (eds.): Public Policy Instruments: Evaluati of Public Administration. Edward Elgar Publishing, Northampton (1998)
16. Salamon, L.M. (ed.): The Tools of Government: A Guide to the New Govern University Press, New York (2002)
17. Leung, C., Rea-Dickins, P.: Teacher assessment as policy instrument: Contra capacities. Language Assessment Quarterly 4(1), 6–36 (2007)
18. UVU Policy Office. Glossary of terms for campuswide policies. Retrieved fr Valley University (UVU) website (2014), `http://www.uvu.edu/p procedures/terms.html` (accessed April 25, 2014)
19. Margetts, H., Willcocks, L.: Information technology as policy instrument in th security system: Delivering an operational strategy. International Review of tive Sciences 58(3), 329–347 (1992)
20. Cohen, M.A.: Information as a policy instrument in protecting the environmen we learned? The Environmental Law Reporter 31(1), 10425–10431 (2001)
21. Ferran, N., Minguillon, J., Pascual, M., Barragan, C., Canals, A., Geser, G., Hornung-Prähauser, V., Schaffert, S., Baumgartner, P., Naust-Schulz, V., Lamminnen, S., Koivisto, A., Väliharju, T.: The concept of open educational instrument for implementing lifelong learning strategies at higher and further e stitutions. In: Proceedings of EDEN Conference, Vienna, pp. 591–597 (2006)
22. Colis, B., Moonen, J.: Flexible learning in a digital world: Experiences and e Kogan-Page, London (2001)
23. Harding, A., Kaczynski, D., Wood, L.N.: Evaluation of blended learning: analysi tive data. In: UniServe Science Blended Learning Symposium Proceedings, pp. 56
24. Lascoumes, P., LeGales, P.: Introduction: Understanding public policy throu

25. Linder, S.H., Peters, B.G.: The study of policy instruments: Four schools of thought. In: Peters, B.G., Van Nispen, F.K.M. (eds.) Public Policy Instruments: Evaluating the Tools of Public Administration. Edward Elgar, Cheltenham (1998)
26. Howlett, M.: Governance modes, policy regimes and operational plans: A multi-level nested model of policy instrument choice and policy design. Policy Sciences 42(1), 73–89 (2009)
27. Riggs, J.: MOOCs, flips, and blends. Huffington Post (2013), http://www.huffingtonpost.com/janet-riggs/flips-and-blends_b_2593733.html (retrieved)
28. Whitelock, D., Jelfs, A.: Editorial: Journal of educational media special issue on blended learning. Journal of Educational Media 28(2-3), 99–100 (2003)
29. Mitchell, A., Honore, S.: Criteria for successful blended learning. Industrial and Commercial Training 39(3), 143–149 (2007)
30. Delialioglu, O., Yildirim, Z.: Design and development of a technology enhanced hybrid instruction based on MOLTA model: Its effectiveness in comparison to traditional instruction. Computers & Education 51(1), 474–483 (2008)
31. Garrison, D.R., Kanuka, H.: Blended learning: Uncovering its transformative potential in higher education. The Internet and Higher Education 7(2), 95–105 (2004)
32. Dowling, C., Godfrey, J.M., Gyles, N.: Do hybrid flexible delivery teaching methods improve accounting students' learning outcomes? Accounting Education: An International Journal 12(4), 373–391 (2003)
33. Broek, S., Hake, B.J.: Increasing participation of adults in higher education: Factors for successful policies. International Journal of Lifelong Education 31(4), 397–417 (2012)
34. Dean, P., Stahl, M., Sylwester, D., Peat, J.: Effectiveness of combined delivery modalities for distance learning and resident learning. Quarterly Review of Distance Education 2(3), 247–254 (2001)
35. Wallace, L., Young, J.: Implementing blended learning: Policy implications for universities. Online Journal of Distance Learning Administration 13(8) (2010), http://www.westga.edu/~distance/ojdla/winter134/_young134.html
36. Snodin, N.S.: The effects of blended learning with a CMS on the development of autonomous learning: A case study of different degrees of autonomy achieved by individual learners. Computers & Education 61, 209–216 (2013)
37. Kemmer, D.: Blended learning and the development of student responsibility for learning: A case study of a 'widening access' university. Widening Participation & Lifelong Learning 13(3), 60–74 (2011)
38. Napier, N.P., Dekhane, S., Smith, S.: Transitioning to blended learning: Understanding student and faculty perceptions. Journal of Asynchronous Learning Networks 15(1), 20–33 (2011)
39. Carter, L., Salyers, V.: E-learning as educational innovation in universities. In: Shavinina, L.V. (ed.) The Routledge International Handbook of Innovation Education, pp. 442–455. Routledge (2013)
40. Ratz, S.: Community language classes: How ready are students for more technology? Journal of Perspectives in Applied Academic Practice 1(1), 3–10 (2013)
41. Kim, K.-J., Bonk, C.J., Oh, E.: The present and future state of blended learning in workplace learning settings in the United States. Performance Improvement 47(8), 5–17 (2008)
42. Precel, K., Eshet-Alkalai, Y., Alberton, Y.: Pedagogical and design aspects of a blended learning course. International Review of Research in Open and Distance Learning 10(2), 1–16 (2009)

43. Werth, E., Werth, L., Kellerer, E.: Transforming K-21 Rural Education thro Learning: Barriers and Promising Practices (2013), http://www.ina cms/wp-content/uploads/2013/10/iNACOL-Transforming-K Rural-Education-through-Blended-Learning.pdf (accessed 2014) (retrieved)
44. McIntyre, S., Watson, K., Larsen, S.: Strategies for large scale blended learnir Training, teaching and management Paper presented at the 4th Internatic Learning Conference, University of Hetfordshire, Hatfield, UK (2009), http://www.unsworks.unsw.edu.au/primo_library/libweb dlDisplay.do?docId=unsworks_7750&vid=UNSWORKS (accessec 2014) (retrieved)
45. Tynan, B., Ryan, Y., Hinton, L., Mills, A.L.: Out of Hours, Final report of th teaching leadership: planning and implementing a benefits-oriented costs mo nology enhanced learning. Australian Learning & Teaching Council (2012), http://www.olt.gov.au/system//resources/_1242__Report .. (accessed April 29, 2014) (retrieved)
46. Russell, C.: Naming and measuring the elephants: Sustainable change for bl ing. In: Proceedings Ascilite Wellington 2012, pp. 809–813 (2012)
47. Rolfe, V.E., Alcocer, M., Bentley, E., Milne, D., Meyer-Sahling, J.: Acaden tudes towards electronic learning in Arts and Sciences. European Journal Learning (EURODL) (2008), http://www.eurodl.org/?p=archiv 2008&halfyear=1&article=313 (accessed April 29, 2014) (retrieved)
48. European Association of Distance Teaching Universities, OpenupEd. (2014), http://www.openuped.eu/ (assessed May 30, 2014) (retrieved)
49. Chen, C.C., Jones, K.T.: Blended learning vs. traditional classroom settings: A fectiveness and student perceptions in an MBA accounting course. Journal Online 4(1), 1–15 (2007)
50. Akkoyunlu, B., Soylu, M.Y.: A study of student's perceptions in a blen environment based on different learning styles. Educational Technology & S 183–193 (2008)
51. Kolb, D.A.: Experiential Learning: Experience as the Source of Learning a ment. Prentice Hall, Upper Saddle River (1984)
52. Tempelaar, D.T., Rienties, B., Giesbers, B.: Who profits most from blend Industry and Higher Education 23(4), 285–293 (2009)
53. Banerjee, G.: Blended environments: Learning effectiveness and student sati small college in transition. Journal of Asynchronous Learning Networks (2011)
54. Benson, V., Anderson, D., Ooms, A.: Educators' perceptions, attitudes ar Blended learning in business and management education. Research in Learnin gy 19(2), 143–154 (2011)
55. Zhu, C., Valcke, M., Schellens, T.: A cross-cultural study of teacher perspectiv er roles and adoption of online collaborative learning in higher education. Eu nal of Teacher Education 33(2), 147–165 (2010)
56. Salmon, G., Jones, S., Armellini, A.: Building institutional capability in e-lear ALT-J Research in Learning Technology 16(2), 15–95 (2008)

Social Media Education: Barriers and Critical Issues

Melani Au, Jeanne Lam, and Radar Chan

Centre for Cyber Learning, HKU SPACE
The University of Hong Kong, Hong Kong SAR, China
melani.au@hkuspace.hku.hk

Abstract. As one of the highest smartphone penetration regions in the globe, Hong Kong has more than 12 million mobile users are capable to access mobile data services. People spend time on their mobile devices for information, entertainment as well as communication. With the advancement of information, communication and technology (ICT) especially in mobile technology, various online social media tools, e.g. Facebook, WhatsApp, rapidly developed in the past decade. The use of these tools is so overwhelming which transformed people's way of communication. Discussions on using social media in education are getting keen. However, regardless of the popularity of social media in Hong Kong, the effectiveness of using existing social media tools to facilitate teaching and learning is not noticeable. This paper illustrates the barriers behind this phenomenon in Hong Kong. Factors from technological perspective, institutional perspective and users' perspective are critically discussed. It is believed that with optimal monitoring, motivation and planning, social media can be beneficial to both institutions, teachers and students in the long run.

Keywords: social media, social network, social media learning, mobile technology.

1 Introduction

In the past decades, the continuous development of information, communication and technology (ICT) brought tremendous changes to human's way of living. With a few clicks on the computers, billion-pieces of information are transmitted through the World Wide Web. People can manage their livings from shopping grocery online, reserving medical appointment to managing bank accounts. As mobile technology is getting mature, use of smartphone becomes very popular. Once the mobile device is connected to mobile data services, people can access to numerous information through mobile apps with only several touches on the screen. The introduction of various social media tools, e.g. Facebook, WhatsApp and WeChat, significantly evolves people's way of communication. Regardless of geographical boundaries and timezone, people can share, comment and acquire information anywhere and anytime. The flow of electronic information has never been that rapid before. As one of the highest smartphone penetration regions with more than 12.1 million mobile data service users [1], accessing to social media tools becomes an integral part of Hong Kong users. Such advancement of ICT and mobile technology also brought impacts on education. Though face-to-face classroom teaching is still popular, integration of online

K.C. Li et al. (Eds.): ICTE 2014, CCIS 494, pp. 199–205, 2015.

learning components enhances the flexibility and effectiveness of learning ing [2]. With the high responsiveness and popularity of social media tools of adopting social media in education becomes keen. Higher education (HEI) in Hong Kong are aware of the strong influence of social media, y concerned of the originality of materials shared and adopted from thes Although the costs of using existing social media tools are low, technologi security and privacy issues may arise. Moreover, the strong emphasis c results in Hong Kong education system cultivates an "examination-orien across the industry. As long as the tools are not related to examinations, b and students are not motivated to participate. Hence, in spite of the wide u media in Hong Kong, its adoption to Hong Kong education is challengin mentative. This paper illustrates the issues that barrier the use of social me Hong Kong education. Factors from technological perspective, institution tive and users' perspective are critically discussed. Suggestions for optim of social media tools are made at the end.

2 Literature Review

Over the past decades, when people refer to the term "social media", they ly think of various social media tools, such as Facebook, WhatsApp, Li MySpace, etc. However, "Social media" is more than just communicatio defined by Ahlqvist et al. [4], social media is built on three elements: co munities and Web 2.0 which users can make use of web technologies to share different forms of contents in social nature. Kietzmann et al. later r cial media employs mobile and web-based technologies to create highly platforms via which individuals and communities share, co-create, discuss fy user-generated content" [5]. With the emphasis on "interaction", "cr "technology", social media evolves the traditional way of people's com Everyone is more willing to share and interact in virtual communities whic graphical boundaries and timezone. Such interactions and collaborations valued in learning and teaching. With the integration of ICT in educatio mid-1990s, its benefits are recognizable in terms of flexibility, dynamic lea ronment and student-centred learning [6]. A European study conducted b et al. stated adoption of social media in European education makes stu more personalized and collaborative [7]. It offers specific opportunities enhancement of innovation and creativity, improving the quality of learnin and fostering learner mobility. However, researchers argued that lack of and improper use of social media brought risks of privacy invasion and rassment [8]. The freedom and openness provided by such social media lead to excessive sharing of information, yet, it is hard to prove if all the i shared is correct.

According to the latest figure from the OGCIO [1], Hong Kong's bro

by a group of Hong Kong researchers discussed that online social networks influenced students' social-academic integration and learning outcomes. Findings indicated that online social networking had a more direct impact on student social learning, while the impact on academic learning outcomes was more steady [9]. Some experimental studies were also performed to provide teachers and students with a designated e-Writing blog for learning and teaching English languages [10]. Though responses from students were somehow positive, results shown that they tended to pay more attentions on personalizing their blogs instead of collaborating with peers for learning purposes. Besides, the sample size was too small to generalize the phenomenon over the region.

3 Barriers and Issues for Hong Kong Education Industry

Hong Kong's ICT infrastructure is one of the best among the world with a high household broadband penetration, it is easy for learners to get access to numerous online resources for learning purposes. The use of ICT in learning and teaching has been widely discussed which both teachers and students recognized its effectiveness in different aspects. Yet, as the trend moves toward learning through collaborations and interactions with Web 2.0 technology, the effectiveness seems gradual. The popularity of social media tools in Hong Kong has no doubt encouraged peer communications and exchange of information, nevertheless, students did not perceive a connection between online social activities and classroom learning [11]. While education institutions in Hong Kong are making efforts to engage social media in learning and teaching, a few factors are needed to be considered before implementation.

3.1 Technological Difficulties

Large Variations of Mobile Devices. The advancement of mobile technology and mobile data services make online access more flexible and efficient. Different social media tools can be accessed solely via mobile devices (e.g. WhatsApp or LINE) or in both desktop and mobile format (e.g. Facebook, Youtube) which fosters rapid communication and collaboration between learners. Though the number of mobile device users is increasing, the configurations, from hardware (e.g. differences in screen sizes) to software (e.g. operation systems), of different mobile devices vary significantly. Compared to desktop version, mobile apps of social media tools are simplified which may not fit into the configurations of all devices. Some of the functions may be disabled and frequent update of software is required. When social media is used as learning and teaching channel, teachers have to ensure the features of the tool are functional so that every student is able to use. Yet, it is difficult and time-consuming to standardize them.

Risk of Security and Privacy Issues. Like all other information technology tools, security and privacy are always the concerns when using social media for learning. When current social media tools are designed for easy communication and sharing of multimedia contents, such "convenience" may put security and privacy at risk. Nowadays,

advanced technology is able to keep tracking of people's online activities. O
Clarke-Pearson mentioned that once Internet users access to the Web, the
records called the "digital footprints", from the websites we visited to the la
we pressed on the Internet, all these actions leave evidence for webmasters
our online habits [8]. Social media developers might make use of those priv
tion for their own benefits without users' consents. As we can see from our
network sites, the developers are able to access for our peers' contact list whi
of spam invitations of online games and promotions were sent to us per r
without the senders' notice.

3.2 Rapid Changing Environment

Loss of Control and Monitoring. Though education institutions encoura
rations among students and teachers to facilitate positive learning outcome
emphasize on control and monitoring on quality of learning and teaching.
many kinds of external open social media sources available in current s
hard for institutions to monitor each tool to ensure learners are using the
Greenhow and Robelia stated that institutions need to have adequate
monitor various the activities took place on social media at the same time,
messaging, wall posts, comments, etc. [11]. Institutions face a dilemma be
"openness to communications" and "control over content posted in social
institutions are afraid of these negativities, why bother to use them? [12
conducted by Seaman and Tinti-Kane on faculty indicated that over 70%
member concerns the lack of integrity of student submissions [13]. Since
information is too easy, the originality of work piece is difficult to be ider
can also explain why faculty is not confident to use social media tools. In
monitoring issue, some of the HEIs in Hong Kong developed social med
their internal use, e.g. learning through blogging in an English course [1
time and money invested in developing the tool are long and huge, comp
benefits bring to the institutions, such massive investment makes instituti
to proceed for their own development.

Changes in Educational Approach. When embedding social media in le
teaching, it requires institutions to deploy new pedagogical approach. The
to re-evaluate their position as a knowledge provider in the community
new strategies, methodologies and tools. Moreover, in order to deliver
learning experiences, training and support have to be provided to teachers,
well as administrative staff [7]. Education institutions need to put huge
terms of money and manpower, to educate users for the appropriate use of
dia, especially issues of intellectual property and rules of conduct. Such ch
impacts to users in all levels which resistance to changes may arise.

3.3 Individual Concerns

ICT usage may be limited to disseminating teaching materials through online learning platforms. Even if social media is used, teachers usually select some multimedia contents, such as videos from Youtube and Podcasts, to be shown during lecture [3]. All teaching approaches are "one-way information transmission" but not really reflecting the value of using social media. When embedding social media into teaching process, the role of teachers no long act as an instructor but a facilitator and a mentor, to guide and encourage students' discussions. As abovementioned, without certain trainings and supports given by the institutions, teachers may not be able to adapt to this new transition [7]. Yan et al. also mentioned that teachers get used to the traditional way of teaching and would not be easy to change [14]. Besides, when the teaching schedule in Hong Kong education system is usually very tight, especially for primary and secondary schools which must follow the syllabus assigned by Education Bureau, teacher would treat "social media teaching" as extra tasks that increase their workload, they would be unwilling to do unless sufficient incentives are given.

Students' Perspective. Teenage students are sensitive to technology changes. Learning to use new IT tools is an easy task for them. However, in students' perceptions, there is a lack of linkage between using social media to their academic learning. Researchers found that students have high activity level in social media for social purpose but are less motivated when it is connected to learning. Some students reflected that social media should not be used as a tool for academic work [15]. Wong also discussed that "the assessment system for Asian higher education institutions is generally examination based while the style of teaching and learning is aimed at helping students to pass the examination" [16]. As Hong Kong students were brought up by a strictly designed education system which public examinations have significant influences on their futures. This "examination-oriented" concept is strongly implanted to Hong Kong students' minds. Thus, Hong Kong students will not have any interest to use social media in their study if it does not benefit to students in their academic assessment.

4 Conclusions

Regardless of the overwhelming use of social media in social context in Hong Kong, integration of social media in learning and teaching encounters a number of barriers and issues. Due to the rigidity of systems for primary and secondary education, there is little room for primary and secondary schools for adopting such tools in education. Relatively, the flexibility is larger for higher education, however, concerns on security and control, changes involved in institutional educational approach discourage such use. Besides, teachers' eagerness on facilitating communication and students' perception of lack of connect between social media and academic learning also raise the hurdle.

In view of the potential benefits which social media can bring to learning and teaching, institutions are suggested to take a step-by-step methodology for integration of these tools. First, use of social media should be positioned as a supplementary tool to propose gradual change in pedagogical approach. Institutions should have a guideline clearly stated the extent of social media usage and institutional monitoring. Over-control

on the use of social media is definitely not recommended as this would
meaning of its use. Social media can be used as a medium for creating qu
answer (Q&A) communities for course content. Both teachers and students
bute to the Q&A which everyone can see all the contents. This also help
teachers' burden for answering the same questions during class and reduce
tance for the change. Intrinsic incentive such as awards or prizes can be g
most contributed teachers to motivate them. Second, once teachers are more
social media learning, they can act as facilitators to encourage students
communicating course content via these tools. A study indicated that when
more involved and self-disclosed in social media, students would be more m
social media learning [17]. However, institutions and teachers have to set
regulations to avoid abuse usage and stated those regulations explicitly to
Again, intrinsic incentive would be a good way for encouraging students to
Furthermore, if students' participations in social media will be taken into
academic outcomes, the effectiveness will be definitely enhanced. This kind
value added to the use these tools stimulate users' interests and motivations
ly, when acceptance of all teachers and students are high, institutions can r
pedagogical approach to embed the use of social media to a larger extent.
focusing on formal academic learning, institutions should be aware of the po
ence from informal learning which can complement, emphasize creativity
tion [11]. There is no doubt that academic knowledge is important, yet, the in
skills that students acquired for searching, sharing and commenting on releva
tion are valuable. Such skills would be certainly beneficial to students in thei

In the inevitably change of ICT and emphasis on lifelong learning in H
institutions, teachers and students should make the most from the use of
tools in learning and teaching, so that they can maximize the benefits and e
competencies in this ever-changing society.

Reference

1. Office of the Government Chief Information Officer (OGCIO): Hong Kong- A cation as an ICT hub. Hong Kong, China: HKSAR Government (2014)
2. Wagner, D., Day, B., James, T., Kozma, R., Miller, J., Unwin, T.: Monitoring tion of ICT in education projects- A handbook for developing countries. The Washington, DC (2005), http://www.sca2006.tic-educa.org/a modulo_2/sesion_7/Monitoring%20and%20Evaluation%20of% 20in%20Education%20Projects.pdf#page=31
3. Moran, M., Seaman, J., Tinti-Kane, H.: Teaching, learning, and sharing: H higher education faculty use social media. Pearson, Boston (2011), http://files.eric.ed.gov/fulltext/ED535130.pdf (retrieved
4. Ahlqvist, T., Bäck, A., Halonen, M., Heinonen, S.: Social media roadmaps: e futures triggered by social media. VTT Research Notes, 2454 (2008), http://www.vtt.fi/inf/pdf/tiedotteet/2008/T2454.pdf (r

6. Oliver, R.: The role of ICT in higher education for the 21st century: ICT as a change agent for education. In: the Proceedings of the Higher Education for the 21st Century Conference (2002), http://bhs-ict.pbworks.com/f/role%20of%20ict.pdf (retrieved)
7. Redecker, C., Ala-Mutka, K., Punie, Y.: Learning 2.0- The impact of social media on learning in Europe. European Commission, Luxembourg (2010), http://www.ict-21.ch/com-ict/IMG/pdf/learning-2.0-EU-17pages-JRC56958.pdf (retrieved)
8. O'Keeffe, G., Clarke-Pearson, K.: Clinical report the impact of social media on chil-dren, adolescents, and families. Pediatrics 127(4), 800–804 (2011)
9. Tian, S., Yu, A., Vogel, D., Kwok, R.: The impact on online social networking on learning: a social integration perspective. International Journal of Networking and Virtual Organisations 8(3/4), 264–280 (2011)
10. Ying, K.-K., Cheung, M., Leung, K., Kwan, R., Lee, R., Wong, K.: Learning through Blogging: Understanding Teacher and Student Perceptions towards English Writing Blogs. In: Lam, J., Li, K.C., Cheung, S.K.S., Wang, F.L. (eds.) ICT 2013. CCIS, vol. 407, pp. 200–211. Springer, Heidelberg (2013)
11. Greenhow, C., Robelia, B.: Informal learning and identity formation in online social networks. Learning Media and Technology 34(2), 119–140 (2009)
12. Reuben, R.: The use of social media in higher education for marketing and communications: a guide for professional in higher education. In: Seminario Académico Tendencias En La Formacion online documento (2008), http://www.ciff.net/ seminarioformancionnonline/DocumentoSeminarioII.pdf (retrieved)
13. Seaman, J., Tinti-Kane, H.: Social media for teaching and learning. Pearson, Boston (2013)
14. Yan, K., Au, M., Chan, R., Tsang, C.: Open Education: Challenges in Hong Kong. In: Lam, J., Li, K.C., Cheung, S.K.S., Wang, F.L. (eds.) ICT 2013. CCIS, vol. 407, pp. 212–226. Springer, Heidelberg (2013)
15. Madge, C., Meek, J., Wellens, J., Hooley, T.: Facebook, social integration and informal learning at university: It is more for socialising and talking to friends about work than for actually doing work. Learning Media and Technology. Routledge, London (2009)
16. Wong, J.: Are the learning styles of Asian international students culturally or contextually based?International Education Journal 4(4) (2004)
17. Mazer, J., Murphy, R., Simonds, C.: I'll see you on "Facebook": The effects of computer-mediated teacher self-disclosure on student motivation, affective learning, and classroom climate. Communication Education 56(1), 1–17 (2007)
18. Silius, K., Miilumaki, T., Huhtamaki, J., Tebest, T., Merilainen, J., Pohjolainen, S.: Students' motivations for social media enhanced studying and learning. Knowledge Management & E-Learning: An International Journal 2(1) (2010), http://www.kmel-journal.org/ojs/index.php/online-publication/article/viewFile/ 55/39 (retrieved)

Computer Literacy and Use of Open Educatio
Resources: A Study of University Students in Hon

Kam Cheong Li and Billy Tak-Ming Wong

University Research Centre, The Open University of Hong Kong.
Good Shepherd Street, Ho Man Tin, Kowloon, Hong Kong SAR, Chin
{kcli,tamiwong}@ouhk.edu.hk

Abstract. This paper reports a preliminary study on the relationship bet computer literacy and use of open educational resources (OER) of unive students in Hong Kong. It reviews the technology infrastructure and Go ment support for enhancement of students' computer literacy, and develop of resources in the city, showing that Hong Kong has laid a foundation for to grow and bloom. However, by reporting the results of a survey cond with university students, it highlights that most students, despite their computer literacy, have a low level of awareness and limited experien OER, and have been exposed to only a few popular types of resources. Th servations call for further institutional and instructional support to enhance dents' awareness of available resources and understanding of their proper u

Keywords: open educational resources, computer literacy, student awarene

1 Introduction

The open educational resources (OER) movement in the past decade has cant implications for teaching and learning. An observable trend, for exar vast quantity of available OER on the Web which allow users to freely re revise, remix and redistribute resources according to the openness of their It is suggested that such engagement of OER enhances teaching and lear tiveness in terms of getting teachers and learners involved in the use and c of resources [2][3][4].

Despite the increasing quantity of OER and benefits of using OER prop existing studies reveal that the use of OER is not as common as expected regions (e.g. [5][6]). Various barriers to the adoption of OER in teachin cerns about the usefulness of resources have been discovered in these s example, lack of network infrastructure has been found to be a commor developing regions (e.g. [7][8]).

Computer literacy has been conceived as another critical factor for wide OER [9][10][11][12]. Its significance is to effectively search and use suitab

skills such as computers with Internet connection and a certain level of computer literacy, which are however not available to many regions.

Hong Kong, on the other hand, is one of the regions with well-established infrastructure on information and communication technology (ICT) and substantial government support for ICT in education. The computer literacy of students in Hong Kong is comparable to European students [14]. However, the use of OER remains unpopular in the tertiary education sector. A survey conducted in 2011 on the use of OER among a cross-section sample of university teachers [15][16][17][18] shows that less than half (43.6%) of them use the resources in class and only 21.1% have ever produced OER as teaching or learning resource.

This paper reports the results of a recent survey as a preliminary study on the relationship between computer literacy of students of the Open University of Hong Kong (OUHK) and their use of OER. It first provides a brief review of the technology infrastructure and government support for enhancing students' technological readiness, and development of OER for their learning. It then describes the study design, following which the survey results are presented and some notable findings are discussed.

2 Technology Infrastructure and Government Support for Enhancement of Students' Computer Literacy

Hong Kong is a highly developed city in terms of technology infrastructure. According to government data [19][20], there were as many as 203 internet service providers and 28,256 public Wi-Fi access points by May 2014. Its household broadband penetration rate has reached 83.2% and mobile penetration rate 236.8% (as at March 2014), both are among the highest in the world. There are 73.2% of mobile users capable of gaining access to data network (2.5G/3G/4G), while enjoying the lowest level of telecommunication charges in the world. In addition, a recent report by Akamai Technologies shows that Hong Kong has attained the fastest average peak internet connection speed at 66 Mbps among 185 regions in the world, nearly three times higher than the global average of 21.2 Mbps [21].

The Government has been providing substantial support for ICT in education. As reviewed by the Education Bureau [14], all schools had been supported to set up their ICT infrastructure on computer facilities and broadband internet connection. There was high extent of ICT use, including the emerging Web 2.0 technology such as Blog, Wiki and Podcast, in different subjects. Needy students are helped to apply for recycled computers from non-government organizations or ICT industries. The Government has also launched the Internet Learning Support Programme to help these students to acquire affordable computers, Internet access services and essential internet skills [22].

With the substantial government support, students' awareness and competency in use of ICT have shown a significant growth over the years. Above 90% of secondary students have computer and internet access at home, a proportion comparable to other leading countries. Their competency in information search is comparable to European students, and in computer operation skills they even exceed that of European students [14].

3 Development of OER in Hong Kong

Different parties in Hong Kong have been actively involved in the devel provision of various kinds of OER. Examples of the major resources inclu the portals developed by the Education Bureau (e.g. Resource Banks,[1] Inte tivities DIY[2] and the Resources Depository in the Hong Kong Educatior site[3]), and by education institutions (e.g. language learning resources[4] p universities in Hong Kong). In recent years, open courseware is being p tertiary institutions such as OUHK and the University of Hong Kong. Nota has been engaged in an open textbook project and has set up a platform fo resources [18][23][24][25]. Massive open online courses (MOOC) are als fered by several local universities, e.g. the Hong Kong University of S Technology and the Chinese University of Hong Kong, though much of content are not open for reuse or revision, not to mention remix or redistribu

As reviewed by Li et al. [16][17], most of these educational resources, ing freely accessible online, do not entirely fulfill the required openne Their copyright licenses mostly do not allow revision of content, remixing bution. Many do not even allow users to retain a backup copy. Students n search for other sources of OER on Internet to suit their learning needs.

It is thus reasonable to review these highly techno-ready students in I for the search and use of OER for learning purpose.

4 Study Design

This study revolves around the use of OER by OUHK students. It aims to (their computer literacy; (2) figure out their familiarity and experience with (3) identify the relationship, if any, between their computer literacy and use

The study adopts the unified theory of acceptance and use of technology model [26] (Fig. 1) as theoretical framework to examine students' use of model has been widely adopted as theoretical ground in studies on the ac OER (e.g. [7][27][28]). It combines eight dominant theories or models of acceptance, including theory of reasoned action (TRA), technology accept (TAM), motivation model (MM), theory of planned behaviour (TPB), a

1 http://www.edb.gov.hk/en/curriculum-development/resourc support/about-resource-support/resource-banks-of-good-educational-practices.html

2 http://diy.fwg.hk/

3 http://resources.hkedcity.net/

4 Some of these resources include *English for Professional Communication* of the En University of Hong Kong (http://www4.caes.hku.hk/epc/), *Learning* the Independent Learning Centre, Chinese University of Hong Kong (https://

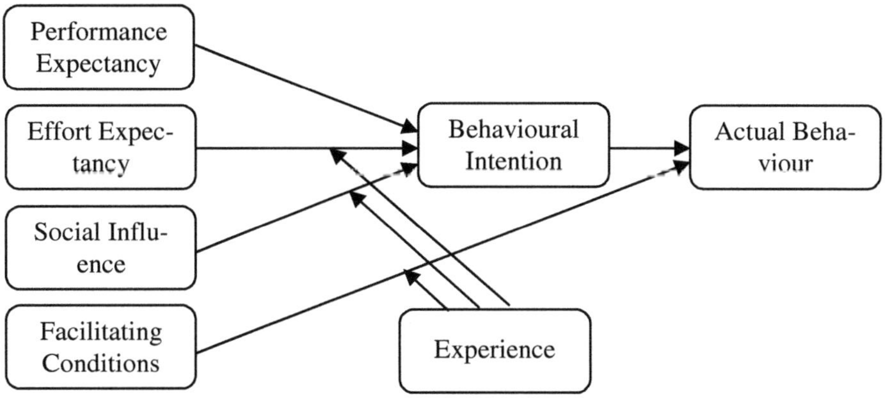

Fig. 1. Adapted UTAUT model for this study

theory of TPB and TAM (C-TPB-TAM), model of PC utilization (MPCU), innovation diffusion theory (IDT), and social cognitive theory (SCT), and is proven to have a better robustness and validity in predicting the acceptance of new technologies than any of its eight component models [26].

According to the UTAUT model, the use of OER (actual behaviour) is determined by facilitating conditions and behavioural intention. Facilitating conditions refer to the degree to which an individual believes that organizational support or technical infrastructure exists for the use of OER. Behavioural intention is determined by three factors, i.e., performance expectancy, effort expectancy and social influence. Performance expectancy refers to the degree to which an individual believes that using OER will help him or her obtain gains in some sort of performance in learning. Effort expectancy represents the degree of ease associated with locating, adapting, and using OER. Social influence is the degree to which an individual perceives as important and others believe he or she should use OER. The strength of effect for three constructs, i.e., effort expectancy, social influence and facilitating conditions, are moderated by an experience variable which refers to users' computer literacy in this study.

The questionnaire is adopted from [26] which is developed on the UTAUT model. Modification is made by rewording items to suit the context of the study, and adding items to cover students' familiarity and knowledge of ICT, and their awareness of OER.

5 Results and Discussion

The questionnaire was administered to 42 OUHK full-time undergraduate students from a broad range of disciplines. Table 1 shows the results of students' computer literacy on a number of common computer skills. Most students indicated that they have excellent or good familiarity with social media such as Facebook and Whatsapp. This is followed by email and search engine, which are both Internet-related computer skills. Students are relatively less familiar with PC operation, and use of word processing, presentation and spreadsheet programs, but still a large proportion of them

Table 1. Students' familiarity of computer skills (percentage)

	Excellent	Good	Average	Fair
PC operation	7.1	35.7	35.7	14.3
Web search	16.7	38.1	28.6	16.7
Email	16.7	47.6	21.4	11.9
Word processing	14.3	38.1	26.2	21.4
Spreadsheet	11.9	28.6	40.5	11.9
Presentation	14.3	31.0	40.5	14.3
Social media	38.1	40.5	9.5	9.5

(40–50%) rated themselves as good or excellent on each item. These resu strate students' high computer literacy especially for skills related to the In

However, students showed a limited degree of awareness of OER, wher them indicated that they had no idea about OER, 26.2% know of it, and 4. how to use it. Only three students (7.1%) stated that they knew how to re and redistribute OER. The limited awareness is also reflected in their frequ of OER. As shown in Table 2, among common types of OER, most stu used Wikipedia (40.5%) more frequently (above 15 times in past three majority of them never used the others, i.e., Wikibook (42.9%), You (42.9%), free courseware (57.1%) and MOOC (76.2%). Students had knowledge of open license at all. These results revealed a sharp contra students' high computer literacy and low usage of OER, which suggests may be no direct relationship between the two.

Table 2. Students' frequency of use of OER in the past three months (percer

	16+	11 – 15	6 – 10	1 – 5
Wikipedia	40.5	9.5	26.2	19.0
Wikibook	4.8	0	23.8	28.6
YouTube EDU	7.1	4.8	11.9	33.3
Online dictionary	21.4	9.5	31.0	26.2
Free Courseware of OUHK	2.4	4.8	11.9	23.8
Massive Open Online Course (MOOC)	2.4	4.8	2.4	14.3

Table 3 presents the values of Pearson correlation among the constructs model. For the two constructs affecting actual behaviour, only facilitating shows a significant correlation (0.391). For the three constructs affecting b intention, both performance expectancy and effort expectancy show a sign relation, i.e., 0.592 and 0.433 respectively. Social influence does not app had any effect on students' intention to use OER. For the three constructs by experience, only facilitating conditions shows a significant correlation (experience.

The findings of this study echo and support the observation that studer

Table 3. Correlation among UTAUT model constructs

	Performance expectancy	Effort expectancy	Social influence	Facilitating conditions	Behavioural intention
Behavioural intention	.592*	.433*	.058		
Experience		.259	-.013	.425*	
Actual behaviour				.391*	.028

*. Correlation is significant at the 0.05 level (2-tailed)

OER is also observed in [29], who finds that confidence in Internet skills does not have a substantial impact on confidence in finding and using OER.

This finding presents another perspective different from some other studies which focus on significance of basic level of computer literacy to use of OER. For example, Richter and McPherson state that "for learners to make effective use of OER, they need to learn basic IT skills" [30] (p. 207), and Birzina identifies computer literacy as one of the key skills necessary for use of OER [31]. Perspectives of different studies may as a whole suggest a unidirectional relationship between computer literacy and use of OER—effective use of OER requires a certain level of computer literacy, but high computer literacy itself does not necessarily lead to use of OER.

The correlation results among UTAUT model constructs show that performance expectancy and effort expectancy exert significant influence on students' intention to use OER. This is consistent with the findings of [28]. Effort expectancy is also found to be a significant factor in [7]. This suggests some general considerations for design and development of OER, that the resources should be able to improve students' learning performance and be easy to use.

Facilitating conditions is a factor showing statistically significant correlation with use of OER in this study, but not in the above two which focus on use of OER in Africa. This reveals the positive impact of well-established technology infrastructure in Hong Kong, a feature which facilitates students to efficiently search and access OER and is not yet available in less-developed regions such as Africa.

Students' poor familiarity and experience with OER highlight their low awareness of OER, which appears to be a major barrier for the use. Without adequate familiarity of available resources, students may not easily locate suitable OER for their learning needs.

Quite a number of students raised the concern about credibility of OER, mostly because of the open nature of resources which allows free modification by the public. They were also concerned about whether OER can be used or cited in assignments, a consistent finding with related studies [3][32] that open online sources such as Wikipedia are deemed to be less academically reliable than books or journals. Students are thus reluctant to cite these sources in their coursework.

Students also commented on the lack of instructional and institutional support for OER, that such resources are never suggested nor used by instructors in their teaching. This is a possible reason that social influence does not have any correlation with behavioural intention in UTAUT model in this study. Students tended to disagree with the items of social influence "*The lecturers and other staff in OUHK are helpful in the use of OER for my learning*" and "*In general, OUHK supports the use of OER in my learning*" in the questionnaire.

As perceived from the suggestions of the students, further promotion a
should be high priority to enhance their understanding of OER, especia
copyright issue and credibility of resources. Recommendations are made th
versity can involve in the development of OER, or help select high quality
and host them for student access so as to resolve the credibility issue.

6 Conclusion

This study reveals that comptuer literacy is not a driving factor for use
Hong Kong. The technology infrastructure and Government support
education in Hong Kong, despite substantially enhancing students' compu
has not demonstrated much impact on students' use of OER. Most stude
unaware of the resources available, not to mention the search and use
resources for their learning purpose.

The findings suggest that the lack of institutional and instructional supp
to be the main reason for students' limited use of OER. Compared with
findings a couple of years ago on the use of OER in Hong Kong tertiary
sector [16][17], the situation nowadays does not show an observable impr
terms of the support from instutitions and teachers to facilitate students
from OER. It is high time for a review on the extent to which efforts and i
on development and promotion of OER have taken effect, and to identify a
suitable support for students towards the goal of improving their engageme
resources.

References

1. Wiley, D., Green, C.: Why openness in education? In: Oblinger, D.G. (ed.)
gers: Education and Information Technologies, pp. 81–89. Educause (2012)
2. Afnan-Manns, S., Medrano, R., Mickelsen, K.F.: OneClick Digital and t
project: OER as content, OER as pedagogy. EDUCAUSE Review On
http://www.educause.edu/ero/article/oneclick-digital-
medrano-project-oer-content-oer-pedagogy (retrieved May 5,
3. White, D., Manton, M.: Open Educational Resources: The value of reuse in h
tion. JISC funded OER Impact Study, University of Oxford (2011),
http://www.jisc.ac.uk/media/documents/programmes/elea
er/OERTheValueOfReuseInHigherEducation.pdf (retrieved)
4. Wild, J.: OER Engagement Study: Promoting OER reuse among academics.
port from the SCORE funded project (2012), http://www.open.ac.u
files/score/file/Joanna%20Wild%20SCORE%20Fellowship%2
20Report%20-%20web%20version.pdf (retrieved)
5. Badarch, D., Knyazeva, S., Lane, A.: Introducing the opportunities and c
OER: The case of the Commonwealth of Independent States and the Balti
Open Educational Resources and Change in Higher Education: Reflections fr

6. Harishankar, V.B.: Establishing OER practice in India: The University of Madras. In: Dhanarajan, G., Porter, D. (eds.) Open Education Resources: An Asian Perspective, pp. 207–220. COL and OER Asia, Vancouver (2013)
7. Mtebe, J.S., Raisamo, R.: Challenges and instructors' intention to adopt and use open educational resources in higher education in Tanzania. The International Review of Research in Open and Distance Learning, 15(1) (2014), http://www.irrodl.org/index.php/irrodl/article/view/1687/2771 (retrieved)
8. Wang, C., Zhao, G.: Open Educational Resources in the People's Republic of China: Achievements, Challenges and Prospects for Development. UNESCO institute for information Technologies in Education, Russia (2011)
9. Knyazeva, S.: IITE OER project: New dimensions. In: Proceedings of the International Conference "ICT in Teacher Education: Policy, Open Educational Resources and Partnership", St. Petersburg, Russia, pp. 137–141 (2010)
10. Mortera-Gutierrez, F.J., Burgos-Aguilar, J.V.: Innovative applications using new technology: The case of the knowledge hub search engine and open educational resources building communities of practice. In: Education and Research Technology (ERT) Forum, California, USA (2010)
11. Sharehu, A.L.: A survey of the level of digital literacy and open educational resources (OER) awareness among teacher educators in Nigeria. In: Proceedings of the 5th Conference on e-Learning Excellence in the Middle East, Dubai, United Arab Emirates, pp. 22–32 (2012)
12. Umar, A., Kodhandaraman, B., Kanwar, A.: Can open educational resources thrive in closed educational systems? Some reflections on OER in developing countries. In: McGreal, R., Kinuthia, W., Marshall, S. (eds.) Open Educational Resources: Innovation, Research and Practice, pp. 193–206. Commonwealth of Learning and Athabasca University (2013)
13. Santos, A.I.: The Discourses of OERs: how flat is this world? Journal of Interactive Media in Education. Special Issue: Researching open content in education, 1–10 (2008)
14. Education Bureau.: Report on the Review Surveys of the Third Strategy on Information Technology in Education (2012), http://www.edb.gov.hk/attachment/en/edu-system/primary-secondary/applicable-to-primary-secondary/it-in-edu/rs2_final%20report_public_eng_clean%2021012013.pdf (retrieved May 5, 2014)
15. Li, K.C., Yuen, K.S.: Development of open educational resources in Hong Kong: A status analysis. In: Proceedings of the Regional Symposium on Open Educational Resources: An Asian Perspective on Policy and Practices, Penang, Malaysia (2012)
16. Li, K.C., Yuen, K.S., Cheung, S.K.S.: Open Educational Resources in Hong Kong. In: Lam, J., Li, K.C., Cheung, S.K.S., Wang, F.L. (eds.) ICT 2013. CCIS, vol. 407, pp. 16–25. Springer, Heidelberg (2013)
17. Li, K.C., Yuen, K.S., Cheung, S.K.S.: Open educational resources in Hong Kong: Status and future challenges. In: Proceedings of 2013 International Conference on ICT in Teaching and Learning. HKU SPACE, Hong Kong (2013)
18. Yuen, K.S., Wong, A.J.W.: Open educational resources in Hong Kong. In: Dhanarajan, G., Porter, D. (eds.) Open Education Resources: An Asian Perspective, pp. 41–51. COL and OER Asia, Vancouver (2013)
19. Office of the Communication Authority.: Key Communications Statistics (2014), http://www.ofca.gov.hk/mobile/en/media_focus/data_statistics/key_stat/index.html (retrieved June 1, 2014)

20. Office of the Government Chief Information Officer.: Hong Kong – A Premier an ICT Hub (2014), http://www.ogcio.gov.hk/en/facts/d Sheet-HK_as_ICT_Hub-EN.pdf (retrieved June 1, 2014)
21. Akamai Technologies.: The State of the Internet: 1st Quarter, 2014 Report (201
22. GovHK.: Internet Learning Support Programme (2012), http://www.gc theme/ilearnathome/news/ (retrieved June 2, 2014)
23. Li, Y.: Constructing and Sharing Open Educational Resources: Policy and C Lam, J., Li, K.C., Cheung, S.K.S., Wang, F.L. (eds.) ICT 2013. CCIS, vol. 407 Springer, Heidelberg (2013)
24. Tsang, E.Y.M., Yuen, K.S., Li, K.C., Cheung, S.K.S.: Designing open textboo tive teaching and learning. In: Lam, J., Li, K.C., Cheung, S.K.S., Wang, F.L 2013. CCIS, vol. 407, pp. 43–55. Springer, Heidelberg (2013)
25. Yuen, K.S., Li, K.C.: An open textbook system to tackle Hong Kong's textboc In: Proceedings of the Regional Symposium on Open Educational Resource Perspective on Policy and Practices. Wawasan Open University, Penang (2012
26. Venkatesh, V., Morris, M.G., Hall, M., Davis, G.B., Davis, F.D., Walton, acceptance of information technology: Toward a unified view. MIS Qua 425–478 (2003)
27. Dulle, F.W., Minishi-Majanja, M.K.: The suitability of the Unified Theory of and Use of Technology (UTAUT) model in open access adoption studies. Development 27(1), 32–45 (2011)
28. Percy, T., Van Belle, J.-P.: Exploring the Barriers and Enablers to the U Educational Resources by University Academics in Africa. In: Hammouda, I., Mikkonen, T., Scacchi, W. (eds.) Open Source Systems: Long-Term Sustain AICT, vol. 378, pp. 112–128. Springer, Heidelberg (2012)
29. Kelly, H.: A path analysis of educator perceptions of open educational resourc technology acceptance model. The International Review of Research in Open a Learning 15(2) (2014), http://www.irrodl.org/index.php/irrod article/view/1715/2836 (retrieved)
30. Richter, T., McPherson, M.: Open educational resources: Education for the tance Education 33(2), 201–219 (2012)
31. Birzina, R.: Open educational resources (OER) as a means for students' learning. In: ECER 2014: The Past, the Present and Future of Educational Europe, Porto, Portugal (2014)
32. Śliwowski, K.: Myths and obstacles Open Educational Resources are fac http://oerpolicy.eu/myths-and-obstacles-open-educatic resources-are-facing/ (retrieved May 23, 2014)

A Thematic Analysis of the Blended Learning Experiences of Undergraduate Students in Hong Kong

Jeanne Lam

School of Professional And Continuing Edcuation,
The University of Hong Kong, Pokfulam Road, Hong Kong SAR, China
jeanne.lam@hkuspace.hku.hk

Abstract. The development of blended learning in Hong Kong has been shifted to using pedagogical driven approach and the adoption of learning theories in blended learning course development became significant. In the past years, HKU SPACE adopted cognitive alignment in outcome-based learning theory for designing and developing blended learning course to the students. This research aims at understanding learning experiences of undergraduate students in blended learning. In this study, qualitative approach was adopted for obtaining in-depth understanding of learning experiences of the students in the blended learning environment. Focus group interviews for students were conducted in an accounting course. The interviews were analyzed by thematic analysis while thematic maps were used for coding and themes identification. The themes in learn via learning activities, learn via collaboration, learn for good assessment result, learning activities helps study and enjoyed most, perceived advantages of online learning, need more learning support, need mobile learning, preference in integrated and non-integrated blended learning, and difficulties in blended learning were identified. With the themes identified, issues on learning engagement, importance of aligning assessment with learning activity, online collaboration and enhancing blended learning experiences were discussed. Finally, pedagogy designs to enhance students learning were recommended. The study contributes to fill the research gap in understanding blended learning experiences of undergraduate students in Hong Kong.

Keywords: blended learning, outcome-based, undergraduate, sub-degree.

1 Introduction

The use of ICT in higher education in Hong Kong has been increased rapidly. The development of blended learning in Hong Kong has been shifted from using technological driven approach to pedagogical driven approach. The adoption of learning theories in blended learning course development became significant. In recent years, the Hong Kong Government has promoted outcome-based learning and a number of learning institutes have implemented it accordingly.

The School of Professional and Continuing Education of The University of Hong Kong (HKU SPACE) employed the constructive alignment theory to design a blended

K.C. Li et al. (Eds.): ICTE 2014, CCIS 494, pp. 215–224, 2015.

learning sub-degree accounting course, Management Accounting (MA). Tang's constructive alignment theory was adopted in course and lesson aligning intended learning outcomes, teaching and learning activities and tasks [1]. A number of learning outcomes were set and in-class and onlin were designed. A research study was conducted with this blended learning

This paper aims at understanding learning experiences of undergraduate the sub-degree blended learning MA course. In this study, qualitative ap adopted for obtaining in-depth data collection and analysis.

2 Literature Review

Outcome-based learning has been widely adopted in Hong Kong. With th ment of outcome-based learning by the University Grants Committee in H higher education institutes have been encouraged to adopt this learning m University of Hong Kong decided to adopt the outcome-based approach in of the new 4-Year Curriculum after analyzing the surveys of students' exp studying at the University [2]. The aim of the decision was to establish a ment which allowed for deeper engagement of students in their studies. The versity of Hong Kong designed a learning outcome tracking system to s development of outcome-based teaching and learning [3].

In the sub-degree sector, the Federation for Self-financing Tertiary Edu gested using Biggs and Tang's constructive alignment theory to align inter ing outcomes, teaching and learning activities and assessment tasks as go in designing sub-degree courses [4]. Education Bureau, Hong Kong Coun creditation of Academic and Vocational Qualifications and Joint Quali Committee issued a handbook for the sub-degree sector on good practices assurance. This sector was where the outcome-based teaching and learnin being emphasized for the provision of quality teaching, learning and learner

The effectiveness of implementing outcome-based learning has not al positive. In Au and Kwan's study, over 90% of university instructors who p in the survey reported that the performance of students did not improve af plementation of the outcome-based learning [5]. Despite of the results of the effectiveness of outcome-based learning, the method is widely accep field of education in Hong Kong.

Nevertheless, outcome-based learning is one of the most popular metho in the field of education. Under this approach, goals and objectives to be ac defined and learning outcomes are measured against the preset objectives. posed the constructive alignment and solo taxonomy for constructivism and alignment in teaching in which activities were designed according to tives and that assessments were carried out to measure the degree of ful objectives [6]. Upon completion of the study and achievement of a certai the learning institutes would issue a certificate as proof of educational attain

methods [1]. Only academic students could achieve high-level engagement under passive student activities required environment but both types of students could achieve it under active student activities required environment. Biggs advocated the use of activities as to lead all students to high-level engagement in learning. Both academic students and non-academic students' level of engagement could be aligned with active student activities in learning. Based on the twin principles of constructivism in learning and alignment in teaching, Biggs' constructive alignment theory states a good teaching system aligns teaching method and assessment to learning activities stated in the objectives so that all aspects of the system act in accord to support appropriate learning. Constructive alignment leads a design of teaching to encourage deep engagement.

3 Methodology

Case study derived from research can be of great value in teaching and learning [7]. In this research, a case study about the learning experiences of the Hong Kong sub-degree Accounting students in the blended learning environment was conducted. This qualitative study was conducted based on Yin's method of case study [8][9].

The purpose of this study was to explore the learning experiences of the sub-degree students in blended learning environment. Stake suggested a number of ways, including observation, description of contexts and interview, to conduct case study research [10]. In this study, the primary data sources were from in-depth focus group interviews of students. The field work was conducted after examination of the MA course in 2013. The following research questions were asked as a guide to address the issues into research statement.

1. How do students study in a blended learning environment?
2. What form does engagement take within blended study?
3. What factors influence the form of student engagement in blended learning?

The students' focus group interviews were conducted in a semi-structured way. An interview guide was drafted and issued in outline form. The interview guide contains purposes, arrangement, introduction and questions in the categories of learning activities, factors affecting students' engagement in online learning, difficulties in online learning, integrated and non-integrated blended learning, collaborative learning, teachers' role and other issues. In each category, standardized open-ended questions were asked as basic questions. There were totally 38 questions in these 7 categories. Besides the standardized questions, the interviewer asked further questions based on students' responses with self-decided sequence and wordings to increase the comprehensiveness of the data collected.

The interviews were tape-recorded and the transcript were then prepared. To let the students express their views with accurate wordings and expression, they were asked to use mother tongue, Cantonese, to answer the questions. The transcripts were then translated into English for analysis. Recurring ideas and themes were identified and illustrative quotations were selected. Qualitative analysis software, Nvivo labeling and sorting segments of text into categories was used for data analy

Consents were obtained from the School and from the students for ethic eration. To ensure the validity and reliability of the study, the interview reviewed by a local expert and 2 overseas experts in blended learning. B transcription and translation of each of the interviews were verified by a st was in the interview.

4 Results and Findings

The transcribed and translated interviews were analysed by thematic ana Coding was performed using Nvivo 10.0 and 15 themes and 160 sub-th identified. Then the initial thematic map, developed thematic map and fina map were created [12]. The final thematic map with 9 themes and 45 sub shown in Fig. 1.

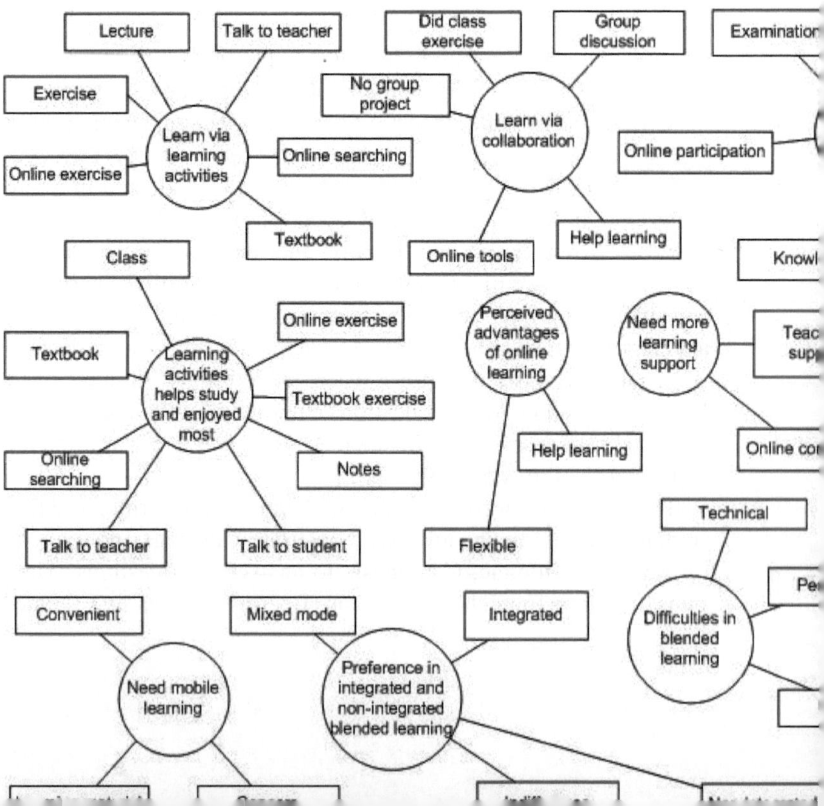

The 9 themes are 1) Learn via learning activities; 2) Learn via collaboration; 3) Learn for good assessment result; 4) Learning activities helps study and enjoyed most; 5) Perceived advantages of online learning; 6) Need more learning support; 7) Need mobile learning; 8) Preference in integrated and non-integrated blended learning; and 9) Difficulties in blended learning.

4.1 Learn via Learning Activities

Students learnt by participating in in-class activities, self-learning activities and online activities. All the students learnt by attending classes which were compulsory for taking the course. After class, most of the students learnt via doing exercises, including exercises in textbook and in online system. Some students preferred doing online exercise as instant feedback would be provided after answer submission.

Some students learnt by reading notes and textbook. Others learnt by searching on the Internet. Students would study and search for additional information in the Internet but not in the library as more resources were available. Students also mentioned they learnt by talking to teacher. Students learnt using combination of learning activities.

4.2 Learn via Collaboration

There were no group projects in the MA course. Sometimes students did exercises and had group discussions in class. Some students mentioned they liked collaborative learning because it helped them learn. They could learn from each other and understand their strengths and weaknesses when working together. However, some students did not like collaborative learning as they liked learning independently which learning time and pace were more flexible. Some did not like trouble-makers in the group. A student worried about being laughed at if his comments were nonsense.

For online communication, they used WhatsApp, Skype, Facebook and WeChat. Normally, they used text to communicate and upload photos for sharing in WhatsApp. For Skype, they used audio and video communication in group of 4 to 10 students. They uploaded and shared files, for example, answers of exercises, onto Facebook.

4.3 Learn for Good Assessment Result

Students attended classes and did online learning with the main reason for obtaining good assessment results. Most students explicitly stated their reasons for learning were passing the examination and obtaining online participation marks which contributed to overall assessment results. Students found calculation important in the MA course for passing the examination and understanding the steps in calculation was crucial. The purposes of getting good assessment results were to graduate, to get a certificate, to further study and to get into university. Two students mentioned that they learnt because they wanted to acquire knowledge.

Some students did online learning because they found online activities were useful for examination preparation. A student mentioned it was important for students as the online activities were related to examination. If online exercises were similar to questions in examination, they would do them more often. A student said that she would learning before examination only if online participation was not for assessm plied students did online learning and looked for learning resources in onlin ment which could help obtain good results in examination.

4.4 Learning Activities Helps Study and Enjoyed Most

Students in general found doing online exercise, doing textbook exercise a ing class were most helpful. Some students found reading notes, talking t talking to teachers, searching online and reading textbook were helpful.

Students found doing online exercise and doing textbook exercise were th they enjoyed most. Some students found they enjoyed attending class, reac talking to students, talking to teachers and searching online. They mentione enjoyed these activities because they were helpful to their study for examinat

4.5 Perceived Advantages of Online Learning

The major perceived advantage of online learning was flexibility. They s learning was convenient and they could learn anytime online. They could learning resources from online system.

Students found online learning useful for them to learn and prepare fo tion. One student found the materials on online platform were more precis student said self-assessment was available as instant feedback was provide activities. When a student had question to ask, he could read online materi the solution instead of sending email to teacher and wait for reply. Besides, resources were available on the online platform and they could assess th self-learning.

4.6 Need More Learning Support

Students needed more learning support. For online resources, they need audio and video of lectures, and video clips in Chinese, to help them learn examination. A student needed more learning contents on application of M life and a student needed more practical contents with real-life case stud students needed more online questions and more detailed explanation in the answers.

Students found teacher support important and they needed to have mo from teachers. They needed to have online classes and online discussions by the teachers to answer their questions. A student needed the teacher videos to explain the answers of online exercises. Two students showed linking with teacher online and face-to-face teaching. They mentioned th could post questions in the online platform for them to discuss and then

4.7 Need Mobile Learning

Students mentioned their needs on having mobile learning to support their learning. Many students said that using mobile devices to learn was convenient. If there was a mobile app for the MA course, they will use it to learn more frequently. They would like use it in class, during self-learning and when travelling to school. A student showed preference on using mobile devices than using computers to learn.

The students had some ideas on how the mobile app could be designed. They wanted the app to contain review materials and exercises. Besides, reminders for doing exercises and reading notes should be sent via mobile phone and links of the learning materials should be provided in the reminders so that they could access the contents conveniently.

However, some students showed concerns on mobile learning as some students did not have smart phones. Moreover, student might be easily distracted by other apps or function of the phone which might affect student's concentration in learning.

4.8 Preference in Integrated and Non-integrated Blended Learning

Nearly all students preferred learning in blended learning mode. Most of these these students preferred the blend with face-to-face learning, online leaning using computer and mobile learning.

About half of the students preferred integrated blended learning because they could learn with differenct ways. They realized that self-displine was important if online learning was complementary to face-to-face learning. One student felt that school fee had to be reduced if physical contact hour with teachers was reduced. The other half of the students preferred non-integrated blended learning as they wanted online learning as supplementary to face-to-face learning. They wanted a teacher to guide their learning all the time and they could ask questions immediately in class. One student found that she could not concentrate when using computer to learn. Two students showed indifference in learning mode as long as marks were obtained.

4.9 Difficulties in Blended Learning

Students found technical problems in using the online platform. The platform was revamped in their year 2 study and they found the change affected their experience. Some students reckoned the online platform as not user-friendly and difficult to use. The system performance was slow especially in examination period and some online activities could not function in different browsers. Some of the contents were found to have errors and not up-to-date. Also the instructions for doing online activities were unclear and some online exercises could not be loaded when using mobile phones. They also found the courses, learning materials and learning activities were difficult to locate.

Medium of instruction was a problem for some of the students. Student found it difficult to learn in English and they could understand more when learning in Chinese. However, they needed to answer in English in examination and so they needed to learn

in English. A student suggested the course providing video clips with Chines
for them to learn the topics again after class. A few students mentioned th
proficiency of their teacher was not good enough.

Some students had problems in self-learning environment, for example,
no time, not self-disciplined and lazy. A student felt isolation in online lea
needed to talk to teacher and students during learning. Some other stude
immediate support from teacher was insufficient during online learning.

5 Discussion

From the results and findings, the following issues are identified regardin
experiences of sub-degree students in blended learning environment.

5.1 Learning Engagement

Students learnt by participating in in-class activities, self-learning activities
activities. Students mentioned 8 types of learning activities in blended lear
helpful. These included doing online exercise and doing textbook exercises,
class, reading notes, talking to students, talking to teachers, searching online
ing textbooks. Student enjoyed 7 types of learning activities and all these
were considered as helpful activities except reading textbook which they fou
and time-consuming. It was found that students enjoyed helpful learning act
they engaged in learning via activities they enjoyed.

5.2 Importance of Aligning Assessment with Learning Activity

Students learnt because they wanted to acquire knowledge and to obtain go
ment results. Their engagement in learning related to how the learning
helped them to achieve their intended learning outcome. They engaged i
activities which they found useful for examination preparation or for a
Therefore, it is important to align assessment with learning activities so th
would like to learn through the activities and could learn through the activ
dents' engagement should be considered during the assessment's design pro

5.3 Online Collaboration

Some students like collaborative learning but some dislike it. Although man
like face-to-face communication more, they also used online communicatio
They did not use the online platform provided by the School for communi
stead, they used popular software or apps in the market, including WhatsA
Facebook and Wechat, to ask questions, upload photos with learning co
share answers to others. They can learn from peers via online collaboration.

5.4 Enhancing Blended Learning Experiences

It is important to understand students' difficulties and needs for enhancing their learning experiences in blended learning environment. The degree of integration of online components and face-to-face components should be appropriate. Updated learning contents, bi-lingual contents and more questions with detailed feedback should be provided. To help students' learning online, immediate online teaching and technical support should be provided. For technical support, user-friendly system and mobile app should be developed to facilitate students' learning.

6 Conclusion

A thematic analysis was performed to understand learning experiences of the sub-degree students in blended learning environment. The themes in learn via learning activities, learn via collaboration, learn for good assessment result, learning activities helps study and students enjoyed most, perceived advantages of online learning, the need of more learning support, the need of mobile learning, preference in integrated and non-integrated blended learning, and difficulties were discussed.

It is recommended to enhance students learning experiences through the following ways. Firstly, the design of blended learning course should align with assessment. The learning activities should be designed both to help students achieving learning outcomes with assessment and help students study for examination. Larger question pool, detailed instant feedback and practical learning should be provided for them to study. Secondly, continuous improvement should be provided for online learning. The online materials should be maintained with updated contents. Besides, new trends in educational technology, for instance, mobile learning, should be considered for providing needed support to students. Thirdly, more online collaboration should be considered for blended learning design. Online classes and discussion forums should be used for collaborative learning in online environment. This can provide an alternative for students to learn from teachers and peers and minimize isolation problem in online learning. Fourthly, more support should be provided to students so that they can get help during online learning. Teachers should respond to students regularly and more frequently in online environment. Technical support on using online platforms should be easy to contact and responsive. Instructions of using learning activities should be more comprehensive.

This paper documented interim results of a doctoral programme research. Further research such us individual interviews for more in-depth analysis will be conducted. The study contributes to fill the research gap in understanding blended learning experiences of undergraduate students in Hong Kong.

Acknowledgments. This paper documented interim results of a doctoral programme research. This is to acknowledge the University of Nottingham, United Kingdom and the supervisors, Dr. Gordon Joyes and Prof. Charles Crook, of the Doctor of Education (Lifelong Education) programme. Their dedication in supporting and guiding the research is much appreciated.

References

1. Biggs, J., Tang, C.: Teaching for Quality Learning at University. The Society fo
into Higher Education & Open University Press, UK (2007)
2. HKU: HKU Website (2010), http://www.cetl.hku.hk/outcomes
approaches-student-learning (retrieved November 20, 2010)
3. Mong, Y., Chan, M., Chan, F.K.H.: Web-Based Outcome-Based Teaching and
An Experience Report. In: Leung, H., Li, F., Lau, R., Li, Q. (eds.) ICWL 20
vol. 4823, pp. 475–483. Springer, Heidelberg (2008)
4. Federation for Self-Financing Tertiary Education: General Education Guide
FSTE (2013)
5. Au, O., Kwan, R.: Experience on Outcome-Based Teaching and Learning. In:
Fong, J., Zhang, L., Lee, V.S.K. (eds.) ICHL 2009. LNCS, vol. 5685, pp
Springer, Heidelberg (2009)
6. Biggs, J.: Teaching for Quality Learning at University. The Open Univer
Buckingham (2003)
7. Wellington, J.: Education Research: Contemporary Issues and Practical A
Continuum, London (2000)
8. Yin, R.K.: Applications of Case Study Research. Sage Publications, Inc., UK (1
9. Yin, R.K.: Case Study Research: Design and Methods, 3rd edn. Sage Publica
UK (2003)
10. Stake, R.E.: The Art of Case Study Research. Sage Publications, Thousand Oak
11. Braun, V., Clarke, V.: Using Thematic Analysis in Psychology. Qualitative R
Psychology 3(2), 77–101 (2006)
12. Braun, V., Wilkinson, S.: Liability or Asset? Women Talk about The Vagina.
of Women Section Review 5, 28–42 (2003)

Author Index

Author Index

MIX
Papier aus verantwortungsvollen Quellen
Paper from responsible sources
FSC® C105338

If you have any concerns about our products,
you can contact us on
ProductSafety@springernature.com

In case Publisher is established outside the EU,
the EU authorized representative is:
Springer Nature Customer Service Center GmbH
Europaplatz 3, 69115 Heidelberg, Germany

Printed by Libri Plureos GmbH
in Hamburg, Germany